LUCKNOW-
Ode To A City

LUCKNOW-

Ode To A City

PC Sarkar

KALPAZ

ISBN: 978-93-5324-643-3

First Published, 2021

Published by

Kalpaz Publications
C-30, Satyawati Nagar,
Delhi – 110052
Ph.: 011-47034999, 9811692060
www.kalpazpublications.com
E-mail: kalpaz@hotmail.com

Printed at: Gyan Press, Delhi.

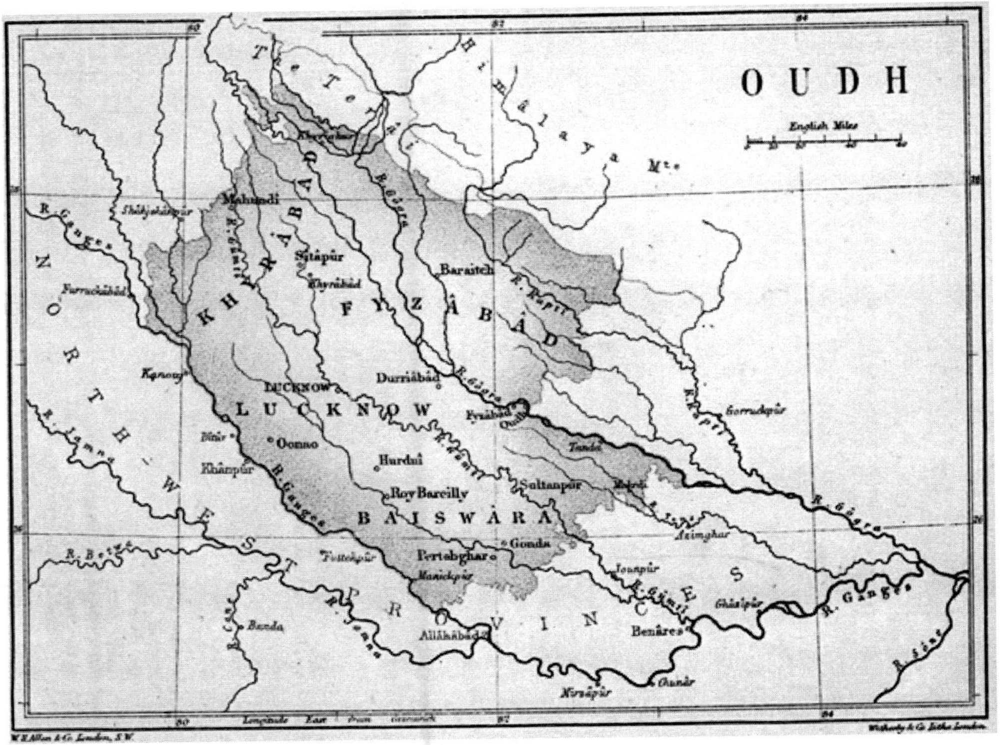

Map of Oudh (Awadh), WH Allen & Co., London (1880)

Contents

Shahanshah Mirza
Wazif Manzil, Park Circus
Calcutta - 700017
Phone: 9831104363; 7003570073, E-mail: s.mirza100@gmail.com

Foreword

Lucknow, the heritage seat of culture, and renowned for its Nawabs and Begums, is not my birthplace, but I share an umbilical relationship with it, as it is the city of my ancestors.

Thus, my joy knew no bounds when Dr PC Sarkar requested me to provide the Foreword for his latest book: *Lucknow - Ode to a City*. It gave me another chance to re-establish the link with a city, which my illustrious ancestor, King Wajid Ali Shah had tearfully left 165 years ago.

Interestingly, this book has not been written by a historian, which adds a twist to the whole approach. On the contrary, it has been penned by an accomplished chemical scientist who is passionate about history and Lucknow. The biggest proof of his passion is that he wrote this book, sitting in Kolkata, about a thousand km away from Lucknow. Being a man of science, his approach is methodical, logical, rational and straightforward. His deep knowledge and insight into historical facts add enough value to this book and makes it an ideal Collector's Collection.

The book takes you on a fascinating journey to the era when Awadh was the nerve centre of the composite *Ganga-Jamuni tehzeeb*, *adab* and etiquette. This book is imaginatively designed and provides a refreshing look at highlighting and preserving the rich heritage of our composite culture.

Altogether in nine Chapters, Dr Sarkar has covered many important aspects of the enchanting city of Lucknow. These Chapters have been chosen very wisely and greatly arouse the interest of readers. He has captured the essence of the bygone era in a fast-paced and lively rhythm, which makes the book unputdownable.

It is clearly evident that plenty of hard work and research has gone into this work, as it has touched the untouched: topics that were never described before, such as the aristocratic property of the Awadh rulers in Shahjahanabad including the *Dara Shikoh Mahal*. It gives the reader access to some hidden facts, in fast and breezy prose. The work also boasts of several vintage and rare images of Lucknow, which further enhances its appeal and is like the proverbial icing on the cake.

I was aware that Dr Sarkar was working on this project, after bringing out a spectacular book, *Lucknow: Buildings, Begums and The British* in 2015, but that it will be ready so soon came as a pleasant surprise to me. He deserves a rousing ovation for this wonderful piece of work, which will generate abundant enthusiasm and pride in the younger generation about Lucknow and its glorious past.

With warm regards and best wishes,

Shahanshah Mirza

Great great grandson of King Wajid Ali Shah

Raja Syed Muzaffar Ali
of Kotwara

7.7. 2021

ODE TO A CITY

I wanted to write a preface which is a bird's eye view of a city and a photographic essence of its description. Exactly what happens when a scientist approaches a book on a city. A city inspired by art, yet a city full of scientists. Nothing can go wrong. I am speaking as a scientist and an artist about a book by a scientist inspired by the art of a city, which puts everything about this artistic city in its logical cause and effect way. This is the alchemy of P. C. Sarkar's book on Lucknow. The city of my art and dreams. Another important factor about this book is the alchemy of the author who belongs to a city, as splendid and as magnificient, steeped in as much art and culture, Calcutta. This is no ordinary confluence of an organic chemistry about defining a city with a past. It is a bridge of understanding cultures. Of describing the science that stands as a backbone to archecture which defines the particularities of a place.

I hope that this book on Lucknow will be first a mirror for its own people who will then prepare themselves to welcome the world as they enter its arched gateways with 'Adab' and respect. Salute Sarkar Sahab.

With admiration,

Muzaffar Ali

Kotwara Studios, Jaunapur Main Road, Mehrauli, New Delhi 110047 India Phone + 91 11 26658614 Fax +91 11 26658615
Kotwara House, Qaiserbagh, Lucknow 226001, Uttar Pradesh, India Phone +91 522 2225332 Fax +91 522 2230706
Anhalwara Palace, Kotwara Raj, Gola Gokarnath, District Lakhimpur Kheri, Uttar Pradesh, India
A 1 Mandar, Juhu Village, Juhu, Mumbai 400049, India, India Phone + 91 22 65891822
Kotwara Lodge, Ayarpata Slopes, Mallitai, Nainital, Uttaranchal, India Phone 05942 237123
muzaffar_ali@yahoo.com www.muzaffarali.com www.therumifilm.com

Acknowledgements

I wish to express sincere gratitude to my family, friends and well-wishers for making this book a possibility. Shahanshah Mirza Sahib, direct descendent of King Wajid Ali Shah at Kolkata, who had always been enquiring about the progress of my second book on Lucknow, provided a very praise-worthy Foreword, for which I am indebted to him. I am equally grateful to Raja Muzaffar Ali Sahib of Kotwara, who, despite his celebrity status and busy schedule, found time to provide the Preface for this humble work of mine. Not to mention the encouragement and help received from Raj Kumar Amir Naqi Khan of *Iqbal Manzil*, Mr Syed Masoom Raza of *Saltanat Manzil* and Mr Masood Abdullah of *Sheesh Mahal*, Lucknow, who have always been ardent supporters of my efforts to project, publicise and document the lost heritage of Lucknow (and Awadh).

Ms Vipul Varshney, a personal friend, celebrated architect, heritage conservationist and INTACH Chairperson, not only provided the architectural drawings in this book - her cheerful demeanour provided the much-needed encouragement, when I tended to falter, especially during the tragic COVID period of 2020 and 2021. Ms Kanak Rekha Chauhan, Co-Founder of Lucknow Expressions Society and Director, Lucknow Literature Festival, had been instrumental in the impressive release of my previous book, *Lucknow - Buildings, Begums and The British*, proved her mettle once again, for which I shall always remain obliged. An ardent Lucknow lover, Mr Inam Abidi of *Jahan-e-Awadh*, located in distant UAE, who affectionately refers to me as a "Jewel of Awadh" was no less responsible for the completion of this book; in fact, his persistent queries on the progress of my writing, motivated me all the more to conclude the project at the earliest.

My (late) brother-in-law, Mr Rajiv Chaube, would have been proud to see the final culmination of my efforts in print; he had always tried to match my zeal and accompanied me in exploring way-off places, including abandoned churches, desolate cemeteries, ruinous monuments and off-bound private properties. May his soul rest in peace.

To cite by name, all my admirers and well-wishers would be a lengthy exercise. But I cannot fail to mention Mr Oliver Frederick of *Hindustan Times*, for his infallible faith in me and in whatever little I know about the heritage of Lucknow. I would like to mention in particular, the contribution of my youngest collaborator, Ms Apoorva Upadhyay of IT College, Lucknow, who enthusiastically toiled in the archives of her college to provide me with source material. Regrettably, I could not include a chapter on ghost stories in this book as suggested by her - for the simple reason that I did not know any more than what I had already narrated in my previous book. Perhaps I will make a special effort to collect more ghostly tales of Lucknow for my next book, *Inshāllāh.*

Needless to say, this book would not have been possible without the active support received from the Editorial and Production Teams of M/s Gyan Books and Kalpaz Publications, Delhi. Thank you all once again.

Tollygunge, Kolkata **PC Sarkar**
July 2021

Introduction

An interesting question often asked is, why another book on Lucknow? To be honest, this phenomenon of books being regularly churned out on this particular city, defies logic. And yet, it is an established fact that Lucknow has a surfeit of books, describing almost every aspect of the city, or at least, what remains of the city and its famed, indolent culture. As a matter of fact, certain cities of India do seem to be an inexhaustible source material, thereby creating an insatiable fascination for authors - Delhi being the leader of the pack, and Lucknow right behind in the race. Ironically, Lucknow, as it stands today, is a strange amalgam of heritage, both Nawabi and colonial, coupled with outcome of the 1947 partition. For the last several centuries, it has managed to retain its status as the second most important city in northern India, after the national capital of Delhi. Lucknow's reputation simply refuses to fade away, and the very mention of the city brings forth the inevitable reference to the *Bada Imambara* (consistently referred to the *Great Emamburra* by our erstwhile colonial rulers) and its *Bhool Bhulaiyya* (labyrinth), its gourmet culture, both vegetarian and non-vegetarian, and the anachronistic *pehle aap* (after you, sir) mannerism of its jaded inhabitants. The discussion then veers off to the city's contribution to the fine arts - dance, drama; the *kathak gharana*, the *ghazal* and the *nazm*, handicrafts such as silver thread work (*zardozi*) and *chikan* (intricate embroidery on fine muslin cloth). Discussions become more and more animated... the remnants of kite flying, pigeon breeding and cock fighting. The elaborate and extended obsequies during Muharram, coupled with the famed fraternity among Hindu and Muslim communities. Of late, Lucknow has also become a favourite location for many Bollywood films and web series. In a nutshell, Lucknow remains an enigma, an anachronism, excessively endowed with both tangible and intangible heritage, the discussion of which cannot be covered by a single book, or even a series of books.

After 1947, Lucknow - caught in the hurly-burly of Indian politics, could not see significant industrialisation or urban development. The city continued to rely on its earlier Nawabi and colonial legacy by way of buildings and infrastructure - while its population bludgeoned, its geographical boundaries expanded exponentially and its demography took a turn for the worse, due to rapid migration of the rural populace into the capital city. Being the nerve centre of politics ensured that the city was always in the news, but it did not ensure concurrent transformation into a modern state capital. The influx of refugees after India's partition also took a toll on the city; however, a discussion on the economic and sociological impact of this man-made tragedy is beyond the scope of this book. Of late, it was realised that the city had gone to seed and several make-overs were put into place, the most significant being Lucknow's *Mayanagri*, in which massive edifices dedicated to Dalit leaders were erected. These complexes, although criticized in some quarters, were no doubt architecturally superlative, giving the city something truly at par with the old Nawabi architectural wonders, which had been put into place roughly two centuries ago. Lucknow now trod upon the path of rapid urbanisation, but somehow, in this advancement, its older Nawabi and colonial heritage started to fade and lose importance. In an age of instant information (*sans* knowledge) on digital platforms, no one really had the time to ponder, research or carry out in-depth studies on the lost legacies of a city, or care to dwell upon the city's historical edifices *which no longer existed in present times*. Similarly, the city, described by various early authors and travellers for its decadence and pleasure-seeking ways, its effeminate traditions, its flamboyance and licentiousness, and yet again, for its deeply ingrained spirituality and elaborate mourning practices, was not all (*lakhauri*) bricks and (*surkhi*) mortar. This seemingly contradictory lifestyle of old Lucknow had been brought about not only by its egalitarian Nawabi rulers and their consorts (described elsewhere in detail), but also by latter-day British officials as well as a diverse range of fortune seekers - from eunuchs to court painters, from pastors to mercenary soldiers. Their names continued to crop up in crumbling tombstones, obscure road names, defaced foundation stones and toppled statues. But personal details of these people were sparse; they remained shadowy figures from a hazy past, although their contributions had been significant in their own unique ways, not so very long ago.

The book is not written in a lyrical style with stanzas; and yet, the sentiments expressed are similar to a formal ode: an exaltation of feeling and style, varying length of line, and complexity of form. It chronicles the writer's thoughts and feelings about a city, through deeply researched details, brought painstakingly together in concise form, for the general reader, as well as the heritage enthusiast. In brief, it is an attempt to analyze and present some hitherto unknown and seemingly ignored aspects of the lost legacy of Lucknow - a humble ode to a city which arose from being a nondescript settlement in the vast Indo-Gangetic plains, and ultimately posed a formidable challenge for a mighty empire, where the sun was reputed to have never set.

किस घर में ख़ुशी होती है, मातम नहीं होता?
क्या सूरमा भरी आँखों में आंसू नहीं गिरते...
क्या मेंहदी लगे हाथों से मातम नहीं होता?

–'रियाज़'

Which home has only happiness, but no mourning?
Do tears not well up in kohl-lined eyes...
Do henna-stained hands not rise for lamentation?

—*'Riyaz'*

History shows that it does not matter who is in power or what revolutionary forces take over the government; those who have not learned to do for themselves and have to depend solely on others never obtain any more rights or privileges in the end than they had in the beginning.

—*Carter Godwin Woodson*

Cities have the capability of providing something for everybody, only because, and only when, they are created by everybody.

—*Jane Jacobs*

Lost Marvels

Well, that's history for you folks. Unfair, untrue and for the most part, written by folk who weren't even there.

— Joanne Harris

History isn't about dates and places and wars. It's about people who fill the spaces between them.

— Jodi Picoult

Chapter - 1

Dara Shikoh Mahal (Shahjahanabad)

The reader might wonder what a Mughal palace in old Delhi has to do with the lost heritage of Lucknow. However, it need not be reiterated that the first three Nawabs of Awadh also had a strong presence at the Mughal capital. This is because they had the responsibility of *Wazirat* or Ministership in the Mughal court, in addition to being a *Naib* or *Nawab* (Governor) of Awadh *suba* (province). Their residence at Delhi was the *Dara Shikoh Mahal* or *Haveli Dara Shikoh*, which exists today as a nondescript museum of the Department of Archaeology of the Delhi Government.

It may be recalled that Prince Dara Shikoh (Shukoh) was heir apparent of Mughal emperor, Shah Jahan. His status granted him the privilege of building his palace right on the river front, north of the Red Fort. After his unfortunate death, the palace came to be occupied by Prince Mohammad Mu'azzam, who would later sit on the imperial throne as Bahadur Shah Zafar - I. Subsequently, *Dara Shikoh Mahal*, after a succession of owners, came into the possession of the Nawabs of Awadh (Srivastava, 1954). The first Nawab, Sa'adat Khan Burhan-ul-Mulk stayed here in 1739, and it is here that he consumed poison and committed suicide. Hence it is sometimes referred to as *Haveli Sa'adat Khan*. The palace seems to have been damaged during Nadir Shah's invasion of Delhi, subsequently restored, but demarcated into two parts (Blake, 1991). Nawab Wazir Safdarjang, who spent more time at Delhi, than in his own capital, Bangla (Faizabad) occupied one portion of the palace. Najib-ud-Daula, the Rohilla chieftain, who was Nadir Shah's nominee at Delhi was also reported to have lived here. Najaf Quli Khan, a noble of Shah Alam's court resided here for sometime. Latif (2010) states that the palace had been the residence of Donna Juliana, a devout Catholic of Portuguese descent, who wielded considerable influence in the Mughal court of Bahadur Shah Zafar - I. This palace had been gifted to Donna, by Bahadur Shah himself, but confiscated by Farrukhsiyar, who later gave it back to her. Donna had also been close to Nawab Safdarjang and his family. Colonel Gentil, a French soldier in Shuja-ud-Daula's court at Faizabad, later married Thereza Velho, the great-grand-niece of Donna. Col. Antoine Polier, another French soldier and adventurer, employed in the court of Shuja-ud-Daula, had also briefly resided in *Dara Shikoh Mahal* (Patel & Leonard, 2011), when he arrived at Delhi, to join the services of Mughal emperor, Shah Alam – II.

It must be pointed out that Sa'adat Khan's original place of residence at Shahjahanabad was a separate entity altogether, among the series of palaces along the Red Fort. Blake (1991), in a topography map of royal mansions and mosques of Shahjahanabad in 1739 shows Safdarjang's mansion as located next to the *Nigambodh* Gate, adjoining which, stands the mansion of Dara Shikoh. The two mansions are separated by the *Qila Ghat* Gate. The map shows the mansion of Sa'adat Khan near the *Kabuli* Gate, geographically opposite the palaces of Dara Shikoh / Safdarjang. The luxurious nature of these palace(s) have also been described, including the snippet of information that Safdarjang's mansion could accommodate five thousand troops and there were stables for five hundred horses. Sada'at Khan's *haveli* has also been described likewise, having six separate gateways, and a bath with five rooms and a dome of glazed glass. While it is more or less clear that Dara Shikoh's palace complex was modified for Safdarjang's occupancy, it is difficult to accept that Sa'adat Khan built a massive, palatial structure for himself at Delhi. Sa'adat Khan was not a builder; historical accounts mention that he was on military campaigns most of the time, and all that he could do for his own capital at *Bangla* (Faizabad) was to erect a mud fort with wooden supports. This fort would get flooded during the monsoons, and had to be demolished and replaced by a proper fort during the times of Safdarjang. Also, on examining the times lines, we see that Shahjahanabad was built and populated during the period: 1639 – 1656. Sa'adat Khan and his brother came to Delhi in 1709; the former was taken into employment as a *Mir Manzil* (Camp Superintendent) by Sarbuland Khan, a *Faujdar* of the Imperial Mughal army (Srivastava, 1954). There was no way that Sa'adat Khan could build a massive mansion adjoining the Red Fort, when the area was already densely populated with Mughal nobility and their families. Although Sa'adat Khan did live in a separate mansion, it must have been outsourced from among the stately palaces built during Shah Jahan. The original owner / builder of Sa'adat Khan's *haveli* is not known. But we are digressing.

David Ochterlony was the first British Resident at Delhi. Immediately after joining his new assignment in 1803, he set about establishing the Residency premises, which would be comparable in status, if not at par, with the establishment of the great Mughals at Delhi. It was an irony that he chose *Dara Shikoh Mahal*. Ochterlony had already spent several decades in India in the Company's service, and had "gone completely native" i.e. become a *White Mughal*, to use a popular term (Dalrymple, 2002). Hence, his choice of a sub-imperial Mughal palace as his official residence was no surprise (Shorto, 2018). Later, Ochterlony would choose another area in Delhi and develop it as *Mubarak Bagh* (named after his favourite wife, Mubarak Mahal), as a sort of personal garden. Again, this garden was the property of a noble from Awadh, who recalled that one of the Mughal Emperors had given it to his family on condition of supplying the Mughal court with baskets of vegetables, fruit, and flowers. Since he could not fulfil the terms, he allowed the enclosure to be partly used as a garden (Villiers, 1913).

Sharma (2005) in her seminal research work, has described the colonial transformation of *Dara Shikoh Mahal* to suit British needs. It needs to be reiterated here that the *Mahal* was not a single building but a sizeable palace complex. The prince's library became the Residency proper; the front façade was provided with an impressive colonnade of lofty columns, which is evident even today. Other additions and alterations included a ballroom, banqueting rooms, enveloping verandas and areas for ancillary functions. (Almost a century later, a similar metamorphosis of a Nawabi residence, *Kothi Hayat Baksh* into a colonial Chief Commissioner's residence, and present day *Raj Bhavan*, through extensive additions and modifications, can be seen at Lucknow). The *tykhana* or underground arcaded rooms of *Dara Shikoh Mahal* remained comparatively undisturbed. The open spaces were landscaped into colonial-style gardens, rather than Mughal-styled ones. With the abolition of the Residency in 1831, the premises were made available to the Delhi College in 1832. It suffered severe damage during 1857, probably due to its associations with colonial ambitions. A district school functioned from the premises during 1858 – 1864. The Delhi College was revived and it subsequently functioned from 1864 – 1877. The district school became the Municipal Board School during 1886 – 1904, after which it became the Government High School. St. Stephen's Mission College came up in the vicinity. Matching with the changing usage patterns, staff quarters, post office, PWD rest house etc. also came up, each gobbling up a part of the original vast grounds of the *Dara Shikoh Mahal*. As of now, the Residency of Ochterlony is still extant, with its colonnaded front, carrying the name of *Dara Shikoh* Library. Inside, one can perceive slender Mughal pillars, cusped arches; the rear of the "library" building has even more obvious Mughal architectural elements. The colonial style lower level chambers, juxtaposed with Mughal style lower level chambers is indeed a sight to behold.

Thomas Metcalf, British Resident at Delhi, during the reign of Bahadur Shah Zafar II, following the footsteps of his illustrious predecessor, had appropriated a Mughal structure, this time the tomb of Mohammad Quli Khan, foster brother of Emperor Akbar, and converted it into his personal retreat called *Dilkusha* in the Mehrauli area. He built his house in layers around the octagonal tomb, which remained essential intact. The structure was damaged during 1857, and as the layers constructed by Metcalf peeled away, the original tomb emerged, rather unscathed. The structure we see today is more or less the original tomb, with scattered additions and follies all around. A portion of a colonial era wall and arch, attached like an incongruous wing to the original edifice, clearly shows the mixture of construction materials: masonry rubble and *lakhauri* bricks juxtaposed together. However, *Dara Shikoh Mahal* may not be so lucky. Firstly, due to its chequered history and usage pattern, most of the original palace has already vanished. The library remains. Even if the colonial superstructure is peeled off, it is doubtful that the original building would emerge. In all probability, the entire structure could come crashing down due to weakened foundations and supports. In the absence of photographs, cartographic details, architectural plans or even sketches, it is impossible to visualise the appearance of the palace in its original form. A sketch of *Dara Shikoh Palace*, purportedly drawn in 1774 by an unknown artist, is available in public domain. It depicts a boundary wall, three bastions and Mughal type *chajjas* and nothing more. It is not even clear whether it depicts the palace or the boundary wall of the palace.

Dara Shikoh's life was a tragedy; he lies in an unmarked grave in the Humayun tomb complex. As a devout scholar, he established several libraries. However, these exhibit a feeling of gloom and despondency now, whether we observe the one at Delhi, or at Agra or even his *Pari Mahal* at Srinagar.

To come back to the Awadh connection with *Dara Shikoh Mahal*, Safdarjang got his son, Shuja-ud-Daula, married to Azmat-uz-Zahra, who would later become famous as *Bahu Begum*. The marriage was solemnised with great pomp and show, with the Emperor himself gracing the occasion (Bhasin, 2018). The marriage took place at *Dara Shikoh Mahal*. Far away from the Red Fort (possibly due to space constraints), Safdarjang, whose actual name was Abul Mansur Mirza Muhammad Muqim Ali Khan, had also built a pleasure garden called *Wazirpur,* for himself and his family. The name *Wazirpur* persists, with traces of the Nawabi garden, four tower-like bastions popularly known as *Burj-e-Mansur* or *Mansur ki Mandaiyan* and a Mughal-style pavilion (Plate 1) near Satyawati College at Delhi. The towers (or bastions) are octagonal in shape, with vaulted roofs, made of lakhauri bricks, granite stones and lime mortar. The pavilion, built with red sandstone is typically Mughal, with no trace of Lucknow's architectural influence. In any case, it was an early Nawabi structure and the Lucknow style developed much later.

Incidentally, Shuja-ud-Daula had been born in *Dara Shikoh Mahal*, just 14 years ago. Shuja-ud-Daula's son, Mirza Amani, was born at Delhi in the same palace on 17th September, 1748. He would later be known as Nawab Asaf-ud-Daula, builder of the famous *Rumi Darwaza* and *Bada Imambara* of Lucknow. Asaf-ud-Daula never re-visited Delhi, and neither did the latter Nawabs of Awadh. The Delhi connection was finally severed by Ghazi-ud-Din Haider, the 6th Nawab of Awadh, who declared himself *Badshah* (King) of Awadh in 1818. The property, however, remained under the ownership of the Awadh royalty, till the annexation of the kingdom by the British in 1856. Subsequently, ownerships became blurred and apparently Wajid Ali Shah, during his exile at Calcutta, had claimed that several properties of his ancestors in and around Delhi, including Safdarjang's *maqbara*, its adjoining gardens, as well as *Dara Shikoh Mahal* (*Haveli Sa'adat Khan*?) be restored to him (Llewellyn-Jones, 2014). That the claim was rejected outright by the British, will come as no surprise to the reader.

Almost half a century later, Sanderson (1915, 1916), who was the Superintendent, Muhammadan and British Monuments, Northern Circle, ASI, had listed several extant structures in *Shahjahanabad,* including those atttributed to Sa'adat Khan. These were broadly classified under *Nahr Saadat Khan* and included an unnamed mosque, a second mosque belonging to a camel driver, several gateways leading to the *haveli* of the Nawab Wazir (the term *haveli*, meaning mansion, was in use in Delhi and Rajasthan, but not in Lucknow), a *baradari* and another mosque built over *Nahr Saadat Khan* built by Jahandar Shah. A photograph of "Dara Shikoh Library", available in Sanderson's *List of Muhammadan and Hindu Monuments,* Vol. 1: *Shahjahanabad - Illustrations* (1915) at Sl. 409, offered no insight of the original structure, as it merely showed the northern terrace of the building, already modified for the Residency.

Chapter - 2

Jalalabad Fort

This derelict fort (not to be confused with a similar-named fort, famous for the First Anglo-Afghan War of 1842) of Lucknow has been referred to in various contexts, by many authors and historians, and yet, it remains shrouded in mystery and uncertainty. Situated in the south eastern outskirts of Lucknow city called Bijnor or Bijnaur (presently in Ashiana colony) today, detailed sketches of the fort by British army officers, Metcham (1858) and Dodgson (1860) are available in the public domain. Both sketches have depicted a moderately large structure with 5 bastions on each side, and a structure resembling a watch tower at one corner. The fort was shown to face a large lake or water body. A hazy photograph of the fort by an

Fig. 1: Painting of *Jalalabad Fort*, Lieut. CH Metcham (1858)

unknown photographer (Plate 2), presumably of the same period, confirms the exterior appearance, as sketched by Metcham and Dodgson. However, the water body, if at all present, is not evident in the photograph, which is of poor quality. Details or descriptions of the fort's interiors are not available anywhere. It is also not clear as to whether the structure was occupied during Nawabi rule, or if it was an abandoned structure. Most authors seem to agree that it was Nawab Safdarjang, the second Nawab Wazir of Awadh (1739-1753), who was the builder of this fort. The area was the scene of intense fighting, as General Outram's forces fought back Indian rebels stationed there in January and February 1858. Later, as the British began to reverse the freedom fighters' initial successes and regain control of Lucknow, their field of activity narrowed and fort was abandoned, serving no further strategic function.

According to Keene (1875), the ruined fort of *Jalalabad*, which was seized by Colin Campbell in his November advance to regain control of Lucknow, was believed to have been built by Shuja-ud-Daula as a defensive post against a possible attack by the British from the eastward. Beg (1911) also wrote that *"The fortress of Jellalabad, now a heap of ruins, is a work of great antiquity. Natives report that it was built by Shuja-ul-dowlah, after his defeat by the British in the Battle of Buxar in 1791."*

The native fortification at *Jalalabad*, however small, with only one regiment (the 71st), 500 *nujeebs* and 1200 *sowars* (of the 12 and 15 Irregular) and 2 guns (Rizvi and Bhargava, 1958) had a strategic location after *Alambagh*, for it was situated on the approach to Lucknow. Dodd (1859) reiterates that Colin Campbell crossed the Ganges on 9th of November, and joined Hope Grant's column on the same day at camp Banthra, six miles short of *Alambagh*. Wishing to have the aid of other detachments which were then on the road, he remained at Banthra till the morning of the 12th, when he started with the force which he had collected with so much trouble. Advancing towards the *Alambagh*, he defeated a party of the rebel soldiers in a skirmish "at a small fort called *Jellalabad*", a little way to the right of the main road, and five or six miles from the city. After this fort being taken and blown up, Sir Colin pushed on and encamped for the night outside the *Alambagh*. Outram's despatches (Forrest, 1893) from February 21 to March 14, 1858 constantly harp on the skirmishes which British troops faced in and around *Alambagh* and *Fort Jalalabad*. Innes (1895) also mentioned that Colin Campbell joined Hope Grant at Banthra on November 9, 1857. They concentrated forces at *Alambagh* on November 12, and afterwards, took possession of the "old fort of *Jellalabad*." Subsequent skirmishes at *Jalalabad* fort has been reported by Innes in the following days, forcing Campbell to move towards Dilkusha on March 2, after taking a wide detour from *Jalalabad*. Wickins (Wickins & Cadell, 1957) reported the same skirmishes when British troops moved further down the Lucknow-Cawnpore Road, from *Alambagh* to *Dilkusha*, where, unfortunately, *Jalalabad* fort was also situated, described as a "an old fort about a mile from the *Alambagh*."

Arthur Moffat Lang, a Lieutenant of the Bengal Engineers, detailed his stay in and around *Jalalabad* Fort in his *Diary and Letters* (Molesworth & Leslie, 1932). *Jalalabad* was described as a village and a fort, about 3 miles from *Alambagh*. The fort had solid mud walls, with flanking defences. In his writings, Lang off-handedly described his stay in the "old crumbling of fort of *Jalalabad*", from the 15th of February 1858, for about a month. The fort was used as commissariat (food stores) and engineer park (engineering equipment and vehicles), and faced period attacks from the "Pandies" (a derogatory term for Indian freedom fighters, originating from Mangal Pande, who had first rebelled against the British in March, 1857, setting off a chain of events, which culminated in Delhi and Lucknow). Much of the action as described by Lang was confined from *Alambagh*, to *Dilkusha*, gradually moving to La Martiniere and Lucknow city. Lang did not describe the eventual abandoning or blowing up (if at all) of *Jalalabad* in his memoirs. James Thornton (1895), a medical officer in the Bengal army likewise described his experiences when posted in the medical garrison at *Jalalabad* fort. A sketch in his book gives a similar look to *Jalalabad* fort, as given in earlier works. Only now, the muddy landscape and water bodies around the fort is evident. Nevill (1922) described the topography of Bijnor and the profusion of lakes (*jhils*) due to the ill drained land, through which the meandering Gomti river and its tributary, the Sai (or Adi Ganga) passed. Nevill reported that almost the whole of Bijnor was studded with numerous *jhils,* interspersed with *usar* (uncultivable, barren) land. This has been reiterated by Qureshi (2005) also.

To come back to the origins of the fort, Fuhrer (1891) had mentioned earlier that "*Bijnor town in tahsil Lakhnau, lat. 26°-44' N., long. 80°-56' E., 10 miles south of headquarters, possesses to the south, the ruins of an old brick fort, and on the west side, the extensive remains of brick tombs built over the Musalmans who fell in battle against the Hindus. The place is called the Ganj Shahidaan, or martyrs' gathering-place. Close to the Ganj Shahidaan is a tomb of immense size, ascribed to Malik Ambar, who, according to tradition, was killed with Salar Masud at Bahraich, but wandered back on his horse, a headless corpse, to Bijnor. The town is said to have been founded by, and to take its name from Bijli Raja, a Pasi, who built the great fort of Nathawan, about a mile to the north of Bijnor; an elevated mound of considerable extent and striking appearance from the wide plains in which it is situated still marks its site. This Raja is said to have possessed 12 forts, amongst which were Kali Pachchhim, Maati, Parwar, Purab, lying to the east of pargana Bijnor, and others whose names are forgotten, but which extended up to Sarsawaan and the Gumti in a north-eastern direction.*" Fuhrer did not mention the *Jalalabad* fort by name, which his compatriots had mentioned fleetingly, during their description of the events at Lucknow during 1857-58. However, Fuhrer's mention of Bijli Pasi, throws up the confirmation that the name and its associated legends have been around for quite some time and is not just a recent phenomenon of Dalit resurgence. Bardic traditions, without adequate epigraphic evidence however, mention the fall of the *Suryavanshi* dynasty of Ayodhya, and the subsequent spread of indigenous tribes in the area, who established their own small principalities. The *Pasis* dominated the area of modern Hardoi, Malihabad and Lucknow, whereas *Bhars* established themselves in Mohanlalganj. *Kurmis* were dominant in Mahona and all of them were said to possess strong mud forts and hold positions of authority in their respective areas of settlement. Later, the Rajputs around Delhi and Kannauj made significant inroads into the territories of these tribes. Amalgamation of different communities also took place. According to local legend, the *Pasi* community desired to have a marriage alliance with a Brahmin girl, for one of their sons. The Brahmin community received help from Jai Chand of Kannauj and Bijnor was laid waste. It may not be possible to describe the Rajput invasions chronologically (Neville, 1904, 1922), but it is certain that with time, the *Bais* of Baiswara established suzerainty over Nigohan, Sissaindi and Bijnor. Similarly, the Panwars, Solankis and Chauhans drove out the *Pasis, Bhars* together with other local feudal chieftains and settled themselves in various demarcated areas.

The first Muslim movement in the area appears to have been during Mohammad Bakhtiyar Khilji in 1202, and what started as a trickle became a regular influx over a period of time. With the advent of the Mughals, Muslim occupation of the territory became the norm, although the Rajputs continued to hold sway in some areas. However, the fortunes of Lucknow were about to change when Akbar reorganised his empire into 12 *suba* or provinces (during 1572-1580), and gave the governorship of Awadh *suba* to Sheikh Abdur Rahim of Bijnor. The descendents of Sheikh Abdur Rahim came to be known as the *Sheikhzadas* of Lucknow. Qureshi (2005) provides an interesting snippet of information about one Saleh Mohammad, Mughal governor of Awadh (after Jahangir's death) having frequent conflicts with the *Bais* Rajputs of Baiswara. Saleh Mohammad developed the localities of Salehnagar and Mohammadi (in his own name) in the area (extant today) and also built a very strong fort near a *jheel*. Qureshi further states that it was confiscated during the reign of Nawab Shuja-ud-Daula and later, Asaf-ud-Daula extricated the wood and stones of this fort, for use in his own buildings. However, Qureshi states that, "*the outlines of the fort and a part of its south-eastern structure with two old wells are very well marked.*" Tandan (2001) states that the *Jalalabad* fort was "commissioned" by Nawab Safdarjang to keep an eye on the powerful *Bais* Rajput chieftains of Rae Bareli district.

Abbas (2009) stated that a ruined stone fort stood in the area around 1937 – 38, as a photograph of the same was available with the Archaeological Survey of India. Recent developments in the area, including the renaming of the ruins of the fort as *Bijli Pasi Qila* and the filling up of the lake to develop the *Smriti Upvan* have created controversies (Shah, 2008), a discussion on which is beyond the scope of this book. Actually, the existence and location of the fort is not in doubt, as it has been clearly shown in several British relief maps of 1857 - 58, which detailed the entrenchment of British troops and also depicted the movement of Colin Campbell during the relief of Lucknow. However, during the Nawabi reign, there was no mention of this fort on the outskirts of Lucknow. So possibly, it was just a ruinous structure even then, otherwise it would have been inhabited and recorded. Logically, it is difficult to believe that Shuja-ud-Daula either built the fort (to counter the British), or even dismantled it for no good reason. The premise that Saleh Mohammad or Safdarjang built the fort to counter the *Bais* Rajputs is stronger. However, Safdarjang's name was Mohammad Muqim, and Shuja-ud-Daula's name was Jalal-ud-Din Haider. So Safdarjang naming the fort after his son, seems rather far fetched. So possibly Shuja-ud-Daula built it. But why would he then dismantle it?

The biggest controversy, however, is whether the present ruins in modern *Ashiana* colony of Lucknow are from one of Bijli Pasi's forts or do they belong to a Nawabi fort? Neville (1922) describes Bijnor (*Pargana* Bijnaur, *Tahsil* Lucknow, Lucknow District) as a town founded by Bijli Raja, a *Pasi*, whose fort at Nathawan, was about a mile to the north of the town; the fort was an elevated mound of considerable extent and striking appearance. He describes Fort *Jalalabad* separately under Lucknow City (Lucknow District) as "a mile further south, beyond a huge *jhil* which forms one of the sources of the Bakh river (*sic*), and to the west of the road is the old ruined fortress of *Jalalabad*, built by Nawab Safdarjang, to protect his capital from any southern invader and to intimidate the rebellious lords of the Baiswara. The fort is a large imposing structure, square in shape, with numerous semi-circular bastions." This matches with the sketches of the *Jalalabad* fort available in literature. Neville does not correlate the fort of *Bijli Pasi* with the *Jalalabad* fort; he discusses them separately. The Bakh river mentioned by him exists today, as a "nala" or drain.

Examining the time lines, Jaichand of Kannauj (with whom the legendary Bijli Pasi had a run-in) ruled during the years: 1170-1194. A mud fort lasting for 900 years (after being besieged periodically, first by the Rajputs and then by the British) seems somewhat far-fetched. It is entirely possible, however, that the present Nawabi fort stands at the same place where one of Bijli Pasi's mud forts stood originally, possibly due to its strategic location and proximity to a water body, which would have served as a source of water (Similar to the premise of *Qila Lakhna* and *Macchi Bhavan* Fort discussed later). Detailed historiographic studies and archaeological interventions are therefore essential before the truth can finally emerge on scientific grounds.

Chapter - 3

Macchi Bhavan

Macchi Bhavan (Plate 3) can be called the Avalon (of Arthurian legend fame) of Lucknow. This is because there are several descriptions of this citadel, few photographs, fewer sketches, many tales, many names and many descriptions given by travellers, historians, soldiers and writers. And yet, there seems to be no unequivocal account of this legendary edifice. Nor are there any signs of it in present times. No one seems to know exactly who built it, what was inside it and how and why it was destroyed. In the following pages, we shall glean historiographic details of the structure, from the various scattered details available and try to derive a conclusive picture of *Macchi Bhavan* in a logical and unbiased manner.

The origin of Lucknow city is itself shrouded in mystery; mythology, religion, fantasy, oral tradition as well as history often get mixed up with outright falsehoods and urban legends, whenever any discussion of the city's origins is taken up. Broadly, it is accepted that the settlement was established by Lakshman, brother of Ram, who ruled from neighbouring *Ayodhya*. In fact, the term, *Awadh* is itself derived from *Ayodhya*. It is not disputed that a hillock called *Lakshman Tila* was the nucleus of the settlement of Lucknow, which was also known as *Lakhshmanpur* or *Lakhanpur*. Later, during the 5th and 6th centuries BC, there is mention that the kingdom of *Kosala* existed in the region, which was later encompassed in the *Magadh* empire. The Gurjara-Pratiharas ruled over the region during the 8th to 11th century AD. The depredations of Islamic invaders started shortly afterwards. In the meantime, the area, loosely co-notated as *Awadh*, (the geographical boundaries of Awadh have varied constantly over time) split up under several small principalities, ruled by indigenous tribes such as *Bhars*, *Kurmis*, *Pasis*, to name a few. The area did not have the flat topography we see today, but even then, the Gomti river was the lifeline of the settlement, much like the

Saryu or Ghagra river, which wound its way in what would later be known as *Bangla* or Faizabad. Geological data, as well as artworks and historical references indicate unequivocally that Lucknow's undulating layout resulted in the formation of streams and water bodies in the area (especially after the monsoon rains), some of them so vast, that they had to be traversed by boat. Hence, another possibility for the origin of Lucknow's name could be due to the presence of *lakhs* (hundreds of thousands) of *naus* (boats) in the area. Although it is doubtful that the meagre population of Lucknow of old would require such a multitude of boats, such suppositions no doubt add charm to the mythos of the city's origins.

If we go by oral tradition, the nucleus of the *Macchi Bhavan* appears to have been laid when the area was thus inhabited by indigenous tribes, and the name, *Qila Lakhna* might be attributed to the person who first established this fortification (Anderson, 1913). In all probability, it would have been a mud fort, but situated on an elevation, and hence holding a commanding position. This commanding landscape was utilised by Sheikh Abdur Rahim of Bijnor, (who had been appointed as Governor of Awadh by Emperor Akbar) for building residences for himself and his sons. Subsequently, this five palace complex came to be called *Panch Mahalla*, with its imposing gateway facing the west, known as the *Sheikhan Darwaza*. Descendants of the Sheikh, referred to as the *Sheikhzadas*, held sway over Lucknow till the arrival of Burhan-ul-Mulk in 1722. Nawab Safdarjang (1739 – 1754), followed by Shuja-ud-Daula are credited to have made additions to this palace complex and the term, *Macchi Bhavan* appears to have been used from then onwards (Rizvi & Bhargava, 1958), with the main gateway now sporting the ubiquitous fish symbol on its spandrels. Thomas Daniell's epic painting (1801) depicts the gateway in all its glory, standing proud but isolated with a steep ramp leading up to its entrance. No battlements, fortifications or walls with are seen, but the ramp itself and the elephant approaching the gateway gives a perspective of the gateway's proportions.

The term, *Macchi Bhavan* has also been attributed to another possible reason: the presence of a building with 26 arches, each arch having an ornamentation of two fishes on its spandrels - giving rise to the term, *macchi bavan* or 52 fishes. However, this theory seems somewhat far-fetched and hypothetical. The extensive use of the fish symbol by Lucknow's Nawabi rulers is also attributed to the *Mahi Maratib*, a high honour in the Mughal court initiated by Emperor Shah Jahan, and conferred to Nawab Safdarjang by Muhammad Shah "Rangila." But there are no instances of it being displayed by Awadh rulers in its actual form as a heraldry i.e. metallic fish head with prominent teeth, mounted on a pole. Another theory, more apocryphal than historical, relates to an incident in which Burhan-ul-Mulk crossing the Ganges at Farrukhabad, on his way to Awadh, had a fish leaping into his lap. It was considered a good omen and its skeleton was treasured in the royal family (Awasthi, 2014) and henceforth, the fish symbol assumed a prominent position in the insignia of Lucknow's Nawabi dynasty. The heraldry of Awadh and the animal connection has been discussed in detail in Chapter 8 of this book.

The *Machhi Bhavan* palace complex remained under constant occupation (and modification) under Awadh nobility, with western writers and artists later referring to it as the palace of Shuja-ud-Daula (1754 – 1775). Joseph Tieffenthaler (1765), a Jesuit missionary who visited Lucknow, wrote about the Five Palaces resting upon a high elevation with walls and high towers overlooking the Gomti river.

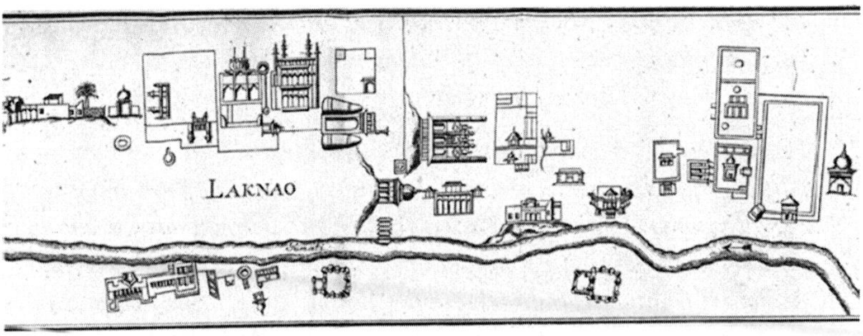

Fig. 2: Plan of Lucknow, Joseph Tieffenthaler (1765)

Nawab Asaf-ud-Daula, who shifted his capital to Lucknow in 1775 initially stayed in the *Machhi Bhavan* (Plate 4), but preferred to establish his own *Daulat Khana Asafi* palace complex later on. Apparently, his additions / modifications in the *Machhi Bhavan* did not find favour with his grandmother, the venerable Nawab Begum, who chose to complain about it to the Mughal Emperor! Other European travellers and artists, who described *Macchi Bhavan* of that period included Laurent de Federbe (1775) and William Hodges (1782). However, British scholar, Francis Gladwin (1785) gave a detailed description of the complex, which is reproduced below:

Gladwin's Account

1. *Is an area called Panch Mahalla, for his equipage and attendants* (referring to Nawab Asaf-ud-Daula). *The entrance to this area is through*

lofty gateways. Over the first is a room called Naubat Khana, or orchestra for martial music, which plays morning and evening.

2. *State apartments encompassing a square garden, together with an external enclosure for smaller rooms, constitute the court, called Bowli* (step well), *from a large well within it, which encloses a staircase and smaller recesses, with openings in the well, from top to bottom. There rooms are calculated* (sic) *for cool retirement during the* (summer?) *months; the apertures through the wall of the well, and the dripping of the waters, renders the air quite refreshing. At the corner opposite the Bowli is an arcaded chamber with a piazza, for sleeping during the summer heats* (sic). *The dimensions of it are about fourteen feet square, with a boarded* (?) *floor. Purdahs (falling curtains) of khus-khus* (species of sweet scented grass) *interwoven fill the arcades. All round the piazza are fountains, falling into a carved marble basin or trough, from where servants continuously sprinkle the purdahs. The hot winds blowing on the purdahs perfectly allay the heat, and sometimes, when violent, renders the cold almost intolerable.*

3. *Parallel to the second court, and at the eastward of it, is a handsome edifice, raised on an arched terrace, entirely of stone. This fabric* (sic), *called Sungee Dalan, comprises a grand hall, surrounded with a double arcade, crowned with four cupolas at the corners, and one at the principal front, covered with copper doubly gilt. At the extremities of the terrace are two wings, for morning and evening resort* (sic). *From both fronts extends a long flower garden, divided into parterres* (a level space in a garden occupied by an ornamental arrangement of flower beds) *by walks and fountains. Along the wide walls runs a corridor, forming one continued arbour of vines, which shades its whole roof. Into this garden are four entrances; one on the north side, through a covered passage, for the access of the ladies; two others through spacious gateways on the east and west; and a fourth from the fourth* (sic), *under another stone building, surmounted also by gilt domes. Within the precinct of the gardens is also a small mosque, with gilt minars, commodious offices, and swings for ladies' exercise.*

4. *To the north of the Sungee Dalan is another garden court, containing public offices, erected by Shuja-ud-Daula, called Mutchee Bowan* (Macchi Bhavan), *remarkable for nothing further than being the first structure of the subahs at Lucknow; for the rest of this palace was built by the present Nawab.*

5. *In a line with the Mutchee Bowan, and to the left of it, lies the zenana. Three heavy piles of unshapely houses, called Sheesh Mahal, Khurd Mahal and Rang Mahal (or generally Mahalsarai), the walls whereof being high, with few windows, and those small and latticed, nothing of course can be discerned within them. From exterior appearance, however, this harem seems fashioned like others of the country, which are, in general, oblong gardens, with fountains, whereof a kind of summer house in the centre. At each end is usually a hall, with four smaller apartments, and as many on the ground floor; the whole fronted with arcades and seah-bauns* (awnings?), *or cloths stretched out from the top of the arcades and supported by poles, in order to shade off the glare of light and heat. Along the side walls within, are offices of female domestics, and without, at the gates, rooms for guards and eunuchs. If the women are numerous, several zenanas are added of the like form. The ladies of family or distinction, or who are favourites, have each their separate dwellings. There being no windows on the outside, the zenanas become often so excessively close in the summer, as to threaten putrid disorders; to obviate which, the women are removed to tents in the country. When they travel, their conveyance is in covered seats on elephants, or in covered palanquins.*

6. *Separated from the palace, by the street only, to the eastward is a flower-garden, called Hussain Bagh, bordering the river; and enclosed with a brick-wall covered with vines. In its front stands three stone bastions, the two corner ones supporting, on arches, two oval-fluted cupolas, covered with copper, gilt. On the centre bastion stands an octagonal summer-house, with a flat roof; within the garden are parterres, fountains, baths and dressing rooms. Before all the gateways of the palace and zenanas, are screens, or small walls, which conceal the entrances.*

After describing Asaf-ud-Daulah's daily routine and habits, Gladwin continued:

Contiguous to the palace is a museum called the Inah Konnah (sic), *an aviary, a menagerie, and an armory, all worthy of observation.*

It is obvious that during Gladwin's visit (1785), Asaf-ud-Daula was still residing within the *Macchi Bhavan* and not in the *Daulat Khana*. If we are to take his narration at face value, the original *Panch Mahalla* palaces were of no great account (by then), but the later *nawabi* rulers had embellished the complex with various impressive architectural additions and gardens. Gladwin describes the *baoli* (step well), but does *not* mention the adjacent grand *Asafi Imambara*, the *Rumi Darwaza* or the *Asafi Masjid*. Warren Hastings had visited Lucknow in 1784 and stayed comfortably in the *baoli* palace complex, and yet, he had also not mentioned about the construction activity in the vicinity, although 1784 is often cited as the year when the great *Imambara – Asafi Masjid* complex was completed (although Asaf-ud-Daula had been apparently short of funds during that time). Keshani (2006), in his seminal paper has cogently pointed out that the above date needs to be re-examined and reaffirmed, as there are enough indications about the complex being actually completed in 1790. Some venerable authors have credited Viscount Valentia (George Annesley, Earl of Mountnorris), for staying in the *baoli* palace in 1803 (during the times of Sa'adat Ali Khan) and describing it in detail. This is patently erroneous, as his memoirs (Valentia, 1809) do *not* mention the actual place of his stay in Lucknow and what he described was actually a Nawabi *hammam* (sunken bath), in all its luxury, the use of which had been provided to him by the reigning Nawab, on the former's request. He described the *Ina Khana* museum (mentioned by Gladwin as above) and its whimsical collection of curios and mementoes procured by Asaf-ud-Daula. In his writings, the Viscount was not in awe of the *Rumi Darwaza*, but expressed genuine admiration for the *Imambara* complex, including its mosque and gateways. He specifically mentioned the "*Bolee* (sic) *palace*" being on one side of the *Imambara* garden and the mosque on the other side.

The Viscount was also singularly impressed by the *Sungi Dalan* (described by Gladwin above), describing it thus: "*It is in my opinion, a very elegant building, perfectly in Eastern style, open in all sides, and supported by pillars. It is, as the name designates, built of stone, but the whole is painted a deep red colour, except the domes that cover the towers at the corner. The center room is large; two narrower on each side make the shape of the whole building a square, with circular towers at the four corners. It is raised one storey from the ground, and a large terrace connects it with a smaller but similar building. A most magnificent musnud of gold, covered with brocade and embroidered wreaths of roses, was placed at one end of the large apartment. We dined in the smaller, on one side, whence we had a view of the bason* (sic) *of water, which extends to the hummaum* (sic) *attached to the palace, where I used to bath. The sides of the bason* (sic) *were covered with coloured lamps; a complete trellis work of the same extended on each side of the walk.*" Indeed, the Viscount was definitely not confused between a *hammam* and the *baoli* palace, and his detailed observations appear quite logical when the time-lines and chronology of construction activity of the complex. are examined. This prompts one to conclude that the *baoli palace* was actually a constituent of the older *Panch Mahalla* complex, which was architecturally incorporated in the later constructions of Asaf-ud-Daula. Colonel Antoine-Louis Henri de Polier (1741–1795) was a Swiss engineer (from France) who spent several years in India, first in Calcutta, and then in the court of Asaf-ud-Daula at Lucknow. However, Llewellyn-Jones (1984) has attributed the architectural marvel of the *baoli* palace to Polier in one of her papers.

To come back to the *Macchi Bhavan* and its wavering fortunes, there is no doubt that Asaf-ud-Daula extended its environs from a fortification to a luxurious palace complex, running parallel to the Gomti river, with bastions and high castellated walls, the *Rumi Darwaza* now being the *de novo* entrance to the palace complex from the western side of his new capital city. The old stone bridge remained at right angles to this immense complex, but as one approached Lucknow, it was still the *Teele Wali Masjid* which appeared from afar, due to its high, prominent position atop a hillock. With the construction of the imposing *Rumi Darwaza*, the older *Sheikhan Darwaza* lost its vantage status, but continued to exist nevertheless, as a sub-entrance to the older palaces, which at one point of time, had also accommodated Nawab Begum and Bahu Begum. As one entered the complex through the *Rumi Darwaza*, he encountered the first courtyard of the *Asafi Imambara*, with its entrance on the right hand side and *jawabi* (facsimile) gate on the left, serving as a *Naqqar Khana* or drum house. Further down, one passed through a rather modest *tripolia* gate (now demolished) and then, came face to face with the smaller *Sheikhan Darwaza*, leading to the older palaces. On the right, unconnected with the *Sheikhan Darwaza* was a vast assemblage of residences, *zenana* quarters (many with awnings described by Gladwin above), pavilions and gardens, the area roughly corresponding with the present day *Hussainabad College* and King George Medical College (now University). Bahu Begum, it seems, now preferred to stay away from her son, in her own palace with a golden cupola, appropriately named *Sunheri Burj* (now demolished), which was situated to the right, almost adjacent to the *Rumi Darwaza*, but outside Asaf-ud-Daula's palace-cum-*Imambara* complex. This overall aspect of Lucknow's palace complex, including *Macchi Bhavan* is possible after perusing through Beato's post 1857 photographs, captured from atop one of the minarets of the *Asafi Masjid* as well as a photograph, by an unknown photographer, available with the National Army Museum Picture Library, London.

With time, the *Macchi Bhavan* palace complex had become neglected and decrepit, but continued to be occupied by lesser nobles of Lucknow's *nawabi* dynasty, as well as widows of former rulers as royalty soon shifted to the *Farhat Bakhsh-Chattar Manzil* complex during the times of Sa'adat Ali Khan, Ghazi-ud-Din Haider and subsequent rulers, culminating in the *Kaiserbagh* palace complex of Wajid Ali Shah. Things, however, rapidly took a turn for the worse, when the British annexed Awadh in 1856 and took radical decisions regarding the occupancy of the former *nawabi* palaces and houses. Now, British officials and soldiers could enter premises hitherto forbidden and off-bound, to decide upon the fate of its inhabitants and the buildings themselves. Thus, many palaces and stately buildings were appropriated for their own use and misuse, to be more specific. For example, the *Kadam Rasul*, an Islamic religious structure, was converted to a powder magazine, with scant regard to the sentiments of the local Muslim populace. Similarly, buildings such as *Taaron Wali Kothi*, *Kothi Hayat Baksh*, *Khurshid Manzil*, the *Chaupar* stables and many others were put to various uses. The *Daulat Khana* became the residence of Brigadier Gray, while the *Sheesh Mahal* palace was converted to army stores. *Musa Bagh Kothi* was occupied by the 4th and 7th Regiments of the Oudh Irregular Infantry. Low paid Company officials, often with unimpressive family, financial and educational backgrounds, could now stay in palaces, strut about palace grounds wearing *sola topis* or canter around on horseback, lording over the local populace – such was the miserable fate of the original inhabitants of the city, in that dark phase of Lucknow's history. It must be kept in mind that *this humiliation of Awadh nobility and the conversion of Lucknow to a militarised zone was much before the 1857 uprising*. Thus, a merciless occupation was imposed, even when the so-called annexation had been totally peaceful, without a drop of blood being shed, and the ruler peacefully leaving his capital city after consoling his subjects. Nothing can be more indicative of the ulterior motives of the British or their hypocrisy (despite crocodile's tears and righteous declarations otherwise), when their indiscretions against a peaceful native populace and its rulers are thus listed and observed critically.

Post 1856, the illegal and unethical colonial occupation of Nawabi property (Jafri, 2020) inadvertently resulted in a few more contemporary descriptions of *Macchi Bhavan*, this time from the pens of British officials and soldiers. John James McLeod Innes, a British soldier, who was active during the defence of Lucknow under the command of Henry Lawrence and later, Henry Havelock, penned his memories in his book (1885), describing the sequence of events which led to the abandonment of *Macchi Bhavan* and concentration at the Residency, after the defeat of the British at Chinhat. Innes describes the *Macchi Bhavan* as an old massive-looking pile, of castellated appearance, about a hundred yards square, perched on a natural eminence about thirty feet above the adjacent streets and roads.

The platform on which it was built was scarped and supported by stout revetment walls, broken at short intervals into the usual Oriental semi-circular bastions, with the city or western front pierced by a gateway in a double-storied guard-house, strengthened by flanking and other defences. All this was close to the masonry bridge and the river, and commanded the city to the west. Towards the east there were two courtyards at lower levels, lined with small buildings and store-rooms, with a gateway at the east end corresponding with the gateway already mentioned at the western face. There were large and airy arcaded halls along one side of the pile, but the remaining rooms were not suitable for use except by natives or for stores. Though much had been cleared out, the whole place was greatly dilapidated, but its chief defect lay in the passages and communications. These and the doorways were so narrow that carts and guns could not pass through the square pile at all, or get from one end of the position to the other. All the roofs were flat, and, like the terraces, were lined with parapet walls.

Martin Richard Gubbins, of the Bengal Civil Service and the controversial Financial Commissioner of Oudh (Awadh) during the uprising, in his memoirs (1858) devoted an entire chapter on *Macchi Bhavan*. He narrated that Henry Lawrence had been searching for a place of strength for stocking ammunition and military stores and considered the *Machhi Bhavan* for such a use, after repair. Gubbins described the approach to the Bhavan as "leading from the Residency towards the *Daulat Khana* and Hussainabad, up and parallel to the stream of the Gomti, one passes under the walls of the *Macchi Bhavan*, which from this and some other positions on the river has an imposing appearance." According to Gubbins, the area comprised three plateaus, of which the lowest was little above the level of the road, and the highest towered above the neighbouring buildings. The high-road skirted the whole length of the position, and followed the level of the ground, which rose naturally from the lowest eastern plateau to that of the highest on the west side. From the road on that, i.e., the west extreme of the position, a short but steep ascent led to the main gateway. The highest plateau was covered with the pavilions originally built by the *Sheikhs (=Sheikhzadas)* of Lucknow, which were in a very dilapidated condition, and contained the modern residence of one of the ex-King's brothers, Nawab Yahya Ali Khan. On the second plateau stood a handsome *baradari* (open arcaded pavilion), and a few smaller buildings. The lower plateau was an open square, surrounded by low ranges of masonry sheds. There was no gate leading directly from the outside into the second plateau ; but two opened into the lower, one at the east end, the second from the main road on the north side. There was no appearance of military defence in the character of the buildings, except in the high and buttressed wall, which rose from the main road to the buildings of the highest plateau. Gubbins further stated that on the south side, the ground was of the same level as that on which *Macchi Bhavan* was built, densely covered with native buildings, which extended upto the walls of the place itself, and completely overlooking, the second and lower plateaus. From the upper plateau, *Macchi Bhavan* had a commanding view of the Stone Bridge and although the *Bhavan* had been the stronghold of the earlier *Sheikhs* (=*Sheikzadaas*) of Lucknow, under the later *Nawabi* dynasty, it had been in use as a store and was in a state of disrepair.

Fig. 3: Sketch of *Macchi Bhavan,* McLeod Innes (1896)

On May 16, 1857, on receiving news of the outbreak at Meerut, *Macchi Bhavan* was fortified by the Light Company of the 13 (400 men, including 100 Europeans) and about 20 guns (Anderson, 1913), with measures taken for its thorough cleansing. Supplies continued to be brought in the *Bhavan* and stored. This was in addition to the Residency which was being garrisoned simultaneously. June 13, 1857 saw increased cases of cholera among the men stationed at *Macchi Bhavan,* which led to the shifting of guns, stores and supplies to the Residency. The *Bhavan* also saw the hanging of four Indian "emissaries" from Benaras and elsewhere who had been charged for conspiracy and sentenced to death. Later, Lawrence inspected the *Bhavan's* premises and ordered men and small ammunition to be transferred to the Residency. Two Indian rebels were again executed at the *Bhavan* on June 23, as Lawrence divided his attention between the Residency and the *Macchi Bhavan* fortifications. Dense clusters of 'native' houses in the immediate vicinity of the *Bhavan* were also either knocked down or unroofed. On the west side of the *Bhavan*, work commenced on construction of a heavy tower under the supervision of Lt. Innes of the Engineering Corps. The aim of the tower was to have a vantage position over the area, including the Stone Bridge, the *Imambaras* and a number of mosques in the vicinity. By July 1, movement between the Residency and the *Macchi Bhavan* had become risky and the only communication possible was by semaphore. Lawrence realised that it was no longer prudent to stretch resources and simultaneously hold on to two positions. Orders were therefore given for the destruction of the fort and its stores, lest it fall in the hands of the freedom fighters. *Macchi Bhavan*'s store of 240 barrels of gunpowder and 594,000 rounds of ball and gun ammunition erupted in a massive explosion, serving the twin purpose of preventing the arsenal from falling in the rebels' hands, and also to shock and awe the native populace.

In his book published in 1896, Innes provided a sketch of the fort's gateway (Fig. 3), as it was in 1857, the comparison of which with Daniell's version (1801) throws up several interesting observations. The gateway is composed of several storeys, the two side wings being of four storeys and the rest being three storeys high. The ground floor had one entrance on each side, with small square windows; the first floor had a triple arched veranda, isolated structure with Innes' sketch being strikingly similar to Daniell's, except (1) the gateway is now a part of a substantial boundary wall with bastions. Inside, one can see a number of tall buildings in a rather congested arrangement and (2) the ground floor and the triple arched second floor have now been blocked, leading to a solid appearance, but devoid of aesthetics. The ramp remains, but is not so steep, because the surrounding grounds are now raised as a sort of glacis. The arched entrance is extant, but now sports a substantial wooden door with iron supports.

The British had not abandoned the fort totally; they had merely blown up their stock of ammunition and firepower, but the battered fort remained and fell into the hands of the freedom fighters, post June 1857, who started to fortify the city of Lucknow by way of trenches, ditches, embankments and upright wooden slats. *Macchi Bhavan* was also fortified, by way of ditches dug deep in the earth, upright teak timbers, and the gateway being bricked up, leaving a small embrasure at the top (Llewellyn-Jones (2007). This is evident from Beato's photograph, post 1857, which shows the ruins of the gateway, the defensive trenches and wooden barricades. More importantly, it shows in detail, some of the buildings *inside* the fort, standing proud and strong, despite the mayhem and destruction all around. The buildings, which were never studied or described, have a distinctive, non-Islamic look, especially the one on the right, next to the broken boundary wall. This particular building repeats the triangular pediment and the two circular mumty rooms (Fig. 10) on the rood, typically found in Lucknow's Nawabi buildings, described in another chapter. On the left, we again see buildings with Lucknow's typical hybrid architecture.

This historic fort of Lucknow, however, survived to see another half a century, before being demolished in phases, again by Lucknow's colonial masters, for setting up of the King George's Medical College in its premises.

Pleasure Gardens and Imposing Gateways

Defaced ruins of architecture and statuary, like the wrinkles of decrepitude of a once beautiful woman, only make one regret that one did not see them when they were enchanting.

—*Horace Walpole*

History is that certainty produced at the point where the imperfections of memory meet the inadequacies of documentation.

—*Julian Barnes*

Chapter - 4

Pleasure Gardens

Lucknow has always been known as the city of gardens. Even in present times, the city has several areas and localities named after gardens, which are no longer extant *e.g. Sundar Bagh*, *Almas Bagh*, *Khurshid Bagh*, *Chand Bagh*, *Chiraya Bagh*, *Bagh Sher Jung*, *Ram Bagh*, *Lotan Bagh*, *Dali Bagh, Phool Bagh, Lalbagh, Wazir Bagh*, *Teli Bagh*, *Mausam Bagh, Nazar Bagh, Buland Bagh, Lotan Bagh, Mehtab Bagh, Mehdi Bagh, Sajjad Bagh* and many others. There is evidence of at least thirty four gardens (Tandan, 2001) in and around the environs of Lucknow, having been commissioned during the Nawabi period. Out of these, twenty four had been apparently established during the 18th century and eleven in the 19th. With time and changing fortunes, many such Nawabi gardens underwent changes (Sinha, 2009) in usage patterns, although the names persisted. During colonial rule, several such Nawabi gardens were appropriated as *nazul* (property escheated or lapsed to the state / confiscated estate), and either parcelled / sold off to buyers (typically *ta'aluqdars*) or converted to public utilities. *Aishbagh* was used for setting up a water treatment and purification plant, together with several industrial units. *Charbagh* was converted to a railway station and *Banarsi Bagh* metamorphosed to the colonial style Wingfield Park. *Badshah Bagh* was converted to a university campus and *Dilkusha* became the new British cantonment. Some *baghs* (gardens) were left to decay, e.g. *Sikandar Bagh* (a portion of which was used for establishing a government horticultural garden, now National Botanical Research Institute), *Vilayati Bagh* and *Musa Bagh*. The former *Mohammad Bagh* or "Prophet's Garden" was razed, gardened (as per colonial norms), bisected with a broad mall, shaded with mangoes and soft sand on ether side. It now housed an elite club (Plate 13) for defence service officers, called *Cantonment Club* (later *Mohammad Bagh Club*), which boasted of a theatre, cricket ground and bandstand, among flower-beds and pergolas sheltering palms and ferns (Cuthell, 1905).

Bandariya Bagh became part cemetery and a school. *Alambagh's* walls and bastions were removed, so that now *Alambagh Kothi* and *Alambagh Gate*, together with the accompanying *Shahi Masjid* stood in isolation, separated from each other, adjacent to Havelock's grave. It's vast grounds were also used for establishing a railway yard. Similarly, the Isabella Thoburn College occupied a major chunk of *Chand Bagh*, for its campus, which shifted from its former premises in *Lalbagh.*

In general, urban remodelling programmes had been initiated by the British to make the city "safe" (from European viewpoint), salubrious and urbane, in tune with the metropolitan ideal of the town-hall / railway-station / museum / menagerie / public park combine. These, with embellishments such as statues, fountains and clock towers, became the new urban landmark. The model had been successfully applied in Delhi (Sharma, 2005). It would also be applied in Lucknow - the two cities being the nerve centres of the 1857 holocaust in north India. A common pattern thus emerged - that of the *Qila Masjid Bagh Haveli* (Fort Mosque Garden Palace) ensemble being targeted, as these were viewed as rallying points for future uprisings. In the name of security, demolitions, coercive seizures and rapid reconstruction were sought to be legitimised, although several places of worship would also necessarily be desecrated in the process (Mancini and Bresnahan, 2015).

Kaiserbagh, of course, faced the biggest casualty, because unlike other *baghs*, which were basically pleasure gardens with pavilions and a building or two, *Kaiserbagh* had been the palace complex and residence of the last king of Awadh, Wajid Ali Shah. *Kaiserbagh* had also been the stronghold of Begum Hazrat Mahal and her band of intrepid freedom fighters, and therefore it deserved to be looted, demolished and trampled upon (Plate 32). To "*level to the ground, as that is the palace where our chief enemies have resided during the rebellion and whence they have issued their proclamations and orders against us*" (Lewellyn-Jones, 1992). Against such popular venomous sentiments, it is indeed a wonder that we can at least see parts of *Kaiserbagh* today (Plate 33), instead of a levelled ground (or mound), because fortunately, the British subsequently and prudently decided to utilise the complex for ensuring the appeasement and allegiance of the landed "barons" or *ta'aluqdars* of Awadh. By 1862, *sanads* (deeds) had been handed out to various *ta'aluqdars* in recognition of their war efforts in support of the British during 1857 (Krishna, 2014). However, it was a truncated *Kaiserbagh* which was handed out; drastic landscaping and large scale demolitions had already been carried out, which had changed the very face of the original complex, dedicated perhaps to Caesar (Cuthell,

1905). A road was now bisecting the premises, the *Safed Baradari* or *Qasr-ul-Aza* had been re-modelled, and the low boundary walls had all but vanished. Many *kothis*, together several gates had disappeared (including the famed *Jal Pari* or Mermaid Gate) described elsewhere. No trace remained of the *Hazrat Bagh*. The *Lanka* or open air pavilion (Plate 31) was allowed to dwindle and finally demolished, to make way for the Amir-ud-Daula Public Library. The *Pari Khana* was replaced by the Canning College building. The tombs of Sa'adat Ali Khan and Khurshid Zadi and the *Roshan-ud-Daula Kothi*, which had been incorporated in the palace complex became free-standing once again. Palaces such as *Chaulakhi Kothi* and *Khas Muqam* (residence of Wajid Ali Shah) vanished. *Zard Kothi* (where Outram had met Malika Kishwar and then Wajid Ali Shah, prior to the annexation) became history. The small, early British-era *Kaiser Pasand cemetery* became disconnected from the palace complex once again. Among the various properties handed out to the *ta'aluqdars*, some were maintained well as per the pre-conditions, some were neglected and started to decay, some were structurally modified to suit individual requirements, and lastly, the titles of few went under dispute, or were transferred, leading to litigation. The British India Association of Awadh or *Anjuman-e-Hind, Awadh* remained the primary stakeholder in the *Kaiserbagh* heritage zone, with the Archaeological Survey of India playing a minor role in repairing and maintaining some structures and the Lucknow Development Authority looking after the green belt. This multiplicity of authorities resulted in overlapping of roles and responsibilities, and the maintenance of the zone became highly skewed over time. What is accepted as *Kaiserbagh* today is generally the central quadrangle, with the parks in the middle, the residential buildings and two gates, Bhatkhande University in the north and Amir-ud-Daula Library to the south. But originally, the quadrangle was but the then nucleus of *Kaiserbagh*. It's reach spread much wider, which was gobbled up by later civic additions and modifications.

So what was the original *Kaiserbagh* like? There are hardly any detailed descriptions of the palace complex-cum-gardens during the times of Wajid Ali Shah. However, few paintings of the period by unidentified artists, do give an idea of the splendour of the place. One painting shows Wajid Ali Shah riding through the quadrangle (Plate 11), with the western gate in the backdrop. Another painting has an aerial perspective of the central quadrangle, with ornate gates on all sides. Ironically, British soldiers are depicted as camping outside; apparently they were not allowed within the premises. It was only after Lucknow had been captured on March 15, 1858 that British soldiers, and later photographers and travellers could enter the place and record their impressions. Few works of art depicting the "loot" or ransacking of *Kaiserbagh* by the British, aided by Sikh soldiers, also reached the outside world, when published in the *History of the Indian Mutiny* by Charles Ball (1858), *My Diary in India, Vol. I* by William Howard Russel (1860) and *Hutchinson's History of the Nations* (1915). Felice Beato, an Italian photographer photographed the ruins of Lucknow in 1858. For *Kaiserbagh*, he used a wide angle view from atop the *Roshan-ud-Daula Kothi*, effectively creating a photographic panorama of the entire palace complex, then in ruins. Other post 1857 photographers too captured the ruins of Lucknow from various angles from their lenses. Russel, special correspondent for *The Times*, who had actually accompanied the marauding British and Sikh soldiers, during the fall of *Kaiserbagh* had perhaps described the palace complex for the first time as a European. Among the mayhem and plunder, Russel noted, "*Imagine courts as large as the Temple Gardens, surrounded by ranges of palaces, or at least of buildings well stuccoed and gilded, with fresco-paintings here and there on the blind-windows, and with green jalousies and Venetian blinds closing the apertures which pierce the walls in double rows. In the body of the court are statues, lines of lamp-posts, fountains, orange groves, aqueducts, and kiosks with burnished domes of metal.*" Beato's panorama revealed the multiple courts, linked *via* gates and most free standing buildings having basements or *tykhanas*. The arrangement was no doubt jumbled but attractive, although not according to the western concepts of aesthetics or architecture. Later writers, including Mookerjee (1883), Ubbas Ali (1874), Keene (1875), Beg (1911), Newell (1934), Hay (1939) and several others would subsequently try and offer a descriptive analysis of the palace complex in their writings.

Authors have been unequivocal that *Kaiserbagh* had many entry gateways, but the one on the north-east (facing the open space in front of *Taaron Wali Kothi*) was the principle entrance (Plate 24), which lead to a court and the *Jilau Khana* or triumphal arch. The buildings of *Kaiserbagh* were painted with a shade of ochre-yellow, which gave an impression of richness and shone like gold in the sun, when viewed from a distance. The complex had several free standing buildings, many of which were subsequently razed to the ground. Two marble pavilions, the *Chandiwali Baradari* and the *Naginewali Baradari* had originally existed within the premises; the former apparently was paved with polished silver, whereas the latter was inlayed with gem stones. *Naginewali Baradari* was later removed and reconstructed in the Wingfield Park (sans its gem stones). The marble *Safed Baradari* we know today was not a place for celebrations; it was called *Qasr-ul-Aza*, a place designated for religious discourse and mourning during Muharram; as per its status from a religious viewpoint, it occupied a vantage position at the very centre of the palace complex (which it continues to do even today).

In all other aspects, the *Kaiserbagh* was literally a private playground for Wajid Ali Shah, lovingly called *Jân-é-Álam* by his subjects. Here, the king gave full vent to his creative talents, from supervising dance forms and classic musical styles to participating in soirees, particularly during the annual *Jogiya Mela*, during which he would himself perform the role of an ascetic. However, *Kaiserbagh* was destined to have a very short life span and meet a tragic end. Architecturally, it has been described as "*the final Rococo phase of Mughal architecture, combined with a gamut of western elements, with a splendid and theatrical disregard for rule.*" Incidentally, *Kaiserbagh* was also inclusive of pre-existing structures built by others. Among the former *kothis* (mansions), it included the *Roshan-ud-Daula Kothi* built by Roshan-ud-Daula (later renamed as *Kaiser Pasand*), *Badshah Manzil* built by Sa'adat Ali Khan, the *Chaulakhi Kothi* built by Azimullah and the *Khas Muqam*. It also encompassed the *maqbaras* (tombs) of Sa'adat Ali Khan and his begum, Khurshid Zadi. The grounds also included a small British era-cemetery, which came to be known as *Kaiser Pasand* cemetery. This cemetery, now in ruins, incidentally has the tomb of Sultan Mariam, also known as *Vilayati Begum*, the third *begum* of Ghazi-ud-Din Haider. A diagrammatic representation of *Kaiserbagh* published in *Tilism* (an Urdu newspaper, *Tilism-e-Lucknow*, was published between July 25, 1856 to May 8, 1857 by Maulvi Yaqub Ansari of *Firangi Mahal*, Lucknow. It serves as an important source of information on the condition of Awadh after the deposition of Wajid Ali Shah in 1856 and the outbreak of the uprising in 1857) clearly shows the *Qasr-ul-Aza* occupying center stage of the palace complex, with double storeyed buildings around it, forming a quadrangle. Behind this quadrangle are the free standing mansions.

William Russel returned to Lucknow in January 1849 (Speirs, 2013). One of his despatches, dated February 14, 1849 stated, "*What is to be done with the Kaiserbagh? A mere shell is all that now remains of rows of palaces. The wind whistles as it lists through unglazed windows and shattered Venetians - through door-less corridors and battered walls. The gardens still remain, but the fountains have ceased to play; the statues - marble and plaster - are all gone. The grand mausoleum of Saadat Ali, the last wise and good Nawab who reigned over Oude, is closed, and the ruin of cannon shot and shell is aggravated by the unresisted effects of rain and wind. A few of the buildings are used as quarters, but by far the greater portion of the palaces of the Kaiserbagh is untenanted*."

When the British ultimately re-landscaped *Kaiserbagh*, the harmony between the buildings was lost, as a result of which, the tombs mentioned above were no longer part of the complex. Similarly, the cemetery, buildings like *Roshan-ud-Daula Kothi* were entirely cut-off from the main complex. Of course, many palaces were demolished, so the *Kaiserbagh* we see today, is but a drastically truncated version of the original palace complex.

Unlike *Kaiserbagh*, not much interest has been evinced in *Sikandar Bagh*, another garden complex attributed to Wajid Ali Shah. *Sikandar Bagh's* origins are unclear; writers surmise that an early Nawabi garden, built by Sa'adat Ali Khan, might have been upgraded as *Sikandar Bagh* by Wajid Ali Shah. Oral tradition has weaved an interesting background story for the origins of *Sikandar Bagh*. In this narrative, the premises had a *baradari* made entirely of wood, in addition to a palace for Sikandar Mahal, a favourite *begum* of the King. Apparently, the *begum* had requested that the garden palace be built for her, after the construction of *Kaiserbagh* was over, which Wajid Ali Shah happily obliged. Unfortunately, the begum had no issue and she died young, resulting in the garden-palace complex being abandoned afterwards. Also, Sikandar Mahal was originally called Umrao, but was given her royal title after Wajid Ali Shah's coronation. Some analysis of this mythos, however, becomes necessary, in a bid to clear the glaring loopholes and chronological errors of this pretty story. Firstly, despite the sheer size of his household, harem and number of marriages, the wives (including *mutah* wives) of Wajid Ali Shah have been well documented. Wajid Ali Shah entered into wedlock with an Umrao Mahal, daughter of Mirza Abdu'llah Beg, as his twentieth wife. Umrao Mahal was born in 1834 and died around 1888 at a ripe old age of 54 years or so. Secondly, as per convention, since she held the title of *Mahal*, she must have given birth to a son, and could not have been issueless as claimed. Thirdly, there is no record to indicate that she was later given the title of Sikandar Mahal. And even if she was re-named, again, the title of *Mahal* would indicate that she was not childless. A parallel story exists in which a Sikandar Mahal married the King, but had no issue. She died of tuberculosis in 1848. If we examine the chronology, it can be observed that Wajid Ali Shah was crowned in 1847 and his *Kaiserbagh* palace complex was completed in 1850, after which, the construction of *Sikandar Bagh* apparently commenced. But why should Wajid Ali Shah construct a palace - garden complex for a woman, who had already died in 1848, even though she was supposed to be his "favourite?" Actually one Umrao, daughter of Umda Khanum had been married to a certain Sayyid Ibrahim Ali, but became a *mutah* wife of Wajid Ali Shah after Ibrahim Ali was pursuaded to award a divorce (*talâq*) to her. This divorce apparently materialised due to the machinations of Wajid Ali Shah himself, when he was still the crown prince. He awarded the title of Sikandar Begum (not Mahal) to her. However, Umda Khanum, the mother petitioned Amjad Ali Shah, that the crown prince had forcefully confined Umrao in his harem. As a result of this, both Umrao and Wajid Ali Shah were summoned before the King, where Umrao agreed to return to Ibrahim, her former husband, rather than go with her mother. This salacious incident was related by Wajid Ali Shah himself in his book, *Parikhana*. It also proves that the creation and naming of *Sikandar Bagh* after a favourite "begum" of Wajid Ali Shah, when he was King, is just another urban myth.

Wajid Ali Shah did marry a Sikandar Mahal, probably *mutah*, as his 355th wife, late in life at *Metia Burz*, Calcutta (Plate 56). But by that time, the fate of *Sikandar Bagh* at Lucknow had already been sealed. On a more logical note, just as the naming of *Kaiserbagh* might have been inspired by Julius Caesar, the naming of *Sikandar Bagh* might have been inspired by Alexander the Great - another example of Wajid Ali Shah's eclectic tastes. Whatever might have been the origins of *Sikandar Bagh*, there is no doubt that its size was considerable. The garden was encircled by high walls with battlements on three sides - the north side having the Gomti river as a natural boundary. Entrance was through a lofty three-storeyed gateway (extant today, but partially re-built), surmounted by four kiosks, two of which were octagonal and two square (with a debased Chinoiserie leaf design, perhaps appearing in Nawabi architecture for the last time). The unique feature of this gateway was the presence of magnificent frescos in it's interiors, depicting delicate floral designs obviously inspired by Lucknow's famed *chikan* embroidery. The ruins inside do not give any indication of the past glory of the premises. Beato's famous photograph called, "Interior of Secundrabagh After the Massacre" had depicted a double storeyed colonnaded pavilion with a prominent triangular pediment, and human skeletons liberally strewn here and there. While the presence of the skeletons had created a great deal of controversy and literary discussion, the building itself was very interesting, as it was neither a palace nor a *baradari*. Also the architecture appeared to be totally European in character. Scattered information about the premises are too scanty, for drawing any concrete conclusion as to what exactly existed within the gardens before it was decimated. *Sikandar Bagh* saw action on November 16, 1857, in which Colin Campbell, accompanied by the 93rd Highlanders, the 4th Punjab Infantry and HM 53rd Foot stormed the premises, resulting in the slaughter of about 2200 Indian freedom fighters after a prolonged assault. The details of this horrific battle have been well documented by several authors and need not be repeated here. In later years, the garden and its ruins were cleared by the colonial government and the "Lacknow Horticulture Garden" was established in a portion of the premises. The gateway was re-built and a new Outram Road, connecting Nishatganj with the city, now effectively bisected the garden into two unequal parts. Post independence, the National Botanical Research Institute was established in the premises, by the CSIR.

Vilayati Bagh stood near to *Dilkusha*, having a slope of about 20 feet (Sinha, 2009), appropriately terraced, which lead down to the meandering Gomti river. Both Ghazi-ud-Din Haider, the first King of Awadh and his successor, Nasir-ud-Din Haider had European consorts. Ghazi-ud-Din's second *begum*, with the title of Muqdara-i-Aliya Izat-un-Nisa Mahal was the daughter of Col. Aish of Kanpur. His third *begum*, Sultan Mariam, also known as *Vilayati Begum*, was originally Mary Short, daughter of Dr. James Short of the EIC. Nasir-ud-Din's third begum, Muqdara-i-Aliya Vilayati Begum was actually Emma, the daughter of a John Hopkins Walters of the British Dragoons. Naturally some controversy arises about the origins of *Vilayati Bagh* - which King had it built for his European wife? In a "Company School" scroll painting (1826) by an unidentified artist (Plate 53), one can clearly see the *Vilayati Bagh* (on the left) and nearby *Bibiapur Kothi*. In the background, a domed structure can be seen, which is unidentifiable. Nasir-ud-Din ruled during 1827 - 1837. From the painting's date, it is obvious that the *Vilayati Bagh* was already in existence, when Nasir-ud-Din Haider had not even ascended the throne.

Russell (1858) described his first view of *Vilayati Bagh* as, "*a walled garden filled with cypresses, summer -houses, plaster statues with kiosks and pleasant walks 'mid orange trees. Beneath it flows the Goomti, about 500 yards from us, coming down with many a curve from the city of Lucknow. It must have been a very pretty spot - opening on the river by a flight of steps, with alcoves, covered walks, orange trees, kiosks, abundant statuary in plaster, a platform for dancing, an orchestra, the ornamented roofs covered with gilded bosses and spires - tall cypresses and tamarinds bordered the orange plantations, and a wilderness of flowers sprang up in their neglected beds. Everything was fast going to decay; the irrigation canals were choked up, the foundations were dry, the statues falling to pieces, the lattices in the kiosks broken.*" One and half decades later, Ubbas Ali (1874) recorded, "*the summer house in this garden was erected by King Naseer-ood-deen Hyder and the grounds laid out by him and planted with European plants, principally; hence its designation. It lies on the banks of the river Goomtee and was, in the King's time, a very handsome pleasure garden. It was a favourite resort of the King, who used to proceed there by water, accompanied by the members of his Court, in pleasure boats by night. The garden is not remarkable on account of any historical associations; it is the station regatta winning post; it has fallen into neglect, but still retains some remnants of its original beauty.*"

It is not known when *Vilayati Bagh* started becoming a derelict, but a little less than a century later, its deterioration was noted by Newell (1934), who wrote, "*a one time famous garden, where ladies of the harem delighted to wander amid rare exotics planted by Nasir-ur-Din Haider. High walls screened their beauties from all eyes save those of the birds and butterflies excepting one on the fourth side, where the waters of the winding Gumti cooled the flower scented air. Now the deserted pleasance guards are nothing more remarkable than a ruined pavilion, while the graves of some soldiers mark the track of the Mutiny.*" Hay (1939), echoed similar sentiments, "*the garden, once so well known, now degenerated into a vast dhobi ghat. The ruins of pillared retreats around the inside of the walls still show traces of coloured stucco embellishments, but nothing remains of the lovely and exotic garden where royal ladies disported themselves, undetected by prying eyes.*" Three hurriedly dug graves of British soldiers exist within the premises, belonging to Henry P Garvey, Act. Mate, Captain Halley Hutchinson and Sgt. S. Newman. Again, contrary to popular myth, none of these three fallen British soldiers were killed during any action within or near the *Vilayati Bagh*. Garvey was killed at *Begum Kothi* on March 11, 1858, whereas Hutchinson and Newman were killed in action at *Musa Bagh* on March 9 and March 19, 1858 respectively. In fact, there is no record of any battle having been fought at *Vilayati Bagh* during 1857 - 58. During colonial rule, the garden was allowed to further deteriorate, because it seems, the premises held no emotional connect, no memories of heroic battles for the ruling British and therefore for its maintenance, there was no provision under a utilitarian (but totalitarian) government.

Badshah Bagh, also created by Ghazi-ud-Din Haider, the first King or *Badshah* of Awadh has been better documented than *Vilayati Bagh*. Erroneously spelled as *Padshah* by western writers, the gardens were enclosed by walls with bastions on three sides, it stretched from present day Hasanganj to Chandganj, with its southern side facing the Gomti river. A detailed and rather flattering account of *Badshah Bagh* was given by Fanny Parkes (1850) as below:

"*We crossed the river to a new house and garden, built by the present king called Padshah Bagh; of which I must give a description, it being the most luxurious palace I have seen in India. A large space has been enclosed as a garden within a high wall; it contains three houses and two gateways; the first house is a most delightful one, all you can wish for in such a climate as this; beautiful rooms, with six fountains playing in them, and everything in fairyland style; then such a hummâm! Or steam baths, containing rooms heated to different temperatures, the heat of each increasing until you arrive at the steam bath itself. The apartments are made of white variegated marble, and the roofs arched; the rooms are so delightful, we felt every inclination to remain in the hummâm, the temperature was so luxurious.*

Crossing from this palace to the center of the garden, we entered another elegant building, supported on white marble pillars, beautifully finished, and adorned and furnished with crimson and gold. On the left of the garden is a third palace, sacred to the ladies of the zenâna; this house if built of marble, and covered with flower-work of pounded tâlk (talc), *which has exactly the same appearance of silver, giving an eastern style to the place. There are two handsome gateways, a steam engine to supply the fountains, and a superb tiger in a cage. Every luxury of life may be contained within the walls of this garden; it is at present scarcely finished, but displays great taste and beauty.*"

Fanny's description pertains to 1831, when *Badshah Bagh* was being embellished and nearing completion. Hence it deserves special attention. The flower-filled garden and shallow lakes of water created a sylvan surrounding for the favourites among the King's harem, which included European women also. However, after the suicide of Qudsia Mahal, (Nasir-ud-Din's favourite queen) in the premises, the King (who was reported to be fickle-minded) apparently lost interest in *Badshah Bagh*, and its upkeep suffered. November 1857 saw the British second relief force under Colin Campbell raked with fire from Indian freedom fighters in the *Kaiserbagh* to the front and the *Badshah Bagh* behind. In March 1858, the British erected a battery at the south-west corner of *Badshah Bagh* near the river Gomti, to bombard *Kaiserbagh* and sanitize it. Russel (1858) passing through *Badshah Bagh* with the relief force, had observed that, "*in the days of its full magnificence, it must have been glorious. Such forests of orange trees, such trickling fountains, shady walks, beds of flowers, grand alleys, dark retreats and summer-houses, all surrounded by a high and massive wall, and forming, as it were, the approaches to a snug little palace of pleasure.*" He described how he had mounted the flat roof of one of the towers, which provided a pleasant view of the "enemy's works." Russell observed that "*in one of the rooms was a portrait of the late King of Oude, which he was permitted to cut out of the frame and carry it off with him - a small bit of loot of very little value.*" Little value indeed, the portrait would have possibly been of Nasir-ud-Din Haider, but it cannot be confirmed. David Scott Dodgson (1860) of the Bengal Infantry had made a sketch of *Badshah Bagh* (Plate 22), which clearly indicated that there was no boundary wall on the south (river) side. Furthermore, a rectangular building was shown with cupolas in the corners. Dodgson had further mentioned that "*Budshur Bagh had fine open pavilion for cockfights and was surrounded by pleasant walks.*"

Half a century later, Beg (1911) described the garden as being of great extent, entry of which was through lofty gateways. He further goes on to state that in the centre of the garden, there was a substantial stone edifice partly two storeyed, with an open arcaded hall at the back, its front having round towers at the angles, which faced south. He mentions a large masonry tank, spanned about the centre by an iron bridge and rounded with gravel walks. On the left of the garden, which was planted with numerous fruit trees and ornamental shrubs, a large building existed which was "*sacred to the ladies of the King's harem.*" Hay (1939) mentioned that at the behest of Nasir-ud-Din Haider, a square house washed in red ochre had been erected for the convenience of the ladies of his harem. She also suggested that the building was used for watching cock-fights and that Zoffany's famous painting, "Colonel Mordaunt's Cock Match" was a scene from this building, which is a unique, if erroneous piece of information. Nasir-ud-Din Haider ruled from 1827 - 1837, whereas Zoffany's work of art was produced during 1784-86, during the reign of Asaf-ud-Daula. Incidentally, Asaf-ud-Daula is also depicted in the painting. There is no way that the painting could have been made in a building which was constructed by Nasir-ud-Din Haider 40 years later.

Badshah Bagh has the unique distinction of housing a battery of Indian freedom fighters, who had bombarded the Residency continuously during the siege, from across the river. The shell which killed Henry Lawrence in the Residency had been fired from this very battery on July 2, 1857.

After the uprising was over, the Maharajah of Kapurthala acquired *Badshah Bagh* for a petty sum of Rs 35,000. Festive gatherings such as picnics were held with the kind permission of his Highness (Beg, 1911). The Foundation Stone of the new campus of Lucknow University was laid in the premises in 1911. Strangely enough, the eldest son of the Maharaja lies buried in the grounds, a pyramidal obelisk marking his grave. The prince had become converted to the Christian faith, forfeiting his right to be a successor, and denied the last rites as Hindu, after his death. The cenotaph is architecturally identical to the one opposite the KDSB stadium, which is dedicated to the memory of Mount Stewart Jackson, Patrick Orr, Lt. Burns, Sgt. Major Morton and several other British women and children, who had been killed in the area on November 16, 1857.

At present, portions of the original walls and bastions of *Badshah Bagh* still stand, bearing cannon ball holes, which were never repaired. Other than the forlorn central tank spanned by a bridge, a massive red building commonly called *Lal Baradari* is extant. The latter, which is in a ruinous state has not quite been documented well. It does not match any of the buildings as described by various writers from time to time. Indeed, it appears that it was neither red in colour, nor a *baradari* (a pavilion with 12 or more doorways) in its original form and function. Dodgson had stated that it was ochre in colour. From its present appearance, it is obvious that it has undergone a number of structural modifications over time, and has lost its original architectural features to a large extent. The original gateways are also extant, but drastically re-structured. Apart from these substantial remnants, there are scattered ruins of what might have been the royal well (Plate 12), and its accompanying enclosure for the "steam engine." The students of the University, busy in their academic pursuits, seem blissfully unaware of the heritage value of the campus in which they study.

Alambagh was an extensive, fortified palace-cum-garden complex, enclosed by buttressed walls, nine feet high, having bastions at the four corners. A British plan of 1857 (Fig. 19), showing the fortification of the garden shows a square, with each wall measuring 400 yards (1200 feet). That means the area of the garden complex was 1,440,000 square feet or about 33 acres. The palace itself was right at the centre of the garden with a single entrance through an impressive European-style gateway, bearing the usual fish symbol on its spandrels. It was named after Alam Ara Begum, the *Khas Mahal* (chief consort / senior-most Queen and mother of the crown prince or heir-apparent) of Wajid Ali Shah, who preferred to reside in her own palace, away from her husband, the King. The *Alambagh Kothi* was situated in the center of the garden, having the usual hybrid architecture, so favoured during Lucknow's Nawabi era. Described as a "manor-like, windowless building" by the British, the building sported a prominent triangular pediment and octagonal turrets at its four corners. The front entrance was through a open colonnaded veranda on the ground floor; the first floor sported arched doorways with fanlights. Strangely, the height of the ground floor was much less than that of the first floor. Although damaged during 1857, a photograph of the *kothi* in 1880 (Plate 8) indicates that it had been repaired and was in reasonably good condition. A decade later, a photograph dated 1890 shows the *kothi* becoming derelict, with some of the arched doorways on the first floor now bricked up. Still, its octagonal towers were intact. Thereafter, it appears that it was allowed to deteriorate on its own (including its gate, photographs of which show a lot of vegetation covering it), but not bombarded with cannons, like *Dilkusha Kothi.*

The British had wrested control over *Alambagh* in September 23, 1857 and subsequently fortified it with picquets on three corner bastions and mounted an 8 inch howitzer and two 9 pounder guns on the fourth bastion (Fig. 19). The boundary walls on the left and right to the main entrance had been pierced and mounted with one 9 pounder each. A 24 pounder and a 9 pounder were mounted on either side of the gateway, across the Lucknow - Cawnpore (Kanpur) road. Outram did not occupy *Alambagh* with his main force. Holding it with a small detachment and a few guns, he pitched his camp in the open, about a kilometre away. He thus occupied a position across the road, extending to the right and left on either side; on the right as

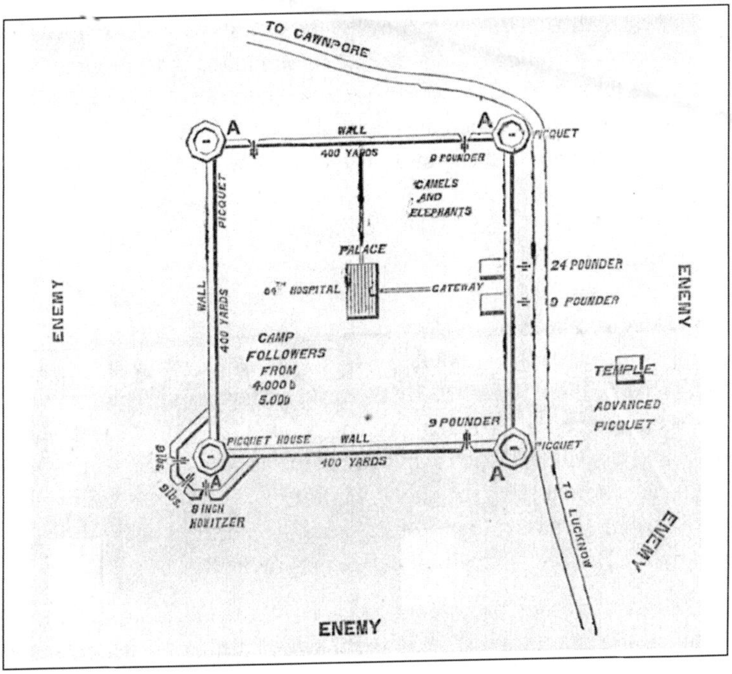

Fig. 19. British Fortification at *Alambagh* (1857)

far as the fort of *Jalalabad*, and covered on all points by batteries, trenches, and *abattis* (made with tree branches). On November 3, Colin Campbell moved from Cawnpore (Kanpur) to *Alambagh* with 3,500 infantry, 600 cavalry, and 42 guns. Hence, it was necessary for them to avoid Kanpur Road (which was choc-a-bloc with native freedom fighters), and this had to be conveyed to Campbell, together with plans of the city and its approaches. Although written descriptions would be useful, they could not equal to what might be conveyed by an intelligent member of the garrison, who had himself undergone the sieze and withstood the blockade. Furthermore, a semaphore (rudimentary telegraph system) had been established between *Alambagh* and the Residency, to exchange messages. Before this could become operational, it was necessary for both sides to have the same code. Thomas Henry Kavanagh, a civilian, volunteered to slip out of the Residency, make contact with the relief force and guide it back through the city. Kavanagh was later awarded the Victoria Cross, the first civilian in history to be awarded this gallantry award. Kannauji Lal, a British sympathiser, who had accompanied Kavanagh on his midnight foray, was disregarded and forgotten in the annals of history; he got what fate usually has in store for traitors of his ilk.

Havelock died of dysentery on November, 1857 at *Dilkusha*. His body was carried to *Alambagh* and hurriedly buried in the open grounds, where there were three mango trees (Plate 9). The letter "H" was carved on the tree, whose branches shaded the makeshift grave. Later, an obelisk, with a plaque was erected on the spot by Havelock's son, Marshman Havelock. The grounds were also used as a cemetery for other fallen British soldiers, including Lt. Henry Ayton, Lt. Dundas Gordon and others. In present times, the cemetery has vanished, but Havelock's grave and obelisk remain within a small enclosure. *Alambagh Kothi* has been patched up partially, but the colonnaded verandah no longer exists; the roof of the ground floor has not been reconstructed, so the building is one hollow, continuous shell from inside (much like other similarly repaired monuments). The gateway has also been spruced up, but remains surrounded by shops, encroachments and randomly parked vehicles. Even its name has been changed to *Chandan Nagar* gate, which is mystifying and unfortunate. It is also known locally as *Phansi ka Darwaza* (gate for hanging) because, possibly, it had been used by the British to hang Indian freedom fighters.

Details of other prominent gardens of Lucknow are sparse. Few sketches are available of *Aishbagh*, which indicate the presence of pavilions with square canopies, and a *baradari*, commonly seen in Nawabi palaces of that era (Plate 7). The gardens had been built by Asaf-ud-

Daula and the marriage of his son, Wazir Ali, had also been solemnised in the premises at considerable cost. Present day *Aishbagh* is a cluttered industrial area; the *baradari* is extant but in a ruinous condition and heavily encroached. According to Mookherjee (1883), *Charbagh* was a congregation of four gardens in the time of Asaf-ud-Daula. There were many large wells, whose water was conducted by way of conduits and fountains. There were innumerable paths, interconnected with each other, together with recesses and pavilions existed in the premises. *Banarsi Bagh* built by Nasir-ud-Din Haider contained a two-storeyed summer house and a circular pavilion known as *Aish Mahal*. Details of its original layout are not available.

The crowded and cluttered *Lalbagh* we see today, with its colonial roundabout mangled beyond restoration, however, has an interesting back story. Apparently, this vast estate was named after Shah Bihari Lal, an affluent merchant from the times of Ghazi-ud-Din Haider. In 1870, his regal house and surrounding grounds were taken over by Isabella Thoburn, under the auspices of the Women's Foreign Missionary Society, from a member of the original owner's family. Strangely, the estate was purported to have buried treasure from the times of Ghazi-ud-Din Haider, described by one Iqbal-ud-Daula in his "Small Book" as follows:

"This is an old garden. To its south is a drain or "nala". Treasure was deposited in this place by order of Ghazi-ud-din Hyder. The details of the buildings which I give are these: Proceed from the western point of the well to the eastern. When you reach the middle of the said garden wall, take the exact centre between East and West points. Dig into the wall there (the centre from the east of western angle of the wall); on reaching the depth of (20) twenty cubits, you will find a door, and opening it, enter the vault which extends to the kothi. Perhaps, in most places, you will find water. Don't mind it until you come to the kothi through the vault. In that place, you will find a sheet of iron in which are given the particulars and the amount of treasures deposited are inscribed. After that you may take every treasure in it. I deeply regret the necessity of giving the traces of these treasures; but what could I do, the command of my grandfather (Fateh Ali Khan) was to this effect, to keep by me the particulars of every treasure.

Among these treasures, there is a thing of very great value: a ruby weighing (2) two tolas, its virtues are these, he who wears it will be safe from harm, from evil spirits, bites of snakes and have no fear of these. This ruby is kept in a silver casket in the vault of the baradurrie. Further particulars are these, when anyone enters the vault, he will first find the iron sheet. On that plate all the contents of the boards and where they are kept are given in detail".

Another Khas-ud-Daula's account of the treasure is as follows:

Under the principal kothi, treasures are buried in (3) three places:

I. Three lakhs of Jypur ashirfis in one place

II. One lakh of Murshadabad ashirfis in one place

III. In one place four crores of only Murshadabad rupees

Particulars of the first - inside the chambers situated eastward is a vault and in that vault in iron chests are the Jypur ashirfis locked and deposited.

Particulars of the second - Under the Principal Baradurie is a wall in which ashirfis are stored.

Particulars of the third - There is a chamber to the west in the vault of which in brass chests rupees are put in.

If by these particulars that I have given any one fancies that he can get these treasures he will find it impossible. Until he consults the Small Book which makes it clear for in that Small Books is written very cautiously that it may not be understood by everybody and until the Book and this book are taken together to the spit and are not most closely compared together because the cardinal points are given contrarily, East for West, West for East, North for South and South for North.

Since the original writings were in Persian, which were translated into English, we can safely conclude that *Jypur* denotes present day Jaipur and *Murshadabad* denotes Murshidabad, erstwhile Nawabi capital of Bengal. Also there is a school of thought that the term *Lalbagh* arose not from the name of Shah Bihari Lal, but either due to the purported presence of a large red ruby as treasure (hence also referred to as "Ruby Garden" by the British), or even because of the fact that there was red roses planted in the garden premises. Esoteric interpretations apart, the *Lalbagh Jubilee Book* (1870 - 1920) also refers to "*the old kothi with its untold secrets of treasure and romance, as well as the taikhana (basement), with its legends of cobras guarding the buried treasure.*" It is clear that the original *kothi* was a single storied structure, "*the building material being of small burnt bricks of which all Lucknow city was built, about an inch thick by four inches square* (obviously referring to *lakhauri* bricks). *This is covered with stucco and washed a drab colour, the cornices being white. The flat roof is supported by large beams, which are not covered by ceilings. It is two feet thick, of brick and earth and plaster well beaten down, and covered with cement. The house has only one storey, and the high thick walls and large rooms add much to the comfort of the inmates during the hot months when so many hours must be spent indoors. Its first room beyond the entrance is so large that one hundred persons have assembled here for teas and prayer meetings, and often an overflow listens from the veranda, on which the doors open. The dining room is almost as large; there is a study, six bedrooms, bath and store rooms. The roof, which is reached by a stairway from within the house, is the general dormitory during the hot, dry nights of April, May and June*."

This *kothi* and its grounds, together with other scattered buildings in the estate served as the nucleus for the later Isabella Thoburn College of Lucknow. With time, many other structures, including a second storey to the original *kothi*, verandas all around, an L-shaped extension and even a clock tower (in 1896) was added to the then school building (Plate 10). It is interesting to note that in 1910, a Hazzard Memorial building was erected for accommodating lecture rooms, study hall and dormitories. However, within five years, it collapsed in September 1915, during "a cloud burst and floods", although the original old *kothi* stood strong. When the college moved out to its larger campus in 1922, the premises remained with the Lalbagh Girls School, presently re-christened as Emma Thompson School.

Details of *Chand Bagh* (including present day *Chand Ganj* and grounds of IT College) are also sparse. Amazingly, Knighton (1921) stated that it was the venue of animal fights, together with neighbouring *Mubaraq Manzil* (part of *Moti Mahal* complex). *Chand Bagh* was situated on either side of the road to Kursi, between Aliganj and the Gomti river. It was a "*large walled-in garden, one of the park places where animal fights often took place. The garden might have been some three to four acres in extent, and was surrounded by a high wall and provided with heavy gates. The garden abounded with a large yellow flower, the African marigold. It had a small lodge, like a country house, with large enclosures in its neighbourhood. A courtyard, about sixty square yards in extent, with buildings all around and a veranda below. Thick bamboo railing was put up in the front of the veranda, as to completely encircle the courtyard, forming a sort of enlarged cage*", inside which ferocious animals were made to fight each other.

18th and 19th century Nawabi gardens have often been criticised as being private enclaves or "pleasure gardens", meant primarily for passive recreation and leisure of the elite. Although Lucknow was a "city of gardens", its ordinary citizens did not have actually have access to these gardens and open spaces. Most of these Nawabi gardens had at least one river front, which allowed access / entry to the boats / barges of nobility; the river side also meant the absence of boundary wall on one side, offering singular views from the pavilions / buildings inside, and also cool breezes during hot summers. The gardens were tended by myriads of workers, including gardeners of foreign origin!! Early Nawabi gardens were inspired by the Mughal gardens of Delhi and Agra, having the usual four square layout. Later, Awadh seemed to have developed its own distinctive style and layout. Instead of a central canal, a Nawabi garden would generally have a raised central tank, surrounded by fountains. The buildings inside would often be heavily westernised and embellished with European motifs. A *baradari* and a mosque would invariably be present; the Awadh nobility, particularly the ladies, seemed to be conscious of their religious obligations, despite being encircled by sylvan surroundings. One or more open pavilions provided the venue for holding festivities (including Hindu festivals such as Holi), as well as cultural sojourns. Statues and gazebos of different mythological origins would be the norm, rather than an exception.

Post 1857, the British created few prominent colonial-style gardens or "parks" in Lucknow. The term "park" denoted that these were public spaces, not confined for use by any particular class of citizens. However, this might be a misnomer, since these parks were meant for use by Europeans and definitely not for Indians. Thus, a new class differentiation had come into play: from the ruling Nawabi elite *vs* ordinary citizen, the demarcation now signified the schism or racial differentiation between Europeans and Indians. The British also sought to re-engineer the demographics of Lucknow, by actively encouraging the rural land-owners or *ta'aluqdars* to buy property at throw-away rates and settle in Lucknow, thereby acting as an effective buffer between the neo-colonial administration and the old decimated Nawabi order. Most *ta'aluqdars* who had generally avoided visiting the Nawabi court in Lucknow in former times, now responded with alacrity to British overtures, although some remained reticent (Oldenburg, 1984, Jafri, 1998). *Kaiserbagh,* the former playground of Wajid Ali Shah and his courtiers, now became the new playground of the Oudh (Awadh) *ta'aluqdars,* who organised themselves under the British India Association, which continues till today.

The design vocabulary of colonial parks included wide expanses of lawn, winding paths, shrubbery and flower beds, curvilinear water bodies and statuary at focal points, with minor variations (Sinha, 2010). The British preferred to preserve the Residency premises as a memorial park, through extensive landscaping. Two colonial parks, dedicated Queen Victoria came up in Lucknow, post 1857. One was in *Chowk*, the old quarter of Lucknow, for which land was retrieved after demolishing scores of Nawabi era structures. Another was a small area, roughly corresponding to the earlier Nawabi *Payn Bagh*, in which a marble canopy over a red sandstone plinth was erected to house the statue of Queen Victoria as a "Victoria Memorial." But their biggest exercise was in the form of the Wingfield Park encompassing the old *Banarsi Bagh* and also portions of the vast grounds of Agha Mir's *karbala*. According to Keene (1875), it was a handsome garden of about 40 acres, with the turf, trees and roads finely varied. The *Nagine Wali Baradari* was translocated in its entirety from *Kaiserbagh* to the middle of the Wingfield Park. Other small marble kiosks were also erected in the premises. The reason for the *Nagine Wali Baradari* being removed from *Kaiserbagh* and reconstructed at Wingfield Park has an interesting back story. As already mentioned, Wajid Ali Shah, during the heydays of *Kaiserbagh*, used to dress up as a *jogi* (mendicant / ascetic) during the annual *Jogiya Mela* and participate in elaborate dance dramas in the premises. The citizens of Lucknow had an intense emotional connect with their deposed King and the venue of his dramatic performances would be a point of gathering for the public, which had to be avoided at all costs - so felt Lucknow's neo-colonial masters. Wingfield Park (Plate 14) was originally laid out by one Reginald Berkeley, whose plans were later modified by M/s Morrison and Hodges, under the supervision of Charles Wingfield, Chief Commissioner of Lucknow and Lousada Barrow, his successor. It later metamorphosed into the Prince of Wales Zoological Gardens in 1926. Presently, its most recent *avatar* is as Nawab Wajid Ali Shah Zoological Garden (although Wajid Ali Shah was not a Nawab).

Chapter - 5

Imposing Gateways

In medieval cities, dramatic gateways were always much more than mere entrances. Often, they represented triumphal arches, translating into pageantry, pomp and show as the ruler, accompanied by his minions, passed underneath them, with the public looking at the spectacle with awe and admiration. Despite differences in their functionalities over time, gateways have always represented symbolic power, due to their spatio-political role (Caliskan, 2010). Interestingly, Lucknow has been included among the three "gateway cities" of the eighteenth century (Kamleh, 2012), the other two being Aleppo (Syria) and Istanbul (Turkey). A partial list of Lucknow's historical gateways has been given in Annexure I. Tandan (2001) listed 52 gateways in Nawabi Lucknow and its environs; colonial Lucknow had at least 30 gateways, or more. Many of the latter gateways are still extant, although barring a few, most are in dilapidated and precarious condition. Lucknow's only Mughal era gateway, the *Akbari Darwaza*, still extant, boasts of no architectural merit. It appears to have been the original entrance to the old city, commemorating Akbar's visit to Lucknow, after Awadh had become a *suba* of the Mughal empire. The later *Panch Mahalla* gateway, built by the *Sheikhzadas* of Lucknow, however, deserves serious consideration. Its architectural features and time-lines have been described in this book's chapter on *Macchi Bhavan*. Although this gateway no longer exists, Daniell's painting of 1801, and subsequent artwork as well as post-1857 photographs gave a fair idea of this gate, its original form and later architectural modifications.

No figures are available on the elevation of the *Panch Mahalla* gateway. But a simple computation based on Daniell's artwork, depicting an elephant with *howdah* approaching the ramp of the gateway, throws up interesting projections.

The common Asian elephant is about 9 feet tall. The central portion of the gateway, (including the three storeys of the side wings) with its arched entrance was about 3 times the height of the elephant (minus the *howdah*) *viz.* the central portion would have been 27 - 30 feet high. The side wings have one additional storey each. If three storeys were 30 feet high, then the 4 storeyed gateway in its entirety, would have been approximately 40 feet high.

Although impressive, it would have been a little more than half the height of the later *Rumi Darwaza*, which stands at an impressive height of 60 feet. A sketch (Fig. 4) of the *Panch Mahalla* gatewayalso appeared in the *Illustrated London News* (May 27, 1858). A similar rough computation of the gateway's dimensions based on the soldier's height standing near the ramp throws up the same approximations of the gateway's elevation being not more than 40 feet high at the most.

Fig. 4. Sketch *Panch Mahalla* Gateway, *Illustrated London News* (1858)

The gateway to the *Daulat Khana Asafi*, commonly known as *Sheesh Mahal* gateway can be discerned in Beato's high-resolution panorama (Plate 36) of *Hussainabad* (discussed earlier), as well as in a photograph of the *Sat Khanda* (Plate 39), by an unknown photographer, post-1857. However, before we examine Lucknow's *Sheesh Mahal's* (now demolished) gateway, we must go back a little in time and examine the gateways (Plate 15) of *Gulab Bari*, the tomb complex of Shuja-ud-Daula in Faizabad, built by Shuja-ud-Daula (1732-1775) himself, during his lifetime. These are composed of single pointed arches, framed within recessed, foliated ones. surmounted by three smaller arches, and a flat roofline. The central arch is flanked by a trio of three, smaller, superimposed arches. All three smaller side arches (on each side) have different architectural designs, with the bottom one being a blind arch and the others being oriel, curvilinear types, the top one having a bay window, supported by corbels. This basic design was to become a prototype (Fig. 5) for later Nawabi gateways of Lucknow, as we shall now discuss.

Coming back to the *Sheesh Mahal* gateway, built more than a decade later by Asaf-ud-Daula, we see the same basic structure described above, with the main arch now flanked by *two* sets of smaller superimposed arches on each side. As with the *Gulab Bari* gateway, the top arch adjoining the

Fig. 5. Prototype of a Nawabi Gateway

main arch is of an oriel window. The additional trio of arches on each side are rather plain, with no notable architectural features. The roof line is flat without any parapet. This prototype would be repeated in the gateways to the outer and inner courtyards of the *Bada Imambara*, but instead of a single main entrance, there would be a *tripolia* gateway, with the trio of (or four) small arches now flanking the *tripolia*. The top flanking arch would again be an oriel window, and instead of a flat roof, with parapet, the roofline would have a perforated arcade, with kiosks having curvilinear heads at the ends. This perforated roof arcade also appeared first in the gateways leading to the outer courtyard of *Gulab Bari*, and would appear recurrently, with minor modifications in many Nawabi structures, last of all in the *Sibtainabad Imambara*, built by Amjad Ali Shah. Thus, it would not be out of place to suggest that it was actually Shuja-ud-Daula, who set the trend for the later Nawabi architecture of Lucknow (and Awadh), although this aspect of his contribution has not been noted by historians and heritage experts.

The architectural features of the *Rumi Darwaza* and gateways for the courtyards of the *Bada Imambara* have been well documented by several authors and need not be repeated here. However, a fact which is often not taken into consideration is that the octagonal bays of the side wings of *Rumi Darwaza* had been obviously inspired by the side bays of the *Panch Mahalla* gateway. Another interesting fact was the existence of a *tripolia* gateway as a sort of *jawab* (or facsimile) to the *Rumi Darwaza*, facing the latter, about 500 meters down the road, leading to the *Macchi Bhavan*. This is confirmed by Beato's photographs as well as sketches of the area, appearing in several early publications. This rather plain structure was similar to the eastern lower face of the *Rumi Darwaza*, with the three large plain arches, framed within pointed, recessed ones, surmounted by 13 smaller ones. The smaller superimposed arches on the flanks and middle were all blind ones. The structure had a plain roof, with a stairway leading to it; the usual Nawabi perforated arcade was missing; a diminutive railing was provided instead. This *tripolia* gateway was apparently destroyed in the colonial cleansing, post-1857.

The *Gol Darwaza* leading into the *Phool Wali Gali* of Chowk is also attributed to Asaf-ud-Daula, with several accompanying urban legends, involving kite flying by the Nawab from its top, or his helping a destitute lady, trying to eke out a living by selling scrap near the gateway. The *Gol Darwaza* is extant, and from its present ruinous condition as well as from a century old photograph of the area, it is obvious that the gateway was not high enough to facilitate kite flying, that too in a densely populated area (Asaf-ud-Daula had control of the vast open *Macchi Bhavan* area, if at all he wanted to indulge in kite flying, but again, it'is a matter of conjecture).The gateway was rather plain, with a central, large semi-circular arch, flanked by superimposed, oval windows, two on each flank. It had an impressive passage way, which opened into the Chowk side proper, the road leading to the *Akbari Darwaza*, from a different era. There was no evidence of the fish motif on either facade of the *Gol Darwaza*, which was unusual, but not uncommon (after all, Asaf-ud-Daula's signature gateway, the *Rumi Darwaza*, was also deprived of the fish motif, due to reasons unknown). In fact, the gateway was devoid of any Islamic characteristics, whatsoever.

From Sa'adat Ali Khan onwards, the European influence became more pronounced on Lucknow's gateways (as with the buildings). The most unique gateway of his time was perhaps the *Moti Mahal* gateway. *Moti Mahal* itself has been described by several authors and also sketched by Dodson (1860). It was called Pearl Palace (*moti* = pearl), because its central dome apparently resembled a pearl. In fact, its premises included palaces such as *Mubarak Manzil* and *Shah Manzil*, and a garden path which led to the river. Strangely, Dodson's sketch does not depict a central dome, but four small corner domes on a rather plain, two storeyed rectangular, arched building. A photograph of the building in 1900 shows an European-style two storeyed building with arched veranda on the ground floor and windows on the first. No pearlescent dome is seen, either at the centre or at the corners. However, it is the gateway of *Moti Mahal* which interests us more in the present discussion. Without doubt, this was one of the most fantastic of all Nawabi structures of Lucknow - its architectural features defied any definition or style. Beato's post-1857 photograph reveals that this three storeyed edifice was composed of three heterogeneous bays, with the central bay bearing the pointed, rather plane main arched entrance, flanked by superimposed, smaller, blind arches. The main arch spanned two storeys, with the top storey having five small arches, the three central ones being open, and the side ones being blind and recessed. The central bay also had a roof line with mock battlements, with a comb-like appearance. The second bays (flanking the central bay) consisted of three superimposed arches of different styles, spanning three storeys of the gateway. The second bays also had two distinctly European-style turrets or towers, more suited for castles in Scotland than a palace complex in Lucknow. These towering turrets are obvious in Dodson's sketch as well as Thomas Barker Jones' epic painting called "The Relief of Lucknow", more popularly known as "Meeting of The Generals", since it depicted the first meeting of Outram, Havelock and Colin Campbell near *Moti Mahal* on November 17, 1857. Interestingly, the painting shows the turret(s) surmounted with a golden cupola, and is not bare, as in Beato's photograph, or Dodson's sketch.

The third, outer bays of the *Moti Mahal* gateway were octagonal, three storeyed structures, each level having arches of different designs. The octagonal bays were surmounted by pagoda-like cupolas, perhaps the first appearance of the Chinoiserie-style ornamentation, which would be refined later. The gateway was damaged during the events of 1857, but was speedily restored, sans its signature Scottish (!) towers during colonial rule, evident from available photographs dated 1863 and 1874. A later photograph dated 1900 shows the gateway in reasonably good condition, but a subsequent photograph (Plate 18) of 1920 shows the gateway (including its boundary wall) in a derelict state, with cracks and obvious signs of deterioration. The gateway finally collapsed during the floods in Lucknow during September, 1923 and was demolished subsequently.

We now move to the *Latkan Darwaza*, which afforded entry to the royal seraglio of the Nawabs (Mookherji, 1883). Its architectural features have not been documented, although sketches (Lt. Mecham, 1857; Major MacBean, 1858; *Illustrated London Times*, 1858) and even photographs of the ruined structure (Beato, 1858) are available. It certainly pre-dates the Baillie's Guard gateway of the Residency, which was built during the tenure of John Baillie, Resident of Lucknow. From the high resolution photograph of Beato (Plate 19), it is obvious that the gateway was a free standing one, at least 40 feet in height. The structure itself was composed of 3 levels, with the lower level having twice the height of the upper one. The gateway had a single pointed arch as an entrance, flanked by two pilasters of the Tuscan order on each side. The upper level was composed of two blind recessed arches on either side, flanking an open rectangular, balcony-like arrangement. The gateway had circular bays on either side, composed of three levels. The bottom and central levels had blind, rectangular arches, whereas the top level had an open doorway. In the absence of any detailed images or descriptions, is almost impossible to visualise what the parapet of the gateway might have been. Innes (1895) in a series of sketches of the Residency's layout depicted the environs of the *Latkan Darwaza* and Baillie Guard Gate also. The *Darwaza* was shown to have a central triangular pediment on top, possibly resembling the later *Sikandar Bagh* gateway. The circular bays on either side were evidently flat, without any crown or cupola. The *Latkan Darwaza* was referred to as the "Clock Tower" or "Pendulum Gate" by British soldiers, due to the image of a clock on the structure; apparently it was devoid of any real clock, which was a source of mirth. Its colloquial name, *Latkan Darwaza* has no explanations, other than it might have been derived from the word "pendulum." The gate was severely damaged during the events of 1857 and subsequently demolished during colonial rule.

John Baillie of the *Baillie Garad* fame (Sarkar, 2015) was Resident at Lucknow from1807 – 1815. He was the nephew of Col. William Baillie, who had been imprisoned by Tipu Sultan in Seringapatam, almost 35 years earlier. The Lucknow Residency complex had originally had been porous in nature, with public roads criss-crossing the premises. John Baillie attempted to secure the Residency from its immediate surroundings and the Baillie Guard Gate, erected in 1814 – 15 was a step in this direction. This led to a protest from the first King of Awadh, Ghazi-ud-Din Haider, since this "lofty" gateway was directly opposite, and even over-shadowed the Nawabi *Latkan Darwaza*. Needless to say that the King's protestations did not cut much ice with the colonial administration. Architecturally, it was a rectangular structure, with a single plain, arch in the central bay and two guardhouses on either side, which, height-wise, came up only halfway to the main gateway. Its outer and inner facade were identically ornamented with oval cartouches near the spandrels and a single rectangular block on top, decorated with a double festoon swag. The arches of the guardhouses were flanked by Ionic pilasters and surmounted by *faux* Adam fanlights. Originally, a pair of huge wooden doors were fitted to the gateway. Baillie's Guard gateway, which was severely damaged during the siege of 1857, was partially repaired, and left to serve as a grim reminder of the siege.

Shahnajaf, built by Ghazi-ud-Din Haider had two gateways, the one on the north side, facing the river, being the main entrance. The south side entrance facing the city, is the one which we are more familiar with. This gateway, which is extant, consisted of a simple arch, surmounted by two lions, ostensibly supporting spears and a crown in the centre. The arch is flanked on either side by (1) a small kiosk with a tiny conical spire and (2) a larger outer pavilion with a typical Islamic dome (Plate 16). The inner courtyards are approachable through extended Nawabi gateways, but without the ubiquitous oriel outer windows. The *Shahnajaf* monument has several unusual architectural features, not commonly found in other Nawabi monuments - the first and foremost being its huge squat dome and fortress-like structure. This dome is ornamented by a festoon swag, commonly found in Martin's buildings. Although *Shahnajaf* is said to be a replica of the tomb of Hazrat Ali in Najaf, Iraq, actual comparison of the two belies this theory. Also, the architecture of this massive structure is somewhat misaligned. Unlike other *Imambaras,* which later served as burial places for their builders, the *Shahnajaf* appears to have been conceived as a tomb, which later metamorphosed into an *Imambara.*

Another gateway from the times of Ghazi-ud-Din Haider is the *Sher Darwaza*, or *Burj-e-Asad*, later re-named as Neil's Gate. This gateway, with a chequered history, served as the entrance to a enclosed compound known as *Imamo ka Dargah*, which had twelve small imitation tombs or shrines in honour of the twelve Imams. There are accounts that the enclosed premises actually had 12 x 2 such shrines, one set built by Ghazi-ud-din Haider and another set built by Badshah Begum, his *Khas Mahal*, or chief consort. A photograph of the devastated area by Beato (Plate 17), immediately after 1857, shows the gateway on the north side and single-storeyed chambers (shrines?) at ground level within the compound walls. The gateway was penetrated by a semi-circular arch, flanked by semi-circular arches, having half the dimension of the main arch, and a flat roof, with pairs of Doric columns on both north and south facades. It is difficult to glean further information from the photograph, as the area is strewn with ruins, but it is amply clear that the gateway was provided with an unusually high parapet wall, possibly with appropriate ornamentation. This parapet would have a place in history, as we shall later see.

September 1857 saw the British forces completely stymied in Lucknow's *Charbagh* area and the number of casualties and wounded were increasing everyday. John Bensley Thornhill, of the Bengal Civil Service and Asst. Commissioner of Oudh, who had been staying in the Residency, volunteered to go out and bring in the wounded, as he was familiar with the area. He collected as many of the injured as possible in *doolies* (palanquins), but lost his way while returning, as a result of which, the long train of *doolies* ended beyond the *Sher Darwaza*. Here, they were set upon by the Indian freedom fighters and put to death. Thornhill himself was wounded and his right arm had to be amputated; he died later on October 12, 1857. Col. James George Smith Neil of the 1st Madras Fusiliers had been active, first in Cawnpore (Kanpur) and then in Lucknow during the events of 1857, under the command of General Havelock; his brutalities towards the native populace had alienated him even from his own fellow officers. On September 25, fierce fighting at the site continued. According to Malleson (1891), "*As our men approached the archway, a tremendous firing opened upon them. Neil, who was leading them, passed through the archway, then suddenly pulling up his horse, he directed his aide-de-camp, Gordon, to gallop back and recall a half-battery which had taken a wrong road. He remained there sitting on his horse, his head turned in the direction from which he expected the half battery to emerge, when a sepoy, who had taken post on the arch, discharged his musket at him over the parapet on the top. The ball entered his head behind the left ear and killed him.*" The area within the *Sher Darwaza* was subsequently referred to as "Doolie Square" by the British, in honour of the wounded in *doolies*, who had earlier met their death within the compound walls of the *Darwaza*. A painting of the Doolie Square massacre by an unidentified artist (Company School) depicts the premises of the *Imamo ka Dargah* as being quite similar to Beato's photograph. Post 1857, during the colonial cleansing of Lucknow, the entire area was razed to the ground, save the actual gateway, which was remodelled and provided with a statue of the "brave, resolute, self-reliant" Neil, whose fanatical exploits would be later detailed by Lewellyn-Jones (2007). Sketches of "Neill's Arch" also appeared in *The Illustrated London News*, December 4 (1886) edition, with appropriate indignation on the condition of the "arch" or gateway. Post 1947, the statue of Neil was understandably removed (although there are several places in India, still named in honour of Neil, including Neil Lines in Lucknow cantonment and Neil Island in the Andamans) and a pair of indifferent masonry lions were erected on the top of the gate, together with the side flanks being extended by walls. Due to repeated carpeting of the road, the height of the gateway now appears somewhat diminished, and so it stands in present times, ignored and devoid of the glory and recognition it understandably deserves.

Nasir-ud-Din Haider is not generally credited for building prominent gateways in Lucknow. His buildings (other than his *Karbala* at Iradatnagar) had significant European overtones; therefore it is no surprise to note that the hospitals built by him in the Chowk area, for *Unani* as well as Allopathic systems of medicine had European architecture, including their entry gates. However, his successor, the venerable Mohammad Ali Shah, certainly deserves accolades for creating a range of architectural marvels at *Hussainabad*, including imposing gateways, during his short tenure as King of Awadh (1837 - 1842). Excepting one (which we shall discuss later), all four remaining gateways are extant, some in very good condition, extensively photographed and well documented. Mohammad Ali Shah essentially moved away from the palace-cum-fortress complex of *Chattar Manzil* and *Macchi Bhavan*, traditionally associated with the Nawabi rulers of Lucknow and created *Hussainabad*, commencing from the western face of the *Rumi Darwaza* and ending with the western gateway of *Hussainabad*. Although he continued to reside within the *Chattar Manzil* complex, the area between the *Rumi Darwaza* and the *Hussainabad* gateway was soon dotted with the *Hussainabad* tank, the *Satkhanda* and a squat building, which later metamorphosed into the Picture Gallery and *wasiqa* / royal pension office we know today. However, Beato's high-resolution panorama of *Hussainabad* (Plate 36) reveals a very different picture of the Picture Gallery (pun intended). The original building was a rectangular structure, with two side wings, the ground floor having plane arched openings, with a simple colonnaded veranda on the first floor, with awnings. Other than small finials on the low roof parapet, the building was devoid of any ornamentation. It was definitely not a *baradari* by any stretch of imagination - most probably, it was the office complex for the Hussainabad Trust set up by Mohammad Ali Shah during his lifetime as a quasi-religious endowment, with the descendants of the royal family of Awadh as its trustees. The present building is an extensively remodelled one, with the arched entrances of the ground floor blocked up (so now we see blind arches) and the first floor sporting urn shaped pillars (of iron) on the veranda. It is not known if the building was originally red in colour, or the present coloration is also an example of British creativity. *Hussainabad* also apparently boasted of a *Meena Bazar*, a *Gend Ghar* (bowling alley) and stables, as mentioned by some authors. Originally, the *Hussainabad* area was apparently known as

Jamunia Bagh, due to the presence of orchards of black plum (colloquial: *jamun*) - deforestation under administrative orders being the accepted norm then, as it is today. However, *Hussainabad* as a whole, was not a walled complex. The walled compound actually comprised of the western and eastern gateways, encompassing an outer court with cubicals ranged on the sides, presumably as a sort of market or *bazar*, and an ornate gateway leading to the *Chota* or *Hussainia Imambara* in the south. The eastern gateway, leading to the outer court of the *Hussainabad* being the most significant, was typically Islamic in character, composed of three arched entrances. This *tripolia* gateway, with a taller cusped central archway and smaller arches on either side had each arch flanked by slender, fluted minarets. The central arch had a turret or kiosk on its apex, surmounted by a fluted cupola with a finial. Like the *Rumi Darwaza*, this gateway too has two storied wings on either side, but as a deviation from the *Rumi Darwaza*, the hexagonal surmounted by gilded cupolas on the octagonal bays at the ends (the bays of the Rumi Darwaza had been devoid of any domes of cupolas). Bands of foliated mouldings were the primary decorative element of the gateway; the archways themselves being composed of three arches each, bedecked with flowery patterns. It is generally accepted that the *Hussainabad Imambara* complex was excessively ornamented, but in a delicate fashion, so the effect was not overpowering. It is clear that the architect meant the inner elevations of both the eastern and western gateways to be very plain, but the outer facades to be impressive and ornate. Another unusual feature was the dissimilarity between the outer elevations of the eastern and western gateways; architectural principles would generally require that the both gateways be similar and matching, to create symmetry and balance, but it was not so in the present case.

The ornate gateway (Plate 21) leading to the *Hussainabad Imambara* has been noted for its grandeur, western influence and similarity with the gateway of Dargah Hazrat Abbas, Rustam Nagar; it is not clear which was the original inspirational one. Another gateway, of the same period, which is no longer extant is, however, of considerable interest. This massive structure (Plate 20) appeared to have led to the neighbouring *Jama* (*Jami Masjid*), but not directly so. It was composed of three heterogeneous bays, with the central bay, two storeys in height, bearing the usual triangular pediment, surmounted by decorative urns, on both north and south elevations. The flanking bays were actually three storeyed circular turrets, with decreasing diameter, bearing pennants like a fort. The central passage way extended beyond the gateway, particularly more so on the south end. From a distance, it resembled the *Alambagh Kothi*, which would be built after a decade. Beato's panorama of *Hussainabad* (possibly photographed from the *Jami Masjid*) revealed other unexplained structures in the area, including a circular diorama, the discussion of which would be beyond the scope of this book. In any case, the gateway in question was at right angles to the *Jami Masjid*, and on one side of a *kutcha* (unpaved) road, so it is highly unlikely that it would serve as an approach to the *masjid*. The gateway appears to have been demolished in the 1890s or later, as it appears in quite a few photographs post 1857.

No prominent gateways are ascribed to Amjad Ali Shah, except the ones leading to the *Sibtainabad Imambara*. These followed the typical Nawabi style, described earlier, with no deviations, typically being large rectangular structures, with three pointed arches, cuspated and superimposed, having a roofline with a perforated arcade, introduced in *Gulab Bari*, Faizabad a little less than a century ago. On the other hand, his son and successor, Wajid Ali Shah can be credited for introducing a plethora of imposing gateways, in around his palace complex, *Kaiserbagh*. By conservative estimates, *Kaiserbagh* could have had 10 gateways or more. Other than the well known *Lakhi Darwazas*, leading into the inner courtyard from the east and west, none of the gateways are now extant. Even the *Lakhi Darwazas* stand as husks of their former glorious existence. From the present remains, as well as from photographs and artworks available from various sources, it is evident that these ornate structures were polygonal in design, with a high roofed passageway and chambers on either sides as well as stairwells to access the roof. The roofs had flying buttresses, inspired by Constantia. The ornamentation contained elements from all earlier Nawabi structures; from *chattris* inspired by *Chattar Manzil* to perforated arcades, first seen in *Gulab Bari*, Faizabad, leading to a truly dramatic effect. Diagonally striped pilasters, liberal use of stucco, richly foliated arches, Chinese friezes, oriel windows and a myriad of diverse decorative elements, including turrets in the shape of the *Badshahi* crown, as well as ornamented mumty rooms perhaps gave an overpowering, but harmonious look to the gateways (Plate 22). Of even more interest are the gateways which were demolished, but the photographs of few of these exist. For example, the north-eastern gateway, as photographed by Francis Frith in around 1860, was a two storied structure, with a prominent rectangular pediment and octagonal side bays. Other than the typical *Shahjahani mihrabs* or cusped arches, there was hardly any oriental feature in the structure. For a change, the windows sported real and not *faux* Venetian blinds!! Other than the octagonal bays, the gateway resembled the so-called China Gate we see today. A photograph of another unspecified gateway reveals a structure which was so richly ornamented with a profusion of exaggerated embellishments that it may be difficult to understand the builder's intentions. But then, Wajid Ali Shah's flamboyant creations were the last that Lucknow's Nawabi rule would see, in terms of architecture, good or bad.

The Mermaid gates of *Kaiserbagh* present another enigma (Plate 23). Although no longer extant, their features can be partly studied from several photographs available, before they were pulled down. While the twin fish motif was well recognised as the heraldry of Awadh, Wajid Ali Shah went a step further and his coins, signage and some of his gateways, sported twin mermaids. The mermaid gateways apparently sported large pea green mermaids on the spandrels, and smaller ones on the pediment. Although the gateways themselves were not very elaborate, Beato's photograph of the damaged gateway, immediately after 1857 also depicted two twisted ramp like structures on one side of the main arch; apparently these led to nowhere, and there have been many conjectures about their true purpose. The main arch was rather plain, flanked by striped columns. An undulating parapet with oval openings and decorative urns, together with rectangular turrets completed the picture. The gateway itself led to several courtyards, each punctuated with further gateways, bearing the Nawabi fish motifs. In all, the mermaid gateways were unique in their own right, if rather bizarre from architectural point of view. During colonial rule, the ramps were demolished and the gateways were spruced up remarkably well. However, as if on an afterthought (akin to many other Nawabi structures), they were allowed to go to seed and were subsequently demolished, possibly in the early 1900s.

It is generally accepted that the main entrance of *Kaiserbagh* was from the north-east side, through a gateway that is no longer extant. A rare photograph of the gateway by Samuel Bourne (1867), shows hazy details of what the main entrance of *Kaiserbagh* might have been. In today's context, as one proceeded west, down Rani Laksmi Bai Marg, the present day China Gate would be on the left, after which a range of buildings of the inner courtyard could be seen, with colonnaded verandas on the ground floor and windows with *faux* Venetian blinds on the first floor, within a common, low boundary wall. The road would lead to a European style gateway (Plate 24), with a flat parapet and minimal decorative elements (unlike the richly ornate *Lakhi Darwazas* inside). The main recessed arch of this gateway spanned two storeys, and was flanked by a pair of free standing columns of Ionic order. The side bays (flanking the central bay) were two storeyed high, with rectangular openings, possibly being stairways.

There was a complete absence of Nawabi architectural elements that one would expect in an entrance leading to the palace. Its proximity to the *Sher Darwaza* / Neil Gate makes it an ideal location for a sniper to climb on its parapet and shoot at Neil's head.

We have earlier discussed *Sher Darwaza* gate in detail, with Malleson's (1891) specific quotation on how Neil died. After discussing the possibility of the NE *Kaiserbagh* gateway being the vantage point from where the Indian sniper took a pot-shot at Neil's head, we shall now discuss a third possibility, after examining a rare photograph of another free standing gateway which stood between *Sher Darwaza* and NE *Kaiserbagh* gateway (Plate 22. This gate or archway stood parallel and west to NE gateway was at right angles to the *Sher Darwaza* (Plate 25). It did not lead to the *Kaiserbagh*; instead it led to the older seraglio of the Nawabs - the *Darshan Bilas* / *Chattar Manzil* / *Lal Baradari* complex, from the eastern side. Being hardly twenty feet away, the parapet of this gate would be much more suitable for the unknown Indian freedom fighter's firing position. Architecturally, it was a typically Nawabi gateway, with a flat parapet, a central, ornamented archway spanning two storeys, which was then flanked by two heterogeneous bays on either side. The inner bays adjacent to the main arch were composed of two storeys, with the ground floor sporting blind arches and the upper floors having oriel windows. The outer side flanks were again built in a dissimilar fashion, possibly being stairways leading to the parapet. Of course, we are discussing the eastern face of this gate; the western elevation will never be known. But from the trends observed earlier, it is entirely possible that the western facade would have been totally different to the eastern one. Perhaps this was the famed *Dar-e-Daulat* gateway. But architecturally, the gateway does not seem to deserve the narrative created around it, as if it had been a gateway to the heavens themselves. Also, in the hurly-burly of 1857, the Indian sniper's position may never be truly determined, although the place of Neils' death under the *Sher Darwaza* is more or less established.

Wajid Ali Shah's other prominent gateways, *viz.* the *Sikandar Bagh* and *Alambagh* gateways also deserve mention. *Sikandar Bagh* gateway (Plate 26) could have been inspired by the quintessential Roman triumphal arch (*cf* the Triumphal Arch of Orange, France built around 27 BC), the main entrance being flanked by heterogeneous bays; the inner bay sporting octagonal projects on the south facade, and the corner bays being stairwells, topped by rectangular Chinoiserie cupolas having ridged tiles. The side bays had three levels, whereas the central entrance arch spanned only two levels. The gateway was embellished with Islamic domes, cusped arches,

European pediments and Corinthian columns. Consistent with Nawabi (Indo-European school) architecture, it managed to present a harmonious, if architecturally dissonant picture. The interiors of the passageway was decorated with intricate stucco, obviously inspired by Lucknow's famed *chikankari* embroidery work.

Originally, the gateway to *Alambagh* (present day Chander Nagar Gate) was a squat, two storied structure, topped with triangular pediments on its north and south elevations (Plate 27). The entrance was composed of double archways, the outer ones being the usual cuspated ones, and the inner ones being plane. The archway spanned two storeys, and was flanked by two heterogeneous bays on each side, and the fish symbol in bas-relief on its spandrels. The inner bays were rectangular, bearing rectangular doorways, the lower ones opening outside on the ground and the upper ones opening on balconies, which ran across both flanks, i.e. a common balcony across two flanks on either side. The tympanum of the pediment was pierced with a circular decorative opening, with the cornice sprouting leafy stucco projections and tiny finials. These leafy stucco projections had first appeared on the extrados of the eastern gateway of *Hussainabad*, then on the Mermaid gateway of *Kaiserbagh*. Both were shorn of much of their architectural features, post-1857, with the Mermaid gate disappearing altogether. The *Alambagh* gateway exists today, spruced up but bereft of many of its original architectural features, including the projecting balconies on the first floor, the decorative stucco petals on the pediment, as well as the tiny projecting finials.

Fig. 6. The Unidentified "Gateway to Lucknow" on Fire - Price's Lighting Tapers (1905)

Any discussion on Lucknow's historical gateways from another era would be incomplete without a mention of an yet-to-be unidentified gateway, which was so prominent that it's image appeared on several diverse platforms in Europe. These images provide clues to this enigmatic structure.

However, we must digress a little and go back to the times of Burhan-ul-Mulk, the founder of the Nawabi dynasty of Awadh. During this period, Sheikh Abdullah or Abdullah Khan had built a fort at Ghazipur (on the border of present day states of UP and Bihar), the ruins of which can be seen today. The entrance gateway to this fort, which is still extant, appears to have served as an architectural inspiration for the unidentified "gateway to Lucknow", because the same shared several common features. A photograph of this gateway to Lucknow first appeared as a photogravure print in 1892, as a typical Nawabi edifice, having a large three-storied rectangular structure. The main entrance was composed of two superimposed pointed arches, the larger and outer one being cuspated, and the inner one being plane. The outer arch had the usual twin fish symbol on its spandrels. The gateway had blind arches on its ground floor, flanking the main arch; the first floor had oriel windows supported by corbels. The second floor was punctuated by a series of windows; the parapet was provided with a balustraded railing and tiny finials. Among the diverse places where the image of this gateway made an appearance, one was on the labels of Guerin-Boutron, Revault, Matte Fils and Hugon brand of Belgian - French chocolates, entitled *La porte de Lucknow, Indes*. The labels even mentioned (in French) that Lucknow had been the site of a terrible massacre in 1857 - 58. The occasion was a French Exhibition in Moscow in 1889. A more dramatic version of the gateway appeared on the back of an advertising postcard for Price's "Lighting Tapers" in 1905 (Fig. 6). In this, the actual scene of war was depicted, with the gateway being on fire, and mayhem all around. It is obvious that Europe was still remembering the events of Lucknow, through several decades. Although the gateway had been already demolished, post 1857. Almost one and half a century before, an artist named Edward Hawker Locker had painted the Ghazipur gateway; if one places the artworks of the Lucknow and Ghazipur gateways side by side, their architectural similarities are quite evident.

Architecture of Lucknow

These are the ruins of our memories, which loom in our minds like the Parthenon, even as they are decayed and weathered by time and regret.

—*Jess Walter*

The ruins often amaze us because we are so arrogant that it is difficult for us to accept the talents of the people of the past.

—*Mehmet Murat Ildan*

Chapter - 6

Euro-Islamic Fantasies

It has been rightly said (Singh, 2001) that the cross-cultural, hybrid architecture of Nawabi Lucknow (and of Awadh, to a lesser degree) has been over-studied and the outcome has usually been *a torrent of criticism.* However, considering the sheer number of scholars and travellers who have described and discussed the same, there is no doubt that there is something fascinating about the subject, even though the grandeur of Mughal architecture was present almost next door to Lucknow, *i.e.* at Agra and Delhi. Lucknow's Nawabi architecture has also been a topic of many doctoral and masters degree dissertations and this book chapter does not seek to duplicate the inferences therein, but to present an analytical narrative, without going into technicalities, which can be of interest to the casual reader, who may neither be a historian or a qualified architect.

While authors such as Llewellyn-Jones (1992), Tandan (2001, 2008) and Fonia (2013), attempted to create a descriptive inventory of the numerous buildings of the Nawabi period, classifying their architectural features and aesthetics, in the social and political context prevalent in those times, Praveen (1989) had described vignettes of life within some of the more popular buildings, in a delightful folksy manner, based on oral tradition and urban legends. On the other hand, Abbas (2009, 2010) painstakingly described the present pitiable conditions of many of these structures, several of which he characterised as "lost" either because the structures had totally vanished or had been modified to an extent that they were no longer recognizable in their original form or purpose. Few prominent structures of Lucknow, including the *Rumi Darwaza, Bada* and *Chota Imambaras* and the *Residency*, have always managed to remain in the limelight; Sarkar (2015) steered clear from this well-trodden path and described several, lesser known unique structures which had escaped public attention and stood today as "silent sentinels" of a lost era. Varshney (2017) lucidly presented the architectural drawings of some of these buildings in present times, juxtaposed with recent colour photographs and brief descriptive write-ups. Of late, several proposals, both academic and administrative, were also put forward for the restoration or rejuvenation, re-adaptation and re-use of some of these buildings, including their appropriate landscaping (Nagpal & Sinha, 2009; Sinha, 2011, 2014, Anon., 2017, Singh & Ahmad, 2019). No doubt, the idea seems very attractive and some work has already progressed in this direction, although a lot remains to be done.

Any discussion on Lucknow's architecture of yore must take into consideration the events after Wajid Ali Shah's exit in 1856, followed by colonial rule, during which Lucknow was re-shaped and "*fairly improved off the face of this earth.*" The source material available on Nawabi structures is therefore very sparse, because due to this colonial cleansing, hundreds of Nawabi creations, belonging to both nobility and ordinary citizens, were razed to the ground, ostensibly to create wide swathes of open spaces. This cleaning exercise started during 1856 - 57 itself in a routine manner and was resumed after 1858, but this time, with a ferocity and vengefulness, not witnessed earlier. The structures which were allowed to remain were structurally modified, their use patterns changed and landscaping re-worked, so that the buildings now stood as isolated entities, instead of being part of a balanced landscape composed of palaces, gardens, places of worship and utilities. For example, the seraglio of Awadh rulers, the *Chattar Manzil* complex had the *Bada* and *Chota Chattar Manzils* facing each other, with gardens, water bodies, a circular diorama and various other structures in between the two palaces. The complex also consisted of the *Farhat Baksh Kothi, Jarnail Kothi*, *Darshan Bilas*, *Gulistan-e-Iram* and *Lal Baradari*, connected underground via tunnels and situated in a planned manner from outside. A gateway, the *Latkan Darwaza* or Clock Tower Gate (so named due to a mock clock design on it), faced the Residency's Bailey Guard gateway on one side, and led to the Nawabi palace complex on the other side. Post 1857, the British opened a road between the two *Chattar Manzils*, demolishing the internecine structures, thereby creating a wide space between the two palaces, which now stood in magnificent isolation. The *Latkan Darwaza* was demolished, although the Baillie's Guard gate was repaired (but shorn of its original ornamentation). Sa'adat Ali Khan's later additions to the *Farhat Baksh Kothi* were removed, and so was the first floor of *Jarnail Kothi*. Due to obvious reasons, the destruction of *Kaiserbagh* was much more concerted (having being the stronghold of Awadh freedom fighters) so much so that today, only scattered information about the palace complex is available, by way of photographs and hypothetical descriptions. It may never be known what *Kaiserbagh* actually was in the heydays of Wajid Ali Shah's rule. Similar was the destruction of Nawabi gardens, e.g. *Sikandar Bagh, Charbagh, Aishbagh, Vilayati Bagh, Musa Bagh, Badshah Bagh*, and to the structures therein. So can any discussion on Lucknow's architecture be really complete without even *knowing* what actually existed within the walls of these now defunct Nawabi gardens? The citadel of *Macchi Bhavan* was also destroyed; a detailed discussion on the historiography of this famed "fort" of pre-Nawabi Lucknow has been discussed in another chapter of this book. The woodlands of *Dilkusha* were appropriated to create a new military cantonment and *Dilkusha Kothi*, now stood isolated from its surroundings. However, contrary to popular belief, the *kothi* did *not* get damaged in the events of 1857-58. It remained in use by the British army, and appears to have been partly demolished by them in around 1870s. Half a century later, Edith Cuthell (1905), wife of Captain Thomas George Cuthell, who had stayed in the Lucknow cantonment observed, *"The ruins of Heart's Delight have been tenderly gardened. Gay creepers clothe the tower and the loop-holed walls, but o'er the sloping mound where the roses bloom. Can it be an old forgotten tomb?"* Thankfully enough, details exist about the structure, including its origins, use, later modifications and architectural features.

Another magnificent building which was shorn of its upper floor, signature half-dome and other unique accoutrements, including domes with parasols, resembling the *Chattar Manzils*, was *Roshan-ud-Daula Kothi* or *Kaiser Pasand*. Not many would know that the *Kaiserbagh Baradari* we see today, originally had small gilded domes on its four corners. One of the domes was damaged during the British bombardment of 1858; thereafter, although the *Kaiserbagh* palace complex was semi-razed to the ground, the *baradari* was allowed to stand, minus its signature corner domes. The so-called *Lal Baradari* within *Badshah Bagh* (now constituting the Lucknow University campus) appears to be a misnomer as it does not have the features of a *baradari* at all. So what actually lay within the pleasure gardens of Nasir-ud-Din Haider? A flattering description is available from Fanny Parkes' writings (1850) and even today, *Badshah Bagh* abounds with scattered ruins of walls with bastions at short intervals, having signs of cannon ball impact, gates of different sizes and architectural features, a deep well, and what possibly constituted a water heating arrangement. The canal, with a small bridge, paved with marble is still extant (now given a coat of paint) but devoid of its original prettiness, as it either remains dry or filled with stagnant rainwater and sludge. Nothing much remains of

Sikandar Bagh (now occupied by the CSIR, for one of its laboratories, the NBRI), excepting it's gate, adjoining mosque, parts of walls with cannon ball holes, and scattered ruins inside. Fleeting descriptions of the Wajid Ali Shah's pleasure garden, are available, particularly with reference to its storming by Colin Campbell on November 16, 1857. The gardens were supposed to have substantial structures inside (where the Indian freedom fighters concealed themselves), which is also evident from Beato's epic photograph post-1857 (Khorakiwala, 2013), which shows a pillared, double storied, highly ornamented Grecian style building, having a prominent triangular pediment and colonnaded verandas. Therefore, we must proceed with this discussion on Lucknow's famed architecture with a heavy heart, knowing that what we conclude is based on a very sparse knowledge base; we will never really know what Lucknow actually possessed, in terms of its architectural marvels, in the heydays of Nawabi rule. To quote an old adage, what we know is little; what we do not know is immense.

Lucknow's pre-Nawabi architecture can be observed from extant structures such as the *Akbari Darwaza*, the *Firangi Mahal* and a tomb complex called *Nadan Mahal*, containing graves of Sheikh Abdur Rahim "Bijnori", his wife, Sheikh Ibrahim Chishti and several others of that period. *Nadan Mahal* is one of the few complexes in Lucknow constructed with stone, in addition to bricks and plaster. The use of Hindu motifs such as elephant heads in the ornamentation indicates a fusion style of architecture in Lucknow, even before the arrival of the Nawabi dynasty from Persia. The most prominent pre-Nawabi structure, however is the *Alamgir* mosque, popularly known as *Teele Wali Masjid*, on account of it having being constructed during the times of Aurangzeb, over a mound, sacred to the local Hindu populace. Adjacent to the mosque is the mausoleum of Islamic scholar, Shah Pir Mohammad who died in 1674, during Aurangzeb's reign. Both the structures are typically Mughal in terms of adornment and architectural symmetry, with no outside influences. The now demolished *Panch Mahalla* Gate was also typically oriental, as evident from its painting by Thomas Daniell (1801) and later photographs. Burhan-ul-Mulk was not known for erecting buildings during his tumultuous tenure, but his successor, Safdarjang is generally known for strengthening the *Macchi Bhavan* and *Jalalabad* forts (discussed elsewhere). The third Nawab, Shuja-ud-Daula, after his defeat in the Battle of Buxar in 1764, settled down in Faizabad and from then onwards, commenced on a building spree, so characteristic of the Awadh Nawabi dynasty. Sometime in 1766, after setting his affairs in order, he made extensive additions to the humble mansion of his grandfather, erected a new and better furnished palace, mud forts, a flower garden called *Angoori Bagh* and an aviary; a wall was constructed around his capital city which was sixty feet thick which had a moat surrounding it (Srivastava, 1945). While *Angoori Bagh* was situated inside the fort, *Moti Bagh* and *Lal Bagh* were in the city. Shuja-ud-Daula's own palace was a magnificent structure on the banks of the Ghagra river; in a coloured etching by William Hodges (1789), the ruins of the palace are depicted in stark contrast against a brooding landscape. Obviously, it had become a derelict place, within a decade of Shuja's death. On the other hand, an 18th century watercolour by an unknown artist, shows the palace in happier times. After the treaty of Allahabad in 1765 and the withdrawal of Shuja to Faizabad, European fortune seekers had started to make a beeline for the then capital of Awadh (which started prospering and gain importance after Delhi). One of these was Colonel Antoine de Polier, who remained active in the court of Shuja-ud-Daula at Faizabad and later, at Asaf-ud-Daula's court at Lucknow. The European influence in the architecture of Shuja-ud-Daula's palace and fort at Faizabad makes one suspect the hand of Polier in its design (Srivastava, 1945). If so, it was certainly the first instance of Euro-Islamic hybrid architecture appearing in Awadh. Other buildings including palaces and tombs of that period in Faizabad, including the tripolia gates remained typically oriental, without any occidental influences. Several works of art from that period, depicting a palace in Lucknow, on the banks of the river Gomti are also available. These include works of Thomas Longcroft, Thomas and William Daniell, William Hodges, William Carpenter, William Simpson, Henry Salt and an engraving by James Fittler. It may be pointed out that Shuja had also stayed in Lucknow for sometime and occupied the *Macchi Bhavan* complex, which, from then on, was referred as the palace of Shuja-ud-Daula in Lucknow. The palace appears to be a two storied fortification, with bastions, pavilions on the roof and the old *Panch Mahalla* gateway or *Sheikhan Darwaza* as the entrance on the west, in all the artworks of that period. However, William Daniell had actually sketched a portion of the palace interiors in question. This sketch, together with a description provided by Rev. Hobart Caunter (1835), provide us with a detailed view of the surroundings, as Caunter had observed:

"The buildings represented in the engraving are merely garden-house, constructed of brick and beautifully stuccoed with chunam; they are raised on chaupoutres (platforms), with steps to ascend from the garden to the first storey. They are spacious, having broad terraced roofs, and at each angle a small cupola covered with the same delicate stucco. Some of them are surmounted by an elegant square canopy with curtains depending from four sides. These canopies are supported upon small pointed arches; and

here is a delightful retreat from the heat of the noonday sun. The interior of the garden houses is divided into apartments, which are occupied by different functionaries to whom the charge of the gardens is committed. Although the exterior effect of these buildings is sufficiently imposing, they nevertheless do not present much attraction to the traveller, except as forming part of the palace of this distinguished city. Though less costly in their structure, it must be allowed that they are more picturesque than some of the grander edifices."

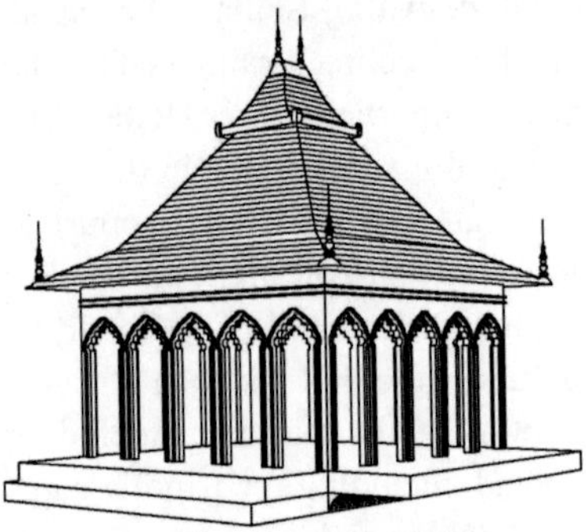

Fig. 7. The Nawabi "Square Canopy"

In many of the old artworks available, the square canopy, so favoured by the Nawabs of Awadh, can be observed from afar, being situated on the terrace of the "palace". Beato's panorama (1858) of the *Macchi Bhavan* also shows same structures with awnings and curtains, but this time, in stark desolation. The square canopy would also appear in the pavilions of *Aishbagh, Vilayati Bagh* and other Nawabi garden complexes later.

Claude Martin, a French soldier, who had sought employment with the English East India Company, had been primarily assigned to carry out survey work in Bengal, Bihar and later Awadh. Martin came in contact with Shujaud- Daula and also Asaf-ud-Daula probably in 1774 at Lucknow (Hill, 1901) and he joined the newly appointed Nawab's services in 1776 as Superintendent of his arsenal, duly approved by the Company. He was granted permission by Calcutta to permanently reside at Lucknow, remain exempt from military duties, hold the rank of Major but draw the allowances of a Captain. Being a man of manifold talents (Llewellyn-Jones, 1999), with time, he not only managed to ingratiate himself to Asaf-ud-Daula, he also proceeded to engage himself in a number of profitable ventures, which ranged from indigo cultivation to casting cannons. According to Tribunus (1908), although Martin was "*a gentleman of talents, intelligence, knowledge of the world, of pre-eminent skill and gallantry in his profession, he was unhappily cursed with an irritation and impatience of temper, as galling to others as harassing to himself. He was naturally imperious and opinionated, conceited of his rank, and presumptuous of his descent.*" Col. Jack Warren (Gamon, 1926) of the EIC wrote deprecatingly about Martin, as one "*who hung perpetually over the Nawab's seat, smirking benignantly when royalty smirked, and anticipating royalty's every wish. His compatriots seemed to regard him with a mild disgust, though they were careful not to let the Captain himself observe it; since the position he had achieved at this court already rendered him an enemy to be reckoned with, if he were offended.*" Martin invested his wealth wisely in land and property - and seemingly ended up owning at least eleven houses in Lucknow (Llewellyn-Jones, 1992), in addition to properties in Calcutta and a "palace" in Biposi, Najafgarh - the site of his indigo cultivation venture, on the banks of the Ganga, near Kanpur. He set up a "Captain Bazar" for providing luxuries and European goods to moneyed buyers (on the south bank of the Gomti, roughly in the area where the Martyr's Memorial stands today). Martin's crowning glory was of course, *Lakhi Pera* or Constantia, which was not completed during his lifetime, and ultimately became his mausoleum. It was never established where he lived during his early years in Lucknow, but he shifted to his "Country House" (later renamed as *Farhat Baksh* by Sa'dat Ali Khan) in 1781. Details of this unique creation have been given elsewhere (Llewellyn-Jones, 1992, Sarkar, 2015) and need not be repeated here. Another detailed account of his country house, published in *The European Magazine* (1790) is reproduced below:

"It is built with brick stuccoed, partly on piers sunk within the current of the river Goomty, which runs with violent rapidity during periodic rains, joining the Ganges about ten miles to the eastward of the city of Benares. You approach the house on the land side through an arched gateway, sufficiently lofty to admit an elephant with its turret; at some distance from this, you enter the shrubbery through a winding walk, ornamented with the richest vegetable productions of India and China, with such of those of Europe as thrive in that climate. On your arrival close to the house, a drawbridge first presents itself thrown over a moat surrounding the building on the land side, communicating with the river, from which it can be filled with pleasure, either for the purpose of cooling the lower apartments or that of defence from the sudden attacks of banditti or rebels. This latter purpose of its construction will not appear very consistent with European notions of modern buildings, and renew our ideas of feudal jealousy. From the bridge you ascend by a few steps to an elegant piazza, commanding a prospect of the pleasure grounds, where you enter a beautiful and spacious hall of an octagon form, with doors leading into various apartments with which it is surrounded on three sides, so disposed as to admit at pleasure a free current of air through them from every corner. This leads to one of the finest rooms in India for size, proportion and finishing, built on the arch in

the river; the prospect from hence over the latter, toward the Faizabad road, does not contain much variety, but is richly interspersed with mange groves and corn fields; that of Lucknow from one of the end windows promises a much finer city than on entering it exhibits. After passing through two smaller apartments, communicating with this room and the octagon hall, you descend to a range on a level with the river, containing baths and fountains - the latter so disposed as to keep playing with advantage in the equal distribution of water against the windows, which when the hot winds prevail during spring months, are kept covered in the day with frames of green brambles; these being kept constantly wet by the fountains, cool the wind in its passage into the apartments, and thereby procure a constant temperature within, proportioned to the strength of the wind abroad, and capacity of the frames to retain the water dripping. The upper apartments, with their terraces and turrets, are principally disposed for the purpose of sleeping in the open air, and recreation during the hot season. The observatory is well supplied with philosophical apparatus."

The narrator then ends his narrative with a supercilious comment: *"We are the more happy in having it in our power to present our readers with the above, as this building and its contents have not a little contributed to impress the less-informed of the natives of that remote part of the country with just ideas of the superiority of European taste and knowledge.*"

European superiority aside, just where did Martin reside, during the period: 1775 - 1781? More importantly, it is generally accepted that the architectural elements appearing in *Farhat Baksh* (or the trimmed *Farhat Baksh* we see today) served as "inspiration" for Lucknow's later buildings. But can we accept this with full conviction? In all probability, Martin resided in the house commonly referred to as "old Martin House" in Khayaliganj area of old Lucknow (Plate 34). This house passed through several ownerships and is presently known as *Kakori Kothi*. It is not that well explored or described, being a private property, but nevertheless, known for its unique colonnaded "circular room" which spans two levels, like a small indoor arena (Plate 35). Some writers have suggested that this space, was actually a cockpit, used for watching cock fights, which seems highly improbable, as not much would be visible of two fighting cockerels, if one took his seat on the first floor and looked down below. Another theory is that Martin was into jewel cutting, and this circular room received natural light from one side or the other, by way of large bay windows on all sides. Again, it seems implausible, as the upper floor has natural light, no doubt, but not the ground floor, which is somewhat dingy.

Whatever might have been the purpose of this unexplained "circular room", if we accept the hypothesis that *Kakori Kothi* was a sort of crucible for Martin's architectural innovations, then we can easily understand the chronology of his innovations being carried forward in his later creations and also to other Nawabi structures of Lucknow. The first and foremost was the presence of a prominent hallway (circular room in *Kakori Kothi*) on the ground floor, with doorways leading off to other rooms in various directions. This could be seen later in the *Asafi Kothi* (now partly demolished), *Farhat Baksh*, Constantia and Barowen (*Musa Bagh Kothi*), albeit in rectangular or octagonal form. *Kakori Kothi* abounds with *faux* windows and Venetian blinds, which appear in innumerable later buildings of Lucknow. It has been stated by some writers that these were specific to buildings which had *zenana* (secluded living area for women) quarters - to give an impression of space and openness, the womenfolk in *purdah* (practice of female seclusion in the middle east and parts of Asia) actually lacking in ventilation and access to open air. But the manner in which this feature got repeated again and again in numerous Lucknow buildings of that period, creates a doubt in one's mind, because not all these buildings had *zenana* quarters. The term "fanlight" had been coined around 1770 in Europe, to describe a semi-circular over-door window, having a number of panes radiating like a fan, from a central floret. Fanlights had evolved at this stage from a plain functional over-door window or "skylight", admitting light to a dark hallway, and these later became both functional and a decorative features of entrances. Martin seems to have introduced this European feature to Lucknow's buildings, including palaces as well as *Imambaras,* which soon started sporting this decorative feature. But Martin went a step further - like the *faux* Venetian blinds, he also introduced the mock fanlights over doorways - for example, these can still be seen in *Kakori Kothi*, in all their fading glory.

Fig. 8. The Festoon Swag

Kakori Kothi has the ubiquitous festoon swag as ornamentation - something which would appear repeatedly in several later buildings, in various *avatars*, from the *Farhat Baksh* to *Badshah Bagh*, *Darshan Bilas*, on the insignificant *Dilaram Kothi* and the water "pavilions" of Sa'adat Ali Khan. Surprisingly, it made an appearance around the squat dome of the *Shahnajaf Imambara* also!!

The swag adorned the original Baillie Guard gate of Lucknow's Residency, indicating that British Residents too were not averse to adopting Martin's designs, if it caught their fancy. Baillie Guard gate, which had been severely damaged during 1857 was partly restored, but this time, without its original ornamentation above. The triangular pediment, which had modest beginnings in *Kakori Kothi* returned with vengeance on the south side entrance of *Farhat Baksh*, and then made appearances repeatedly, from the *Gulistan-e-Iram* to *Taaron Wali Kothi*. And to the *Hussainabad* gateways. If one closely observes Beato's picture of the ruins of *Macchi Bhavan* of 1858, a tall European-style building, with the usual prominent pediment situated behind the ruined gateway, becomes obvious. An insignificant, never before discussed aspect of the architecture of this period, again attributed to Martin, is the humble iron drain pipe for waste water. Jutting out from the buildings, the opening of these iron pipes were marvellously fashioned, or cut, so that they resembled the open mouth of a serpent or dragon. These drain pipes can still be seen in *Kakori Kothi*, and elsewhere, including the *Lal Badardari* at *Badshah Bagh.* Another of Martin's creations, the three roof-top pavilions of *Farhat Baksh* subsequently made an appearance atop the *Darshan Bilas,* albeit in a modified form. Martin's flying buttresses of Constantia were duplicated in the *Kaiserbagh* gateways, and much later, in the gateway leading to Butler Palace.

During the initial stages of his presence in Lucknow, Asaf-ud-Daula had resided in the *Macchi Bhavan* fort-cum-palace complex, described elsewhere in this book. However, he was also responsible for building the *Daulat Khana* (*Daulat Khana Asafi*) between present day *Hussainabad* and the Gomti river. This palace complex was accessible through a gateway, commonly known as *Sheesh Mahal* gateway, which shall be discussed in detail in another chapter. *Daulat Khana* apparently consisted of a range of palaces, out of which *Sheesh Mahal* was one. *Asafi Kothi* was another. It is not disputed that Martin had an significant contribution towards the architecture of the palace complex. However, details are sparse. A high resolution photograph of *Hussainabad* by Beato, post-1857, is very informative in this regard. On the left of the photograph, almost contiguous with the present day Picture Gallery (in its original form), one can see the *Sheesh Mahal* gateway leading to the *Daulat Khana*, which in itself, was not very extensive, being hemmed-in by the Gomti river from the north. Immediately behind the *Sheesh Mahal* gateway, a wholly Europeanised, single storey building existed, having a semi-circular, colonnaded portico in front and triangular pediments (possibly on both sides), with a hipped roof over the central bay. This was possibly the *Gol Kothi*. Beyond this, a little to the right side, was a very ordinary, single storey rectangular building with an arched veranda and a flat roof, without any architectural pretensions, almost like a latter day, colonial-style school building - supposedly the *Sheesh Mahal*. A double storey building lay beyond it, with a semi-circular, arched portico, and a semi-circular colonnaded veranda on the first floor, topped with a bulbous dome in front, and a much smaller dome at the rear. The windows of this building had triangular pediments; the roof was devoid of any substantial parapet. This domed building had minimal ornamentation but was comparatively more in line with being a "palace" as compared to the other two buildings described above, and was possibly the *Asafi Kothi*. *Daulat Khana* was a walled, gated complex, but not fortified. The single storey building with the arched veranda is extant today (in parts). The complex also had few scattered buildings, one of them (near the entrance) resembling a *baradari*, and the others being of no consequence. *Daulat Khana* also had a small arched gateway on its eastern side. Other than the *Sheesh Mahal* gateway, none of the three main structures described above had any Islamic overtones; they were purely westernised, from an architecture point of view. Other structures to the left of the main buildings, do not appear in the photograph. However, we do know that a small tank, the *Zenana talab* existed (which is extant today), as well as a ball court called *Gend Khana*, together with randomly placed gardens and pavilions. The *Daulat Khana* also had a six-storied tower, which does not appear in Beato's photograph, but does so in a photograph by Bourne & Shepherd (1860s). Surprisingly, this tall tower has never been documented by historians, and only a fleeting reference of this "*Dowlat Channah* (sic), with the pagoda" is found in the *Asiatic Journal* (1816).

Earlier, Thomas Longcroft, a renowned "British Old Masters" artist had visited Lucknow in 1784, and had produced a series of detailed water colours of the city, then developing under Asaf-ud-Daula. Although his "views" of the city streets and common people were less than flattering, he had actually depicted the construction of the *Asafi Masjid* in one of his artworks. This is unequivocal evidence that the *Asafi Imambara* complex was actually completed in around 1790 and not 1784 (this aspect is discussed in detail in the Chapter on *Macchi Bhavan*). More importantly, Longcroft produced four artworks depicting views of *Daulat Khana* from across the river. From his depiction (Plate 5, 6), we come to know that the complex was flush against the Gomti river, surrounded by a low running wall, punctuated by single as well as double storey pavilions. While we are all familiar with Martin's *Farhat Baksh* jutting into the river proper, with the water flowing through the portico, the latter serving as a pier, we see that some of the pavilions of *Daulat Khana* too jutted out into the river, with the water flowing through the lower floors. Plates 50 and 54 depicting *Panorama of Lucknow* by an unidentifed artist confirm the same premise.

Longcroft also depicted *Asafi Kothi* with its twin domes under construction, with the accompanying scaffolding. In one of his artworks (not included in this book), he clearly depicted a bridge of boats across the river, reaching directly to an entrance gateway in the boundary wall of the palace complex. He indicated that in places, the boundary wall reached till the river bank, but in other places it was a little behind; the space between the river and the boundary profusely covered with *sarpat* grass (*Saccharum munja*, a tall grass so commonly found along river banks in India). More importantly, in one of his artworks, he depicted the six storey tower (or pagoda discussed above) (Plate 6), which was apparently not free standing, but appeared to be a part of a single storey *baradari* or pavilion type building. The tower, although resembling the latter date *Satkhanda*, was not tapering. It was topped by a gilded dome, small in size having an arcade below it. In fact the dome and an arcade had approximately half the circumference of the other levels. The representations of buildings which Longcroft made, were almost as accurate as latter day modern photographs would be (Manners & Williamson, 1920).

Sa'adat Ali Khan was appointed as sixth *Nawab Wazir* of Awadh in July, 1798. Having being exposed to western influences for considerable periods during his youth, he went a step ahead of his half-brother, Asaf-ud-Daula, in building palaces and mansions across Lucknow, with unabashed European influence, the most notable being the *Dilkusha Kothi* (Plate 37). Sadat Ali Khan's *aide-de-camp* Major Gore Ouseley designed the building based on the plan of the Seton Delaval House in Northumberland, England. But it was not a straightforward copy, as stated by some writers. One of the earliest "views" of *Dilkusha Kothi* by artist Seeta Ram in 1814 (Losty, 2015) shows the building without its characteristic Chinoiserie pagodas having stylised leaf canopies with spires, on the angular corner staircase towers of the *kothi*. Fortunately, enough photographs, architectural details and even modern-day computer-aided projections and floor plans are available for *Dilkusha*, and it is almost certain that the structure underwent a major make-over during the reign of Nasir-ud-Din Haider, around 1830, giving it the look we are familiar with, *i.e.* the Chinoiserie pagodas

Fig. 9. The Chinoiserie Pagoda

on top of the staircase towers and the removal of the hipped roof and pediment, which crowned the top of the central bay. Indeed, the usage of *Dilkusha Kothi* also changed from being a country house to a hunting lodge. *Dilkusha* never had a *zenana*; it had real windows and none of the *faux* ornamentation, so popularised by Martin. But its architectural features served as inspiration for several later buildings of Lucknow. The Chinoiserie pagodas appeared in the *Darshan Bilas Kothi*, but that is understandable, since *Darshan Bilas* was meant to showcase the palace architecture of Lucknow at a single place: *Barowen* in the west, *Farhat Baksh* in the middle and *Dilkusha* in the far east of the city. The pagodas are visible in an unidentified building in *Hussainabad* (now demolished); their last appearance was on the gateway of *Sikandar Bagh,* but instead of being circular, these were now squat and square.

In addition to Sa'adat Ali Khan's various talents (and shortcomings), it seems that he was also an amateur architect, as mentioned by Valentia (1803). To quote the Viscount:

"April 1- At half after five, Mr (Henry) *Salt and I set off on elephants to visit the Nawab at one of his country seats, situated about three miles beyond the palace. We arrived there in a little more than an hour, and found his Excellency waiting for us. It is called Baroun, and was built by himself after a plan of his own. The architecture is an imitation of Grecian, with many faults, yet a very fine portico, rising the whole height of the house, gives a considerable degree of grandeur to the front. It is a vast pile, but contains only one large room on each floor. The furniture is European and the walls are ornamented with portraits of his English friends, and the different Generals who have visited this place. On the roof is erected a range of small rooms, which occasionally serves as zenana, being surrounded by a high parapet wall. It is hardly finished, and has not yet been inhabited."* In this narrative, we get another first hand description of *Musa Bagh Kothi* or *Barowen*, with the startling revelation that it had been designed by Sa'adat Ali Khan himself. The name *Barowen* (or *Baronne*) was possibly derived from the name of the village called *Baraun* or *Baraoun* (Tieffenthaler, 1786), where the building was situated. Observing the features of *Musa Bagh Kothi* (Plate 38), it has been generally accepted by writers that the building had been designed by Martin, with several architectural features freely borrowed from Kedleston Hall, an English country house in Kedleston, Derbyshire. On examining the time lines, the chronology of the building's development becomes less hazy. Sa'adat Ali Khan became Nawab in 1798 and *Barowen* was not yet complete in 1803

Fig. 10. The Nawabi "Mumty"

(according to the Viscount's description above). Martin died in 1800, so it is not likely that he got to see the *kothi* completed, if at all he had been associated in its building plans. So the premise that Sa'adat Ali himself designed the *kothi* is not so incongruous, as it seems at first instance. *Barowen* hardly had any oriental features - it was heavily embellished with Martinisque fanlights - festoon swags, the usual triangular pediments, octagonal and circular cartouches, accompanied by Corinthian pilasters. The building faced the river, and was flush with a substantial boundary wall, with bastions at its two corners, topped with a Chinoiserie pagoda each. Although *Dilkusha* was built earlier, *Barowen* was the earliest building to sport these Chinoiserie pagodas, which would then be repeated on the *Dilkusha* at a later date, followed by other buildings of Lucknow. Another novel feature - drum-like, ornamented mumty rooms appeared on the roof, where the two stairways of the *kothi* ended on the south side. These mumty rooms sported pennants, as evident from Capt. Robert Smith's sketch (1814) of *Barowen*. This drum-like mumty would become a recurrent feature in later Nawabi architecture, ranging from the *Darshan Bilas*, to an unidentified building in the *Macchi Bhavan* complex and lastly on one of the *Kaiserbagh* gateways itself. Since the *Macchi Bhavan* buildings are considered to be of an earlier date, compared to Sa'adat Ali Khan's buildings, maybe such a mumty appeared in the *Macchi Bhavan* first, and was copied in the *Musa Bagh Kothi* later. Such possibilities result in a fascinating scope for further research and discussion, since neither the *Macchi Bhavan* buildings nor the entire *Musa Bagh Kothi* are now extant, courtesy our former colonial masters.

During his life time, Sa'adat Ali proved to be a prolific builder, second only to Asaf-ud-Daula. He managed to dot Lucknow's landscape with several buildings, some of them architectural oddities (like the *Dilaram Kothi* on the north bank of the Gomti and the fishing pavilions opposite it, in the midst of the river), or the mini castle-like *Khurshid Manzil*, complete with turrets and a moat.

However, the next building which would serve as an 'inspiration' for Lucknow's builders was the parasol palace or *Chattar Manzil* of Ghazi-ud-Din Haider, the seventh Nawab and first King of Awadh (1814 - 1827). *Chattar Manzil*'s architect has never been identified with unequivocally.

This massive structure, with four storeys towering above the ground and two floors underground, connected to the *Darshan Bilas* and other buildings of the seraglio, *via* underground tunnels, continues to throw up challenges for conservation architects and historians alike, as excavation work of the palace continues, till the time of writing this book. The dome-with-gilded-parasol would be repeated in a number of later buildings, particularly the *Chota* or *khurd* (smaller) *Chattar Manzil*, *Darshan Bilas* (both commissioned by Nasir-ud-Din Haider, second King of Awadh), the *Roshan-ud-Daula Kothi* or *Kaiser Pasand*, in the *Chota Imambara* complex and on some of the gateways of *Kaiserbagh*. Although the parasol feature was more oriental than occidental, the larger or *Bada Chattar Manzil* was itself a quaint mixture of European and Islamic styles: its north facade, with a prominent triangular pediment with a wholly European appearance, whereas its south front (facing the *Chota Chattar Manzil*) was Islamic in character with a profusion of *Shahjahani* cusped arches and doorways. The rather unattractive central dome of the *Chattar Manzil* we see today (*Chota Chattar Manzil* is no longer extant) is not the palace's original one. The building suffered heavily during 1857-58 and its domes were also damaged likewise. However, the building (and other buildings in the vicinity) were patched up (not unattractively) by the British, and put to various uses by the colonial government. Several decades on, repairs were again carried out on earmarked buildings.

Sporadic excavation and restoration works carried out by the UP government from the year 2015 onwards reveals that the structures had been repaired in the year 1902 (from the dates on the excavated bricks), as evident from the view exposed after peeling of layers of plaster: *nawabi* bricks juxtaposed with modern bricks and recast ornamentation. Usage patterns changed once again after 1947, and some of the buildings continued to be used (and misused), *e.g.* the *Chattar Manzil*, while others were left to decay, e.g. the *Darshan Bilas* and the *Gulistan-e-Iram*. The present unattractive dome we see on the *Chattar Manzil* is possibly a result of the second phase of repairing under British rule in the early 1900s. There is no record of major repair or modification work having being carried out on the *Chattar Manzil* post-independence. Similarly, the main gateway of *Sikandar Bagh* had suffered extensive damage during 1857. Earlier, the open arcades on the side flanks had been walled-up as a fortification measure by the freedom fighters. During the intense bombardment by the British, the circular domes had been blown off. As there was no immediate use of the premises, no subsequent attempt was made to repair it like some other structures which had suffered similar damage. The damaged gateway was allowed to remain, covered with vegetation (like the Residency premises) after completely demolishing the shattered front domes. Much later, possibly in the 1890s, the front circular domes were re-built and the walled fortifications removed, so that the gateway now resembled its former self. Thus, we see a classic example of the Theseus paradox in Lucknow's Nawabi buildings: just how much of the building that we attempt to study or re-create as a Nawabi building is actually Nawabi?

Chapter - 7

Historiographic Battles
(and Indo-Saracenic Styles)

The Nawabi buildings of Awadh have generally been classified (Sharma, 2000) on the basis of their use patterns, *viz.* (1) *Imambara* architecture, (2) Mosque architecture (3) Tomb architecture and (4) Palace architecture. In this narrative, the Temple architecture of the Nawabi period is often ignored, although there are stunning examples of Hindu temples, with detailed ornamentation, particularly in the older areas of the city and its outskirts, *e.g.* the old Aliganj Hanuman temple, the Krishna (*Dwarka Dheesh*) temple in Chowk, the Shiva temple adjacent to the *Tikait Rai ka Pul*, the Lord Jagannath temple in Chinhat, the Shiva temple (Pathakganj), Malihabad and several others. Despite the Hindu motifs, the Islamic effect was obvious in many such temples, with the multi-foil cuspate arches and the entrances bearing the usual twin fish symbol of Awadh. The temple at Chinhat even sported an Islamic crescent symbol on its dome, instead of the usual *trishul* (trident) or *chakra* (symbolic wheel of fate), as pointed out by Sinha (2016).

The *Imambaras* were spacious congregational buildings, generally rectangular in nature, with a main central hall and other halls on the flanks or even at the back. The rulers of Lucknow, being *Shi'as*, promoted the holding of *majlis* (religious gathering), mourning the martyrdom of the Imams, Hasan, Husain and their family at Karbala in Iraq, during the observance of *Moharrum*. Often the ruler, who built the *Imambara,* would be buried in the central hall of the *Imambara* itself. A water tank (*hauz*) would be present near some of the larger *Imambaras*, to facilitate the process of ablution or ritual cleansing (*wazu*) of the devoted, before prayer. *Imambaras* generally stood on elevated platforms, and were quite ornate inside. As long as the basic purpose was served, considerable architectural freedom was available in designing and decorating these *Imambaras*; for example, they could be domed or flat-topped, with or without parapets etc. The most well known *Imambaras* of Lucknow are the *Asafi (Bada) Imambara*, the *Hussainia (Chota) Imambara* and the *Amjad Ali Shah (Sibtainabad) Imambara.*

Mosques of Lucknow, typically served to accompany the *Imambaras*, as many of these (but certainly not all) would be built side by side, to complement each other. The mosques would be situated on elevated plinths, flanked by two minarets, with a central fluted dome and two lesser domes on the sides. The interiors would be vaulted and provided a spacious prayer hall with negligible ornamentation. The well known mosques of Lucknow are the *Asafi Masjid*, the *Jami Masjid* and the *Teele-Wali Masjid.* The *Asafi Masjid* has been criticised in some quarters for being disproportionate; nevertheless, it towers over the *Bada Imambara* complex in its own right and is an extremely impressive edifice. The nearby *Jami Masjid*, adjacent to the *Chota Imambara* has several unique features: it was supposed to have *four* minarets, but only the two front ones could be completed, and that too, long after the death of its builder, Mohammad Ali Shah. The rear minarets remain incomplete and are now mistaken for octagonal turrets. The front facade was obviously borrowed from the *Rumi Darwaza,* and presents an attractive appearance, if somewhat over-ornamented and excessively coloured. The *Alamgir Mosque* or *Teele-Wali Masjid* is a *Sunni* mosque, being several generations older than the Nawabi mosques of Lucknow - the latter being pre-dominantly of *Shi'a* faith. Situated on a natural elevation, it was the first structure visible from afar, when one approached Lucknow during medieval times. Crowned with three domes and tall, slender minarets having balconies at three cardinals and domed cupolas, the mosque has an unusual balcony above the central arch, accompanied with domed pavilions, unexpectedly indicating significant Rajasthani influence.

Tomb architecture in Awadh remained traditional, with the main edifice being situated on an elevation, in a four-square Mughal-style garden. The domed Nawabi era tombs of Safdarjang at Delhi and of Shuja-ud-Dauala and Bahu Begum at Faizabad are typical Mughal-inspired structures. In such tombs, the actual grave was almost always below the level of the ground and inaccessible. Unfortunately, Safdarjang's tomb, built by Shuja-ud-Daula, has been criticised on several fronts, but we shall avoid semantics for the moment. In Lucknow, the most attractive mausolea are undoubtedly those of Sa'adat Ali Khan and his begum, Khurshid Zadi. Both were erected by their son and heir, Ghazi-ud-Din Haider. The tombs are extremely graceful, provided with turrets, alcoves and kiosks, with the tomb of the Nawab being bigger and squatter and the tomb of the begum being sleeker and more "feminine." The tombs are not massive structures, nor are they provided with extensive gardens, and yet, they present a very balanced and appealing appearance to the viewer. Architecturally, there is little left to be desired, except a better building material like stone or marble (Chatterjee, 1957).

Ghazi-ud-Din Haider's tomb called *Shahnajaf* was apparently inspired by the tomb of Hazrat Imam Ali's tomb at Najaf, Iraq. Although *Shahnajaf* hardly bears any architectural resemblance to the latter, it is a unique structure nevertheless. It had a riverside entrance (now blocked) and also through a gateway, surmounted by masonry lions, on the city side (Plate 16). The building itself resembled a mini fortress, with a large squat dome over a vaulted hall, the entire structure being enclosed within a wall, complete with battlements. *Shahnajaf's* sturdiness was commented upon by several British soldiers, who observed that despite continuous cannon bombardment, the structure could not be brought down or even substantially damaged in 1857. However, the most striking feature of this building is Martin's festoon swag on the central dome – the first example of this kind of European ornamentation appearing on a religious structure-cum-funerary structure of Nawabi Lucknow.

In Lucknow's context, a *Karbala* is a place primarily designated for the burial of *Ta'zîyas* on the 10th day of Moharrum and may later serve as a burial spot for *Shi'a* Muslims. The unfinished *Karbala* built by Nasir-ud-Din Haider is an unusual domed structure, one drum-type dome larger than the other; the domes have small balconies or *chajjas* inside, for ventilation and light. Inside, there are two main halls, with cloisters on the sides and two graves, one belonging to Nasir-ud-Din Haider himself and the other of Qudsia Mahal, his favourite begum. Two unfinished chimney-like minarets, without parapets stand, one on each side of the main entrance. The minarets have spiral stairways inside, through which the roof of the structure can be accessed. The roof is not flat but consists of barrelled type undulations, the purpose of which is not clear. The other famous *Karbala* of Lucknow is at Talkatora, which is a single storied edifice; three sides are cloistered, with the main entrance being on the fourth side. Two towers with pinnacled kiosks and an attractive dome complete the exteriors. On the inside, there is a central hall, encircled with an arched veranda.

The so-called *palace architecture* of Lucknow has been the most reviled, and also, the most admired, due to various factors, which we shall now try to unravel in the subsequent pages. The early "palaces" of Nawabi Awadh were truly devoid of any "hybrid" style; they were inspired by Mughal architecture, which can be seen in Faizabad and Lucknow. With increasing French and the British presence in the Awadh court, European influences started creeping in, so much so that the Nawabs themselves became adept at suggesting architectural designs in later creations. In addition to the ornamentation, the buildings became compact as a whole, without an open interior courtyard, especially suited for the *zenana*. Such compact buildings include the *Dilkusha, Chattar Manzil, Darshan Bilas, Gulistan-e-Iram* and many others of that period. They exhibited significant European influence, often possessing triangular pediments, fluted pillars, turrets, kiosks, Grecian arches, combined with typical Islamic domes, arches and other architectural features, giving rise to the term, "hybrid architecture." Less flattering terms were also used, including "debased", "detestable", "vitiated", "bastardised", "corrupt", "degenerate", "grotesque", "ridiculous", "execrable", "absurd", "puerile" and other similar epithets. After all, what could be expected from the profligate court of Awadh, and its rulers, who were themselves "weak", "languid", "effeminate", "dissolute" and "incapable", sunk deep in vice and debauchery?

If we are to understand the root cause of this intense aversion towards hybrid Nawabi architecture, examining its historiography would not be out of place. That the British had arrived on the shores of the Indian sub-continent, ostensibly as traders, but actually to colonise the area and cannibalise its assets, is no secret. Indeed, in some quarters, it is a matter of pride even today. Colonialism was the new normal then – nations of Europe sending their adventurers to far-off shores in search of land, wealth (often ill-gotten, through loot, plunder and unethical trading practices), slaves and natural resources. Although the East India Company operated under the garb of 'trade', it cannot be denied that their actions were under close scrutiny of the British Parliament (Anon., Oudh Papers, 1856), and approvals had to be sought at various levels for decisions taken. In today's jargon, the EIC operated as a sort of proxy or shell company for the then British government, in terms of overseas operations. Unlike previous invaders, who had preferred to return immediately after gathering the spoils of war, or else, assimilate themselves in the local environment, the ambition of almost every British army officer and civil servant was to ultimately retire to England in due course of time, with the wealth acquired from India (Finn and Smith, 2018). Initially, on arrival at Indian shores, they were appalled at the state of the natives, in terms of the latter's social mores, religious beliefs / practices and personal languid lifestyles. In fact, all aspects of native life invited derision. The latter were basically black heathens and idolaters, who needed to be proselytized and put to work either as "coolies" or at best, as petty clerks, for their white masters, in this god-forsaken land, which was seemingly cursed with a terrible climate and infested with vermin and disease.

With the passage of time, British "trade" metamorphosed to "rule" and after 1857, with India officially becoming part of the British empire, this "colonialism" finally transformed to "imperialism." Architecture also acquired different interpretations as per the march of time. Early British architecture, in the three Presidency towns of Calcutta, Madras and Bombay, often implemented by British army engineers, was based on classic European elements from back home. Even Lucknow, despite a sizeable British presence, did not have any significant or impressive structure built by the British before 1857. Lucknow was the second most important city of north India after Delhi, and it received a steady stream of visitors from Europe, who had heard about this mysterious oriental city, famous for its skyline, its riches and its decadent life-style. Travelogues of Tieffenthaler (1786), McPherson (1764 – 1787), Forster (1808), Valentia, (1809), Lumsden (1822), Ali (1832), Mundy (1833), Archer (1833), Spry (1837), Fanny Parkes (1843), Orlich (1845), Heber (1849) and several others, reveal that contrary to expectations, the travellers seemed to have been sorely disappointed with what they actually encountered at Lucknow. They had been possibly expecting something similar to the *Arabian Nights,* akin to the heady earlier artwork of Longcroft, the Daniell brothers, Captain Robert Smith, William Hodges and Alexis de La Grange, Or as WH Russel (1860), a correspondent for *The Times* had waxed eloquent, "*a fairy tale city, more vast and brilliant than Paris; a vision of palaces, domes azure and golden, cupolas, colonnades, long facades of fair perspective in pillar and column, terraced roofs - all rising up amid a calm still ocean of the brightest verdure... spires of gold glitter in the sun. Turrets and gilded spheres shine like constellations.*" Almost without fail, different visitors and travellers would describe their journeys on elephant, meetings with one Nawabi ruler or the other (depending on the period of their visit), the cordiality of the ruler, the exchange of gifts, the invariable breakfast together, the invitation to witness animal fights and the inevitable departure. Bishop Heber was unimpressed by the royal palaces "*which were neither very large nor striking.*" That in which he was received by the King consisted of "*a cluster of mean courts, with some morsels of shewy architecture intermingled, like the offices of a college.*" The *Macchi Bhavan* was described likewise as "*a large and handsome, but dull and neglected-looking pile; called the Fivefold Palace*

(Palais Quintuple), situated at a short distance from the southern bank of the Goomty, on an elevation; built in the form of a castle, fortified with walls and high towers. There is a very lofty gate, and an immense fore-court, which is before a high building, supported by arcades, where they beat the drum."

Most European visitors expressed respect and admiration for the *Rumi Darwaza* and the *Bada Imambara*, as also the delicate ornamentation of the tombs of Sa'adat Ali Khan and Khurshid Zadi. But invariably, almost all such travellers were highly critical of the city's home-grown hybrid style of architecture, which defied convention. Without exception, all were critical of Martin's *Constantia*, a building which enjoys cult status in present times for its unusual architectural features. Overseas visitors at Lucknow were flummoxed on seeing statues of every shape, design and mythological origin, including those of animals, female figures and other decorative motifs and imagery, not normally associated with a "Muslim" city. These travellers derided the squalid condition of the city proper (not without good reason) and marvelled at the gumption of the rulers for erecting palaces which looked impressive from afar, but proved to be rather cheap imitations at close quarters. They could not accept the fact that the classical Greek orders of architecture could be so casually applied and also contaminated by this random and irrational pick-and-choose technique, exhibited by Lucknow's builders. If we accept the interpretation of Srivastava (1997), this could basically be a fall-out from the historiographical battle, which was then being waged in Europe, regarding the purity of Hellenic architectural elements and the extent of their contamination by the Ottomans, who were regarded as Eastern barbarians. The latter had ruled over Greece in the early part of the nineteenth century and had influenced its art significantly. This was unacceptable in England, where admiration for authentic Greek architecture was an inseparable mark of taste and knowledge in art. The British sought to reinforce the purity of Greek antiquity which contrasted against the incomprehensible labyrinthine network of pre-colonial Muslim settlements in Lucknow. The Nawabs of Lucknow had ancestral and religious ties originating from Persia and extending throughout the Muslim world, which also included the Ottoman empire. So unconsciously, the Nawabs' unconventional architectural forays represented the undesirable influence of Islam over Greek antiquity, which was anathema to the British. No wonder, Anton Fuhrer, a German Indologist, who had also worked for the Archaeological Survey of India, was dismissive of Lucknow's architecture "*as being the result of a depraved oriental court and its politics.*" James Fergusson (1876), a Scottish born architectural historian, who was an important personality involved in the 19th century re-discovery of ancient India had gravely remarked, "*The modern palaces of the Nawabs of the Carnatic, of the Rajas of Ramnad* (sic) *or Travancore, are all in the bastard Italian style, adopted by the Nawabs of Lucknow and the Babus of Calcutta. Sometimes, it must be confessed, the buildings are imposing from their mass, and picturesque from their variety of outline, but the details are always detestable, first from being bad copies of a style that was not understood or appreciated, and also generally from their being unsuited for the use to which they were applied. To these defects must be added, that the whole style is generally characterised by a vulgarity it is difficult to understand in a people who have generally shown themselves capable of so much refinement in former times.*" Ferguson also concluded that Martin's creations had a most remarkable effect on the sovereigns of Oudh (Awadh), for although "*their tombs, their mosques and Imambaras were still erected in the debased Saracenic style prevalent, all the palaces of Lucknow were henceforth erected in this pseudo-Italian style.*"

Ferguson was contemptuous of Indian "natives" who "*could not understand either the origin or motive of the various parts of our Orders – why the entablature should be divided in architrave, frieze and cornice – why the shafts should be a certain number in diameters in height, and so on.*" He concluded that "*fashion supplies the Indian with those incentives to copying, which we derive from association and education; and in the vain attempt to imitate his superiors, he has abandoned his own beautiful art to produce the strange jumble of vulgarity and bad taste we find at Lucknow and elsewhere.*" So in a nutshell, Ferguson effectively summed that: (1) the Greek orders of classical architecture were sacrosanct and universally applicable, be it any country or culture, (2) Europeans were superior to all other races and (3) any form of deviation, hybridisation, fusion or innovation in architecture was completely unacceptable. His was a pretty one-dimensional view of the world, but it reflected the opinions of most Europeans of that age, and therefore needs to be taken seriously.

So while colonial India was scattered with architectural "oddities" due to the love of native rulers for hybrid architecture – something which could never be accepted by the purists, it is indeed surprising that post-1857, this very hybrid architecture, under the unlikely name of "Indo-Saracenic" architecture made rapid inroads in the Indian sub-continent. Did colonialism have a different set of rules from imperialism, although the masters and the slaves were the same? The principal characteristics of the so-called Indo-Saracenic architecture (Sheeba and Das, 2018) included bulbous domes, overhanging eaves, arches which would be pointed, cusped or scalloped, vaulted roofs, kiosks with domes, pinnacles, towers or minarets, open pavilions and pierced arcades. This "fusion" style combined elements of "native" architecture, with European styles *viz.* Victorian, Gothic, Palladian and Baroque. The term, "Saracens" generally denoted people who lived in tents, *i.e.* nomadic Arabs. In the eyes of the British, during the eighteenth and early nineteenth centuries, Saracens were synonymous with the Muslims. So if Indo-Saracenic broadly meant a fusion of native Indian (= Hindu / Buddhist) and Islamic styles (although the Muslims in question did not live in tents), wherefrom did European style appear in this mix? Surely not in the term itself!! Also, architecture of the Indian sub-continent had no specific form, as styles varied widely from region to region, period to period and from religion to religion. For example, a 'native' Buddhist structure in the north of the sub-continent would be drastically different from a 'native' Hindu structure in the south of India (Deccan for *dakshin* / south) in those days). So where would all this lead to?

From the above discussion, it is clear that during the colonial period, the British had been harking on Western classical models, "eternal principles" and ordered beauty (Sheeba and Das, 2018), with an anathema for anything hybrid. However, it would be of interest to note that the obelisk or *Lath* at Constantia or La Martiniere Boys' School, Lucknow, had been built in 1815, long after Claude Martin's death. Architecturally, it would serve as an inspiration for the Ochterloney Memorial, to be built later in the *Maidan* of Calcutta in 1828. Both shared common "hybrid" features, having a rare combination of three Eastern architectural styles: the stylobate and pedestal (base) being Egyptian, the column Doric, while the dome being typically Turkish. Both stemmed from a common design of Charles Knowles Robinson, put into practice by JP Parker. In fact, oriental-style architectural oddities had already started appearing in British Calcutta long before 1857. For example, the so-called Gwalior Monument in Calcutta, erected by Lord Ellenborough in 1847, in honour of British casualties during the Gwalior campaign was a curious edifice in itself. Often called as *Ellenborough's Folly*, it was designed by Col. Goodwyn of the British Engineers and constructed by Jessop & Company, Calcutta. The two storied, octagonal structure had a base of white marble, leading to the second storey having a marble cenotaph. The bronze dome, supported by bronze pillars, was obviously inspired by the Mughal "*chattri.*" Fusion architecture once again. So despite their anathema for anything hybrid, the same was already being put into practice, by the British, long before the Indo-Saracenic style would formally make an entrance. Later, with the Indian sub-continent becoming part of the Empire, it was suddenly important to create a *nouveau* building style, which would be Indian in appearance but western in function. Fusion styles were no longer impermissible or disallowed; after all, Indians were now part of the *Raj*, and their diverse building styles were no longer taboo. Votaries of the fusion Indo-Saracenic approach now looked back freely upon the architectural output of not only medieval but also ancient Indian builders for "inspiration." British public and government buildings came to be rendered on an intentionally grand scale, reflecting and promoting a notion of an unassailable and invincible British Empire, which ostensibly encompassed myriads of cultures of the Indian sub-continent. Clock towers, courthouses, railway stations, banks, educational institutions, museums and post offices were built on a grand scale, all sporting a hybrid style, which would have been otherwise denigrated and criticised few decades ago, by the very same symbols of authority. Indeed, imperialism had changed the very goal-posts of the game.

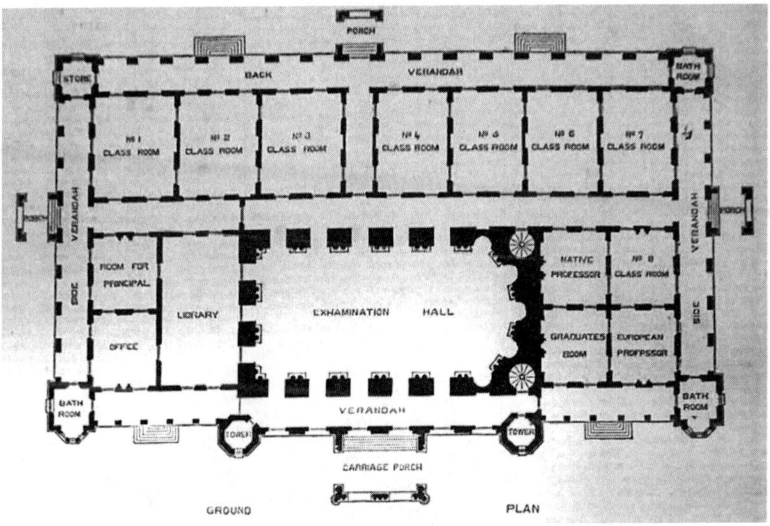

Fig. 11. Ground Floor Plan of Canning College, Lucknow

The buildings erected by the British in Lucknow after 1857, reflected their immediate needs, *i.e.* places of worship, the railway station (Plate 48), hospital and the new cantonment. The churches were invariably Gothic (Plate 40), while the new cantonment did not boast of any architectural style; it was populated by soulless barracks and bungalows (Plate 42), the latter inspired by native, thatch-roofed "*banglas*." The railways came to Lucknow in 1865. The original railway station of Lucknow (Plate 48) has been described as "*a low, unimposing, barrack-like structure of red brick, quite devoid of any architectural feature of note. Access to the platform was gained through the booking hall – a gloomy, cheerless chamber, and with its iron railings, more suggestive of a prison than a railway station.*" Balrampur Hospital, designed by Sydney Cruickshank (1869) was a sprawling complex without any architectural merit (Plate 44). The Indo-Saracenic style appeared quite late in Lucknow, although the Foundation Stone of the Canning College building (now housing the Bhatkhande Music Institute, a deemed University), had been laid by the Viceroy, Sir John Lawrence, on November 13, 1867. Its construction was actually completed

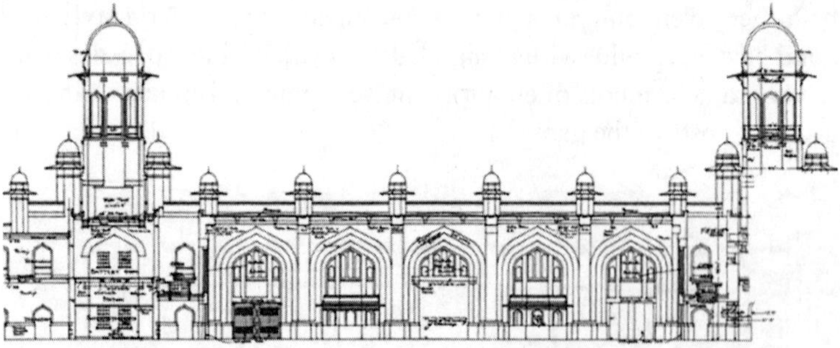

Fig. 12. Elevation of Charbagh Railway Station, Lucknow

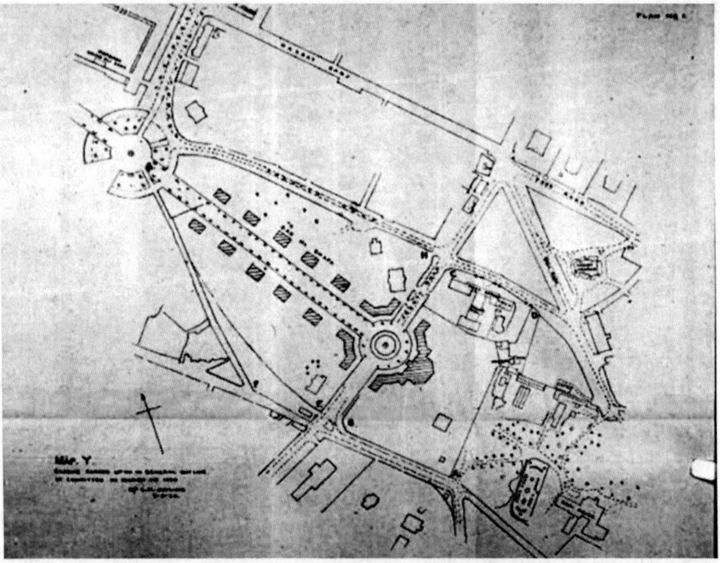

Fig. 13. Plan of Council Chamber, Lucknow

much later, after demolishing the erstwhile *Pari Khana* of Wajid Ali Shah at *Kaiserbagh*. The college building was designed by Tika Ram (1881), of the Office of the Engineer in Chief, Rajputana State Railway. Sir Swinton Jacob, who was also stationed as Chief Engineer in Jaipur, later designed *Lalgarh Palace*, Bikaner (1902 – 1926). Canning College appears to have been the first ambitious project of the then Imperial government at Lucknow, based on the now emerging Indo-Sarcenic style, which combined Nawabi, Rajasthani (primarily comprising of *chabutras*, *chajjas* and *chattris*) with European styles in one package, later serving as an architectural inspiration for the *Lalgarh Palace* at Bikaner. However, before the Canning College building had actually materialised, a colonial clock tower at *Hussainabad* had already come into existence in 1881. Towering over neighbouring Nawabi structures, this 68 meter high tower, designed by Richard Roskell Bayne had been erected in honour of Sir George EW Couper, the first Lt. Governor of the NW Provinces and Chief Commissioner of Awadh (1877 – 1882). Inspired by the *La Giralda* minaret (Sarkar, 2015) of Seville, Spain, its square plan, horseshoe-shaped arches and dome was of obvious Moorish descent. March 31, 1900 saw the laying of the Foundation Stone for the Judicial Commissioner's Court building, which would later become the premises for the Lucknow Bench of the Allahabad High Court. The style of architecture was "*Muhammadan made to suit the requirements of such a building*", drawn up by WG Wood, Executive Engineer and PA to the Chief Engineer, NWP and Oudh.

The Indo-Saracenic style now proliferated rapidly in Lucknow in the early 20th century, with the Victorial Memorial (Plate 49) designed by Sir Swinton Jacob (1904), King George's Medical College (Sir Swinton Jacob, 1906) at *Machhi Bhavan*, the *Kotwalis* at Hazratganj and Chowk (Lebanti, 1909), the new campus of Lucknow University (Sir Swinton Jacob, 1911) at *Badshah Bagh*, the new Railway Station (JH Hornimen, 1914) at *Charbagh* and the Government Arts College (S. Cruickshank, 1917). Some non-governmental buildings in Lucknow also adopted the style, e.g. Lucknow Christian College, Colvin Taluqdar's College, Butler Palace, *Rifa-e-Am* Club, Amir-ud-Daula Library and Carlton Hotel (Plate 45), to name a few. Marris Market in *Kaiserbagh*, envisaged as a modern, hygienic market for Europeans went a step further: it sported the twin fish motif at its entrance, a symbol of the erstwhile Nawabi rulers! However, not all buildings adopted the Indo-Saracenic architectural style. Isabella Thoburn College (Plate 41) in *Chand Bagh* (Martin & Company, 1922) was totally European in character, its architecture unabashedly inspired by the Parthenon (Greece).

A renewed interest in Renaissance and Baroque styles could be seen in buildings of a more "serious nature" such as the Council Chamber (Lanchester & Rodick, 1928) / present day *Vidhan Sabha*, which resembled the Central Hall of Westminster in its conception (Plate 43). Before finalisation of the design, General Cruickshank had provided the ground plans of the Delhi Council Chamber and offices, for reference. The Nawabi *Begum Kothi* (now demolished, in present day Janpath Market area) had functioned as a Post Office for quite some time (Plate 46). It was eventually replaced by the Imperial Post & Telegraph Office (now GPO) building, with its lofty tower, also designed by Lanchester and Rodick (1931 - 32), in consultation with Geoffrey Clark, the Post Master General. To dispel another urban legend of Lucknow, it needs to be clarified that the present GPO was *not* the former Ring Theatre *(sic)*. The area on which the Lucknow Council Chamber and the Imperial Post Office were constructed was mostly open space. Additional space was acquisitioned *vide* executive resolution of the colonial government dated March 9, 1920, for taking over the nearby *Rink Theatre* and the YWCA, after paying appropriate compensation, together with parts of *Darul Shafa*, (which was already government property and no compensation needed to be paid). Earlier, the Post Master General's office (Plate 47) had been designed on a typical European template by J Begg (1917).

Patrick Geddes, an eminent Scottish town planner had visited Lucknow in 1914 (Volker, 1999), and had been appalled at the town planning which had been imposed on the old quarter of Lucknow, half a century ago after 1857, at the behest of Robert Napier, a military engineer. Napier's plan to create spaces by demolishing native buildings left and right, thereby creating wide open swathes, had been accepted and implemented by the Imperial government with alacrity. The creation of Victoria Street in *Chowk* area was a result of this massive exercise, which had effectively resulted in the razing of 70% of old Lucknow. Geddes returned to Lucknow in 1916, and proposed the rectification of Victoria Street, by introducing green belts and more significantly, arcades for the commercial areas, which would benefit both the owners of the aforesaid buildings, due to additional floor space, as well as the public, who would be sheltered from the natural elements, while going about their daily pursuits. Some of these proposals and architectural plans were implemented in due course of time, but the character of the old city was essentially gone. Napier had succeeded in re-constructing Lucknow, based on military considerations, (like most war torn cities all over the world of that era), whereas the contribution of Geddes, with his noble ideas of 'real re-construction' coupled with the renewal of social life, were too little and came too late.

Walter Burley Griffin, an American architect from Chicago, who had earlier designed the Australian capital city of Canberra arrived at Lucknow in 1935, having won a commission to design the Tagore Library of Lucknow University. Although his design never saw the light of the day due to administrative complications and financial issues (contrary to popular belief, the Tagore Library (Fig. 14) we see today was designed by Mr Narwekar, an Indian architect and not by Griffin), the American architect was inundated with new commissions including the Lucknow University Student Union building, a library and museum for the Raja of Mahmoodabad, a *zenana* (women's quarters) for the Raja of Jehangirabad, the Pioneer Press building, municipal offices, several private homes, the stadium, numerous pavilions, rotundas, arcades and towers for the 160 acre United Provinces Exhibition of Industry and Agriculture, due to open in Lucknow in December 1936. Griffin designed the site plan of the numerous temporary pavilions using a variation of the local building method of bamboo and plaster. Of his private assignments, the Bir Bhan Bhatia house at Lucknow, has been widely appreciated. Griffin is also credited for designing the canopy for the statue of King George V, opposite the GPO (presently housing the statue of Gandhiji), and the Capitol theatre opposite to the canopy.

Fig. 14. Tagore Library, Lucknow University by Unidentified artist

After 1947, and into the early '50s, the Indo-Saracenic style gradually petered out, to be replaced by the less ostentatious and more functional Art Deco building style, first popularised in Paris. The hey-days of Indo-Saracenic fusion architectural style had finally come to an end.

Of Men and Menageries

Every sensitive person carries in himself, old cities enclosed by ancient walls.

—*Robert Walser*

A country without a past has the emptiness of a barren continent; and a city without old buildings is like a man without a memory.

—*Graeme Shankland*

From ancient to modern times, the human animal knows how to find fighting.

—*Brad Meltzer*

Chapter - 8

Animal Farm

The Heraldry of Awadh

The symbolic association of a pair of fishes with the state (later kingdom) of Awadh remains unexplained till date. A popular story narrates the river voyage of Burhan-ul-Mulk from Farrukhabad to Lucknow by boat, when a pair of fishes leaped from the water of the Ganga and landed on his lap. Although Islam strictly forbids any form of symbolism, the newly appointed Governor chose to accept it as a good omen and incorporated the fish symbol in the heraldry of Awadh *suba.* Although the story may be apocryphal in nature, there is no doubt that the honour of *Mahi Maratib* (Order of the Fish) had been awarded to Safdarjang by the Mughal ruler, Muhammad Shah, as a recognition of his distinguished services in the Mughal court at Delhi. *Mahi Maratib* was considered to be the highest honour to be granted to highly valued allies of the Mughal empire. It had originated in Persia, possibly during the reign of Khusru Parvez and reached the Mughal rulers at Delhi in due course of time. The symbol consisted of a grinning fish head, with prominent iron teeth and a tongue made of red cloth. Mounted on a pole with a streamer, it was carried during processions and battles, as a symbol of dignity (and aggression). There is no doubt that the twin fish symbol gained prominence during the reign of Safdarjang onwards. But the armies or royal processions of Awadh never carried the *Mahi Maratib* in its true form. Also, the honour was not confined to Awadh alone. It had been conferred generously to both Muslim as well as Hindu rulers, who were loyal or at least subservient to the Mughals. Examples of these were the Nawabs of Murshidabad (Bengal), the Nawab of Arcot, the Rathore dynasty of Ratlam, and Maharaja Anup Singh, Maharaja Gaj Singh and Maharaja Ratan Singh of Bikaner. However, other than Awadh, no other kingdom or principality gave the fish symbol so much prominence. So there might be another angle to this unsolved mystery.

The term "Awadh" is derived from Ayodhya, the kingdom of Lord Rama described in the Hindu scriptures. King Suro's tomb in Gimhae (near Busan), South Korea, has a gate with twin fishes carved on its apex. According to legend, Suro's wife was from the Indian country called *Ayuta* (Ayodhya?). The existence of the twin fish symbols on several old buildings of Ayodhya, unconnected with Nawabi rulers, indicates that perhaps the symbol had been in use from times immemorial. That too, not only in India, but in other ancient civilisations, including China and Japan. They were said to represent life, happiness, material wealth, fidelity and unity for Hindus, Buddhists and Jain. In fact, the twin fishes could have actually represented the holy rivers, *Ganga* and *Yamuna* or lunar and solar principles in the *chakra* (wheel) of life itself. It is interesting to note that the ancient Pandya dynasty of Madurai (12 - 14 century CE) also had a pair of fishes as their royal insignia. Similar fish symbols could be seen in early Christian tombs in Galatia and Rome. Going further back in time, the symbol had also appeared in ancient Egypt and Mesopotamia, as a symbol of rebirth and regeneration.

Fig. 15. Twin Fish Symbol of Awadh (one of many)

Coming back to the heraldry of Awadh, the twin fish symbol (Fig. 15) became the *de facto* insignia for the Nawabi dynasty, with each ruler adding his bit, which was obvious from the coinage, flags and ornamentation on different buildings from different periods of rule. Robert Home, court artist of Ghazi-ud-Din Haider, who had designed the crown of the newly crowned King, tried to incorporate the fish symbol in the carriages (equipage), boats, furniture and other regalia for the now royal court of Awadh. With each successive ruler, the twin fish symbol acquired a different connotation; from the easily identifiable carp, the fishes became more and more elaborate and exotic, some even sporting whiskers like catfishes, to ultimately becoming winged mermaids, during the rule of Wajid Ali Shah. Their usage also became wider, appearing in such diverse platforms such as silver fruit bowls to being embroidered on *chikankari* garments. Private homes, and even temples sported the fish motif on the spandrels of their entrance arches. In his detailed sketches (1814), Captain Robert Smith had depicted the fish shaped marching equipage as well as the grinning crocodile boat and other boats with exotic mast heads, belonging to the rulers of Awadh.

The United Provinces of Agra and Oudh of British India, in short, the United Provinces existed between 1902 to 1947. Its official logo, composed of the twin fishes of erstwhile Awadh, a bow and arrow signifying Lord Rama and three waves marking the confluence of *Ganga*, *Yamuna* (signifying a composite culture) was adopted in 1918, after some delay. Post Independence, this logo was adopted *in toto* for the Uttar Pradesh government, with minor modification. The twin fish symbol was also incorporated in the official logos of many departments and agencies of the UP government, e.g. UP Police, the Provincial Armed Constabulary (PAC), the King George's Medical College (now University) and the University of Lucknow.

A Venice in Awadh

In 2020, heritage enthusiasts, and particularly, heritage enthusiasts of Lucknow, were electrified over the find of a 42 ft long boat, buried in the debris of the *Chattar Manzil* Palace at Lucknow. It was indeed a significant find - particularly so, because the palace complex had thrown up several exciting finds during its excavation in the recent past. Carbon dating techniques at the Birbal Sahni Institute of Palaeosciences, Lucknow, indicated that the excavated structure could possibly be 200 years old, although the findings were yet to be validated. If the boat actually belonged to the early 1800s, it roughly corresponded to the rule of Sa'adat Ali Khan (1798 - 1814). Generally speaking, carbon dating a 200 year old sample of wood can have an error of around 3 to 10 years. So it could be from the reign of Ghazi-ud-Din Haider also (1814 - 1827), who is credited for building *Bada Chattar Manzil*. However, travelling by barges was not confined to the Nawabi rulers of Lucknow. There are "company school" artworks which show barges and ferries, having with decorative mast heads of horses, peacocks etc. even in the times of Shuja-ud-Daula at Faizabad. The use of the term "gondola" for the excavated barge appalled many purists, who felt that the term was exclusive for the boats in the canals of Venice, and nowhere else. In all fairness, it must be mentioned here that the memoirs of Captain Leopold von Orlich (1845) had been translated from German to English by an H Evans Lloyd, who had used the term "gondola" for the King's (Amjad Ali Shah) boat:

"The river exhibited a scene of uncommon activity, traffic boats, small barks, and fishing boats, were rowing backwards and forwards; the King's gondola, adorned at the forepart with two horses leaping from the jaws of a fish, was steering to the Dilkusha Park, in case it might be his Majesty's pleasure to come back by water."

Orlich had also described Nasir-ud-Din Haider's boat thus:

"*The sovereigns of Oude have arrived at splendour and luxury, in everything about them. Naseer-ud-din Hyder procured, in 1820, the first steam boat for excursions on the Ganges, but this did not satisfy him, and therefore he obtained from Calcutta, at great expense, a yacht built on the model of a man-of-war. On board this handsome vessel, the King has hisown apartment fitted up in a costly manner; but which, as well as the vesselitself, is now in a very dirty and neglected state.*"

That the Gomti river was the artery of Nawabi Lucknow is beyond doubt. It served as a means of communication and transport, as well as of leisure. It is for this very reason that the palaces of Nawabi Lucknow stretched on the river front, from *Musa Bagh* in the extreme western end to *Vilayati Bagh* in the east. Claude Martin's creations, *Farhat Baksh* and Constantia also had river fronts. So had Asaf-ud-Daula's *Daulat Khana*. Sa'adat Ali Khan erected octagonal pavilions in the river, a little beyond the *Chattar Manzil* to the west, two on the river banks on either side and one in the middle of the river, where he reportedly spent his leisure moments in fishing (fish again!!). No wonder, most of these palaces along the river had water gates for easy access to these luxury boats. Even the Residency had a water gate, which later become defunct, as the river shifted course. Various photographers, including Beato, Ahmad Ali Khan as well as Mushkoor-ud-Daula had captured the ruins of Sa'adat Ali Khan's river pavilions. These could be seen as two-storeyed (at least the ones on the river banks) structures, with the usual Nawabi ornamentation e.g. triangular pediments and festoon swags. But early 18th century "scroll art" depicting the panorama of Lucknow along the Gomti river in Company School style (e.g. the one available with the Yale Center for British Art, Paul Mellon Collection), actually depict the pavilion in the middle of the river sporting a dome, very much like the one atop the *Chattar Manzils*. The middle pavilion also had regular quay, equipped with a chain as well as metal stairways, leading to the structure!! The scroll also depicted several fish-shaped boats cruising down the river - boats which actually emulated fishes, complete with scales, and golden in colour, and not just normal boats with fish-shaped mast heads.

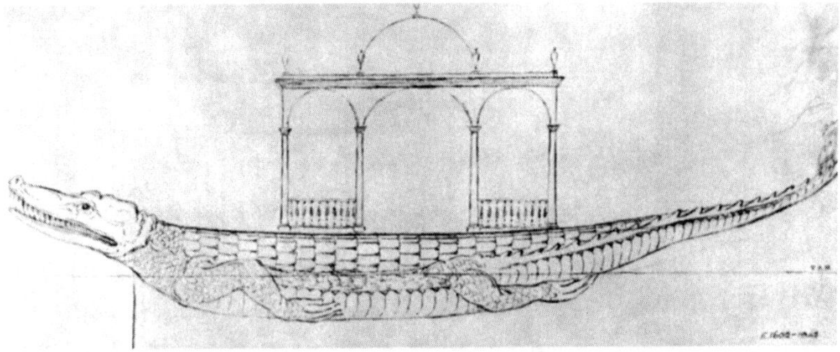

Fig. 16. Nawabi barge designed by Robert Home (1820)

Thomas Daniell, one of the earliest European painters (1786 – 93) who visited Lucknow, painted a long barge with a rearing horse's head, being rowed down the Gomti, (near the *Sunheri Burj* palace of Bahu Begum), close to present Daliganj bridge. Other artists like Ozias Humphry, William Hodges, Robert Home and Capt Robert Smith also produced sketches and paintings of Nawabi boats cruising down the Gomti river. Robert Home, the court painter of Ghazi-ud-Din Haider, did not confine himself to painting portraits. In fact, he is credited for other "zany" creations, including a lengthy barge in the form of a grinning crocodile (Fig. 16). On its scaly back sat a howdah-like pavilion to accommodate the first King of Awadh. Sir Edward Paget, the British army Commander-in-Chief in India had once observed that Ghazi-ud-Din Haider was "*an extremely good and kind hearted man, but like myself preferring anything and everything to his business. Accordingly, instead of attending to affairs of State, he spends his time in boat-building and house-building, in turning, in printing, in collecting European and especially English commodities of all sorts, descriptions and kinds, and, in short, idling.*"

Nasir-ud-Din Haider, 2nd King of Awadh commissioned a luxury barge called "*The Sultan of Oude*", which was brought from Calcutta and retro-fitted for the King and his family. A range of jalousied windows stretched along one side of the fish, and presumably the opposite as well, giving its passengers a measure of privacy, which surely must have been welcomed given the vessel's bizarre appearance. Perhaps this fish vessel is the very one described by a 19th-century eyewitness. He wrote of a fish-shaped pleasure boat "*made of cedar, for the harem ladies, covered with scales of silver, each the size of a rupee though not so thick. The interior was more luxuriously fitted ... [and] there were jalousies through which the fair and dusky occupants, without being seen, could themselves look upon a city as naughty as Nineveh.*"

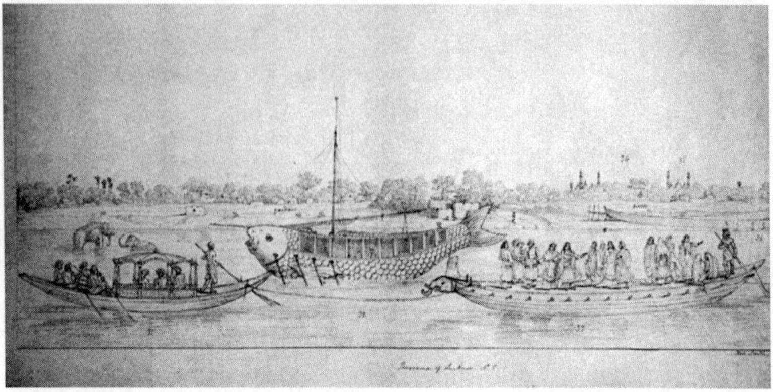

Fig. 17. Sketch of a fish-shaped barge at Lucknow, Capt. Robert Smith (1832)

One English resident of Lucknow in the 1850s recalled a royal boat shaped like a dolphin and brilliantly enamelled (Anon., 2011). Another boat, shaped like a peacock, popularly known as *Mor Punkh*, was in operation, from the days of Sa'adat Ali Khan. Captain Robert Smith was a military engineer with the East India Company and was in India from 1805 to 1833. In his series of sketches (1832) on Lucknow (Lucknow Panorama), he had depicted both the barges, one shaped like a grinning crocodile, and the other shaped like a huge fish (Fig. 17), indicating that both were in operation during the reign of Nasir-ud-Din Haider.

Fanny Parkes, an Indophile, who had travelled across India and wrote about her impressions in her book, *Wanderings of a Pilgrim in Search of The Picturesque* (1850), wrote that a large pleasure boat belonging to his Majesty (she had visited Lucknow during the reign of Nasir-ud-Din Haider) was sailing up and down; *the boat was made in shape of a fish, and the golden scales glittered in the sun.* Was this the "Sultan of Oudh" which ended up on the banks of the Gomti in a ruinous condition, post-1857, so poignantly captured by Beato in his photograph?

Men and Menageries

There are no records of menageries or animal-based sports during the times of Shuja-ud-Daula or his predecessors. However, after the Nawabi rulers were grounded by the British, and active warfare became a distant dream, Lucknow's nobility seemed to have developed a unique, if rather peculiar pastime - that of maintaining menageries, and also enjoying animal-based sports of various kinds. Although, the Lucknow Nawabi dynasty was not known to have been particularly cruel or bloodthirsty, compared to earlier medieval rulers (even the benevolent Akbar had executed Adam Khan, his foster brother, by having him thrown from the ramparts of the Agra fort, not once but *twice*), they seemed to satisfy their blood-lust with such violent pastimes and also proudly invite important guests (= read Europeans) to witness these, for entertainment. Many travellers gave vivid descriptions of such events, which are an eye-opener for readers of today. Lucknow of yore had no gladiators or arenas, but it certainly had make-shift courtyards where animals (and not man and animal) fought each other, often to their death. The first description of a formal menagerie under Asaf-ud-Daula, was by Thomas Twining, a civil servant of the EIC, who had occasion to visit Lucknow in 1792 during the former's reign. According to Twining, "*In one of the courts of the palace, I saw a small collection of wild animals. There was a tiger of extraordinary size, confined to a square wooden cage, which appeared rather clumsy than strong. The top was very low, merely leaving enough room for the tiger to stand without touching it. Upon my expressing my surprise at this, the keeper said that if the top was higher the tiger would spring against it with such force as to be likely to break it, or force it up, whereas, at present, he had not room to take his spring.*

I also saw two wild buffaloes, the only ones I had seen in India excepting the herd which I had passed in my journey from Santipore to Guttaul. I was struck as before with the size and strength, and apparent agility of these animals, and comparing their powers with those of the tiger who was near, I had no difficulty in conceiving their superiority over the latter. There were also two large rhinoceroses, animals less common in this part of India than in the forests and extensive jungles of Bengal, particularly in the vicinity of the Burrumpooter. An officer once descending that river saw before him a line of rhinoceroses extending entirely across the stream and into the forest on each side. They formed a dam across the river, and the officer was obliged to stop his boat till they had passed. Lastly, I saw, not far from the wild animals, a tame one, a countryman too, which in size surpassed them all. It was a large English dray-horse. Being kept as a curiosity for his extraordinary bulk, he was fed unsparingly, and had in consequence, become enormously fat and unwieldy. It appeared too that he was as much confined as the other great animals I had just seen. It was not surprising that his natural perfections - his beauty, symmetry, vigour - should be all lost. Two other horses of the same large species, which had accompanied him from England, had lately died, most probably from their extreme obesity and want of exercise; a fate which seemed to await this also in the ensuing hot season. These horses were said to have cost the deluded Vizier an immense sum. I understand that the Nabob had nearly a thousand elephants, and about the same number of saddle-horses. As the greater part of both had accompanied his Royal Highness (ref. Second Rohilla War) *to the field, I did not visit the royal stables. The Nabob himself was still absent from Lucnow, having with him more than a hundred of the many hundred ladies of his seraglio, and many thousand pigeons, a fact which left no surprise that his Highness should have been so far in the rear, when the army of Sir Robert Abercromby fought the Rohillahs... "*

It is certain that Asaf-ud-Daula enjoyed cock fights, and apparently maintained an aviary housing 'an uncommon number of birds' and thirty-five keepers. In 1790, a rhinoceros reached Britain. It was actually a present from Asaf-ud-Daula to Henry Dundas, the President of the Board of Commissioners for the Affairs of India, who sold it off for a princely sum of £700.00; ultimately, the rhino came in the possession of a Gilbert Pidcock, who had a touring menagerie. Later, the unfortunate animal dislocated its right front leg, and eventually died; its skin and horn were auctioned off in 1810.

The Rev. William Tennant (1803), a Chaplain of the East India Company had criss-crossed several Indian cities and towns during 1796 - 1799, starting from Calcutta, including Benaras (Varanasi), Allahabad, Cawnpore (Kanpur) and Lucknow in his itinerary. On March 15, 1799, he visited Sa'adat Ali Khan's menagerie, which "*consisted of different birds and quadrupeds.*" To quote the Chaplain:

"*A considerable number of tigers are kept in different apartments near the palace, but so mean and nasty in their appearance that a considerable tax is laid upon your patience in going to view them. To their keepers, the tigers are so tame, that they allow them to stroke them on the back, as a cat, and like that animal, seem gratified by your attention. The rhinoceros is the most remarkable animal in this collection; the only one here is about twelve years old, and seems not to have attained its full growth, being of a much less size than the species generally attains. His strength and ferocity are prodigious; no elephant dares to attack him; for his horn proves at first stroke fatal: it is a large protuberance growing exactly upon the snout, and sharpening into a point, and with it he can rip up the belly of the largest elephant. The rhinoceros is protected by a thick horny substance, studded over like a shield; from which its hardness and thickness must protect the animal from any foe. A sword would make no impression upon this singular hide, and where it overlaps, it would probably repel a musket ball.*

Of the sheep there is a great number, and some variety; but the Cabul (Kabul) *breed seems to enjoy the largest share of the royal favour. They are in general very fat, and distinguished by a large protuberance on the rump far exceeding that of the Cape sheep. This excrescence is semi-circular in form, and of nearly half the size of the whole body. Some of these sheep are painted in different colours to gratify the fantastic taste of the natives, a practice which they follow with their bullocks and horses. When they intend to appear very fine, they go so far as to gild the hoofs and horns.*

The stables of the Nawab (possibly he refers to the famed cruciform *Chaupar* stables of Sa'adat Ali Khan) *consist of a large square court of buildings, supported on brick pillars, with a view to the admission of air: these consist of more than one range; that which I examined contained about four hundred stalls, almost all filled with excellent Persian horses. There are separate studs for mares; but breeding does not seem the favourite pursuit here: I saw but four foals; probably the confinement in which they are kept is unfavourable to the dam and the colt. A park of mares and colts is deemed in England a very agreeable object, but in India, it is unattainable, the fields being parched for nine months a year; hay is unknown; grass roots scraped up with a sharp trowel, being the substitute for this provender* (fodder) *is often procured on places which you would declare absolutely bare earth; everything above ground being completely burnt away.*

A very large breed of Guzarat (Gujarat) *bullocks is kept in a cow-house near the stables: the introduction of this breed among the peasants, one would imagine would prove of great advantage in a country where the draught cattle are so small and pitiful as those of Oude. But the ryut* (ryot), *if he gets his labour done, cares not in how slovenly a style it may be executed; or even how small the quantity performed. This is the nature of the race even where it is fully protected; what then we can expect here, where nothing is secure, and where a good teem* (sic) *of cattle would be a kind of attractive bait, to bring the robbers to a farm, or an Aumil* (*Amil* = revenue collector) *from the Court, both equally addicted to plunder?*

One of the curiosities of this place is a mixed species of the goat and deer, which is spotted, and neater in its form than the ordinary goat. The variety of horned cattle, horses, and sheep, is much greater than in Europe. Here are kept a few buffaloes in remarkably fine condition: they are not fully tamed; and by some means or other are much handsomer than the common domestic kind. Apes, monkies and a variety of the tropical animals, make a part of the raree shew (sic) *exhibited at this Court: one of the former is taught to make a genteel salaam to his visitors. The natives of*

India are very fond of these accomplishments; many of them spend whole days in teaching parrots to speak a few Persian words. The management of the menagerie employs a great number of people; and although their allowances have been much curtailed since the commencement of the present reign, the department must swallow up large sums. Many crores of pigeons are kept at public expence (sic), *and elephants and camels to a large amount. The food bestowed in this manner would remove want from the city, if not from the kingdom of Oude."*

It is interesting to note that Tennant collectively refers to the Indian sub-continent as "India", even though there was no such country in those days. Also he referred to Awadh as the kingdom of Oude, although under Sa'dat Ali Khan, Awadh was still a *suba* (state) of the Mughal empire; his court was not an independent royal court.

Viscount Valentia (1809) who had paid a visit to Sa'adat Ali Khan's court in Lucknow had observed that "*collection of birds were few, and not curious*." However, a large number of different goats were present, "*fantastically painted*." Few deer, a tiger, tiger-cat (sic) and rhinoceros were also there. But the most interesting sight was several goats from Kashmir. Apparently, the Nawab had tried to procure the breed for their fine wool, but not succeeded. The Viscount also described an elephant fight, the animals being in *musth* (a periodic condition in bull elephants are characterized by highly aggressive behaviour, accompanied by a large rise in reproductive hormones), and prodded by spears, further increasing their aggressiveness.

Bishop Reginald Heber had landed in India in 1823, and proceeded for a tour of the "Upper Provinces" in 1824. While his judgemental attitude, coupled with an ecclesiastical bent of mind can be excused as a sign of those times, his detailed descriptions of his travels do form an important source of information on the then prevailing condition of the Indian sub-continent. All this, from the eyes of an European, determined to belittle native customs and life-styles. Of the menagerie of Ghazi-id-Din Haider, he had the following to say:

There is a menagerie, with a greater number of scarce and curious animals, but in far worse order, than that at Barrackpoor; and on the other side of the river Goomty, in a well wooded park (Heber was possibly referring to *Badshah Bagh* here), *is a large collection of different varieties of cows, camels, and deer, and five or six very large rhinoceroses, the first animals of the kind I ever saw, and of which I found that prints and drawings had given me a very imperfect conception. They are more bulky animals and of a darker colour than I had supposed, and the thickness of the folds of their impenetratable* (sic) *skin much surpasses all which I had expected. These at Lucknow are gentle and quiet animals, except that one of them has a feud with horses. They seem to propagate in captivity without reluctance, and I should conceive might be available to carry burdens as well as the elephant, except that, as their pace is still slower than his* (sic), *their use could only be applicable to very great weights and very gentle travelling. These have sometimes had howdahs on them, and were once fastened in a carriage, but only as an experiment which was never followed up. There is on the same side of the river, a poultry-yard of beautiful pigeons; and on the river itself is a steam-boat, a vessel fitted up like a brig of war, and other things which show the king to be fond of mechanical inventions. He has indeed a very skilful mechanist an English officer* (Here, Heber is possibly referring to Robert Home), *in his service, and is himself said to know more of the science and different branches of philosophy connected with it than could be expected in a person who understands no European language.*

The last paragraph relates more to the fish boats of Awadh discussed previously, although Heber's opinion that science and philosophy were confined to people adept in European languages appears somewhat ill-conceived. Heber also narrated that, "*About 3 miles from the city, the king had a summer palace called 'Di-koushar'(Dilkusha), surrounded by a park with not only neelghaus* (Nilgai = *Boselaphus tragocamelus*) *and the common Indian deer, but some noble red deer.*"

Captain Mundy, who had toured parts of the Indian sub-continent under the auspices of Lord Combermere, had documented his travels (1833), including a visit to Nasir-ud-Din Haider's court at Lucknow. His reminiscences and impressions were no different from that of other Europeans' who had performed similar travels. However, he did provide detailed descriptions of the animal fights he witnessed, both within enclosures and as open air events, as a form of entertainment. To quote Mundy:

"*We were next conducted to the King's aviary and menagerie; in the inclosure* (sic) *of the latter we were entertained with a ram-fight, which is not a very interesting spectacle, though the combatants are regularly trained for the arena, and meet each other in the lists with true chivalrous fury.*"

Next day, the King conducted the European party to a short distance out of town, where an arena had been prepared for "field sports." Mundy found the proceedings uninteresting and cruel as "*five or six antelopes were brought out of cages, so stiff and weak from confinement that they could barely stand, and abandoned to the mercy of cheetahs and lynxes, which pulled them down without their making any effort to escape. The hawking was little better, the birds turned out having been too long encaged to show any sport. An* (sic) *hyena was next turned loose, and pursued and brought to bay by an heterogeneous pack of about twenty large dogs; and when I arrived near enough to see the fight distinctly, I found the unfortunate animal was muzzled, and was therefore, unresistingly mangled for nearly ten minutes. The next victim was a bear, who, having had most of his teeth extracted, was bullied by a troop of yelping curs, none of them venturing near enough to get within bruin's embrace.*"

Mundy and his entourage had been eager to see the wild beast fights, which "were celebrated" on a grand scale at Lucknow, and the King did not fail to oblige. Accordingly, "*Early in the morning, therefore, the whole party, including ladies, eager for the novel spectacle, mounted elephants, and repaired to the private gate of the royal palace, where the King met the Commander-in-Chief, and conducted him and his company to a palace in the park, in one of the courts of which the arena for the combats was prepared. In the centre was erected a gigantic cage of strong bamboos, about fifty feet high, and of like diameter, and roofed with rope network. Sundry smaller cells, communicating by sliding doors with the main theatre, were tenanted by every species of the wildest inhabitants of the forest. In the large cage, crowded together, and presenting a formidable front of broad, shaggy foreheads well armed with horns, stood a group of buffaloes sternly awaiting the conflict, with their appuyé against the bamboos. The trap-doors being lifted, two tigers, and the same number of bears and leopards, rushed into the centre. The buffaloes instantly commenced hostilities, and made complete shuttlecocks of the bears, who, however, finally escaped by climbing up the bamboos beyond the reach of their horned antagonists. The tigers, one of which was a beautiful animal, fared scarcely better; indeed, the odds were very much against them, there being five buffaloes. They appeared, however, to be no match for these powerful creatures, even single-handed, and showed little disposition to be the assaulters. The larger tiger was much gored in the head, and in return took a mouthful of his enemy's dewlap, but was finally (as the fancy would describe it), 'bored to the ropes and floored.' The leopards seemed throughout the conflict sedulously to avoid a breach of the peace.*

A rhinoceros was next let loose in the open court-yard, and the attendants attempted to induce him to pick a quarrel with a tiger who was chained to a ring. The rhinoceros appeared, however, to consider a fettered foe as quite beneath his enmity; and having once approached the tiger, and quietly surveyed him, as he writhed and growled, expecting the attack, turned suddenly round (sic) *and trotted awkwardly off to the yard gate, where he capsized a palankeen which was carrying away a lady fatigued with the sight of these unfeminine sports.*

A buffalo and a tiger were the next combatants; they attacked furiously, the tiger springing at the first onset on the other's head, and tearing his neck severely; but he was quickly dismounted, and thrown with such violence as nearly to break his back, and quite to disable him from renewing the combat. A small elephant was next impelled to attack a leopard. The battle was short and decisive; the former falling to his knees, and thrusting his blunt tusks nearly through his antagonist. On our return from the beast fight, a breakfast awaited us at the royal palace; and the white table cloth being removed, quails, trained for the purpose, were placed upon the green cloth and fought most gamely, after the manner of the English cockpit. This is an amusement much in fashion among natives of rank, and they bet large sums on their birds, as they lounge luxuriously round (sic), *smoking their houkahs.*

Elephant fights were announced as the concluding scene of this day of strife. The spectators took their seats in a long veranda. The narrow stream of the river Goomty (sic) *runs close under the palace walls, and on the opposite bank a large, open space, sandy space presented a convenient theatre for the operation of these gigantic athletes. The elephants educated for the arena are large, powerful males, wrought up to a state of fury by constant feeding with exciting spices. On the spacious plain before us we counted several of these animals parading singly and sulkily to and fro, their mahouts seated on their backs, which were covered with a strong network for the driver to cling by in the conflict. In attendance upon every elephant were two or three men, armed with long spears, a weapon of which this animal has the greatest dread. We soon discovered two of the combatants slowly advancing towards each other from opposite sides of the plain. As they approached, their speed gradually increased, and at length met with a grand shock, entwining their trunks, and pushing, until one, finding himself overmatched, fairly turned tail, and received his adversary's charge in the rear. This was so violent, that the mahout of the flying elephant was dislodged from his seat: he fortunately fell wide of the pursuer, and escaped with a few bruises.*

Five or six couple (sic) *were fought, but showed little sport; the sagacious animals instantly discovering when they were over-matched. I had long been ambitious of witnessing the far-famed wild-beast fights of Lucknow, and having enjoyed an opportunity of seeing them, which few have had, it would hardly be fair to say that I was disappointed."*

Lt. Col. Davidson (1843) had penned his experiences of touring North India, including Oude (Awadh). He described an old Arab horse in the King's stables (possibly Nasir-ud-Din Haider), which had originally belonged to Hakim Mehdi, and was now forty six years of age, yet still in fine condition. Davidson also came across an English horse which had been presented by King George IV to a former King of Awadh (possibly Ghazi-ud-Din Haider). This horse, which had a particularly vicious nature, was fastened to its stall by strong chains and kept blinded with clothes. Subsequently, however, this horse was turned loose in a courtyard, to fight a hungry royal Bengal tiger. The horse kicked the tiger to death, although its own entrails were torn out resulting in its own death.

Fig. 18. An Elephant Fight in Lucknow, Fanny Parkes (1850)

Orlich (1845) described Amjad Ali Shah's menagerie being a large square court, surrounded by piazzas, where he was shown thirteen tigers, many monkeys, rabbits, fighting antelopes and rams and fighting quails. He rued the fact that the value of this menagerie had been very much decreased by the removal of several animals - six rhinos and several other remarkable animals, which had been taken away to adorn various "sepulchral monuments." Orlich further informed that British officers stationed at

Lucknow were frequently invited to breakfast and dinner parties, when they were entertained with combats of animals, and also encouraged to go for tiger hunts. One such tiger hunt during Orlich's stay yielded *forty* tigers. *Dilkusha* Park, an artificial wilderness was well stocked with antelopes, peacocks and jackals. He witnessed a combat of elephants, organised by the King in honour of General William Nott; the latter was British Envoy during 1843 - 45, having joined the Court of Awadh, after his victories in the Afghan wars.

Fanny Parkes (1850), the iterant Indophile's first hand experience of witnessing an elephant fight (Fig. 18) was thus:

"The animals exhibited at first no inclination to fight, although urged on by their respective mahawats. At length, two elephants, equally matched, were guided by the mahawats on their backs to some distance from each other, and a female elephant was placed midway. As soon as the elephants turned and saw the female, they became angry, and set off at a long swinging trot to meet each other; they attacked with their long tusks, and appeared to be pressing against each other with all their might. One elephant caught the leg of the other in his trunk, and strove to throw his adversary or break his fore-leg. But the most dangerous part appeared to be when they seized one another by their long trunks and interlaced them; then the combat began in good earnest. When they grew very fierce, and there was danger of their injuring themselves, fireworks were thrown in their faces, which alarmed and separated them, and small rockets were also let off for that purpose." Apparently, "*the animals were rendered furious by giving them balls to eat made of wax of the human ear, which the barbers collected for the purpose*!" Parkes hilariously continued further:

"When the elephant fights were over, two rhinoceros were brought before us, and an amusing fight took place between them; they fought like pigs. When the rhinoceros grew fierce, they charged the crowd, and it was beautiful to see the mass of people flying before them."

She described in detail, as to how within an enclosed court (arena?), she witnessed combats between tigers, hyenas, wild buffaloes, bears and rams. Indeed, it must have been a wild, primeval sight, in an Oriental court, which cannot be visualised now. Parkes' account of *Badshah Bagh* and its tiger enclosure, as well as *Dilkusha* park being filled with game: deer, blue bulls, antelopes, bears, tigers and peacocks is indeed an eye opener.

William Knighton, Assistant Commissioner of Awadh, during the reign of Nasir-ud-Din Haider, had given vivid descriptions of various animal sports in the royal court in his rather scandalous book, *Private Life of An Eastern King*, which was first published in 1855. While many of his rants cannot be taken at face value, his detailed, albeit supercilious descriptions cannot be ignored totally. In the very beginning of his book (page 2), he correctly described the location of the King's menagerie, the extent and the variety of which apparently exceeded his expectations. The menagerie was populated with "*elephants in scores, tigers, rhinoceros, antelopes, cheetahs, lynxes, Persian cats, Chinese dogs, all sunning themselves in the park, either in their cages, or stretched listlessly on the grass, as commonly as sheep and cows in an English meadow*." Knighton narrated the shooting of wild fowl in the *Dilkusha* and deer hunt in Misrikh (Sitapur) beyond Lucknow, including the use of trained hawks and a captive cheetah for hunting purposes. Knighton described in great detail about the fight between *Burrhea*, a favourite tiger of the King, with other animals. *Burrhea* was named after a village, at the foot of the Himalayas, from where he had been procured. The King generally not allow him to fight with others tigers or with elephants; he was more of a pet, only allowed to enter contests with animals whom he could vanquish easily. But the fight that Knighton witnessed was between Burrhea and a man-eating tiger who had been ravaging the country side around Lucknow and had been ultimately captured by the King's soldiers. "*It was not a scene to be forgotten: the King and his attendant females gazing intently above; the European courtiers straining with eye and ears to catch every moment and every sound; the man-eater in the centre of the courtyard, slowly turning as the tiger turned, his head and ears and neck ever the same; the tiger stealing along, so cat-like in aspect, and yet so gigantic in strength. Not a sound was audible but the grating of the man-eater's feet, as they were raised and lowered again - not a sound other; but all was mute expectation and anxious gazing.*" Unfortunately, the man-eater managed to break the jaw bone of Burrhea. The man-eater also succeeded in defeating three wild buffaloes in another fight, this pleasing the king, who ordered that instead of being killed, the man-eater should be caged and taken care of.

The animals of the Lucknow's royal menagerie were disposed off at a pittance, after the British formally annexed Awadh in 1856. Edward Blyth, the Curator of the Museum of the Society of Bengal, Calcutta was present in Lucknow during that dark period. He opined that, "*the tigers were the finest caged specimens in the world*", so he tried to buy the entire collection, supposedly at his own expense, with the help of a German friend, who was possibly an international animal dealer (Rookmaaker, 1997). 18 magnificent tigers were sold at Rs 20 per head. Some casualties occurred on the passage down the river, but his collection, when exhibited in Calcutta (possibly in Barrackpore park) contained sixteen tigers, one leopard, one bear, two cheetahs, three caracals, two rhinoceroses, and a giraffe. It is an irony that the animals, after a long and arduous journey, had eventually reached the vicinity of their former owner, Wajid Ali Shah, who was residing along the river, about thirty miles to the south. Some of these animals were later re-purchased by Wajid Ali Shah for his upcoming palace complex, including a menagerie in *Metia Burz*. Calcutta (Fig. 56).

During his stay at Lucknow, Wajid Ali Shah had duly maintained the collection of animals, which he had inherited from his ancestors. He seemed to have a particular fascination for pigeons and had made elaborate arrangements, based on bamboo poles, for their perching and nesting in his *Kaiserbagh* palace complex. The *Kabootar Wali Kothi* (present day Oel House) was also constructed during his reign, although it is doubtful that it was meant to house pigeons. However, after the events of 1857 were over, and he had finally settled down at *Metia Burz*, the deposed King returned to his old pursuits, including the rapid development of a vast menagerie, which entailed the services of eight hundred attendants. A commodious open space in front of the *Noor Mahal* palace was inhabited by spotted deer and wild buck roaming free. One could see partridges, ostriches, turkeys, cranes, geese, herons, ducks, peacocks and hundreds of other varieties of birds in and around a marble water tank. Monkeys, tigers, lions, bears, hyenas, wolves and leopards were housed in cages. Another long and deep tank, with sloping edges, housed hundreds of crawling snakes in their natural habitat. Exotic birds from across the world were kept displayed in cages, some with wire netting. A Bactrian two-humped camel and a pair of giraffes were the pride of the King's collection. As in Lucknow, the King took keen interest in pigeon flying, and was reported to own not less than 25 thousand birds in his personal collection. An interesting, if somewhat hilarious incident involved the escape of a tigress from the King's menagerie, which swam across the river and entered the Botanic Gardens situated on the other side. Although the tigress was eventually killed, it led to an uproar from the public, which wanted the royal menagerie to be shut down. Their demand could not be satisfied, and till his last days, Wajid Ali Shah continued to devote more time and shower more affection on his animals, than on his family members.

After his death in 1887, the British government wanted to tactfully, but speedily remove all traces of the royal legacy of Awadh, including the menagerie. The palace buildings, barring few were auctioned, mostly to shipping companies. As for the collection of animals, these were listed and disposed off, either by auction or by way of private sales. An era of men and menageries had come to an end.

Dramatis Personae

I can only note that the past is beautiful because one never realises an emotion at the time. It expands later, and thus we don't have complete emotions about the present, only about the past.

—Virginia Woolf

The most effective way to destroy people is to deny and obliterate their own understanding of their history.

—George Orwell

That men do not learn very much from the lessons of history is the most important of all the lessons that history has to teach.

—Aldous Huxley

Chapter - 9

Tinker, Tailor, Soldier, Sailor

Abdul Halim "Sharar": Abdul Halim was born on January 10, 1860 (this date is debatable) at Lucknow. By then, Nawabi rule followed by the events of 1857 were already over, and the people of Lucknow were trying to adjust to a new normal, under British masters and *ta'aluqdars* from the hinterlands of Awadh. In this depressing scenario, Abdul Halim lived out the first nine years of his life, before moving to Calcutta to join his father, who had earlier accompanied Wajid Ali Shah to *Metia Burz* in 1856. As a young boy, he spent his initial days in academics and learning languages such as English, Persian and Arabic. However, Abdul Halim's association with indolent and frivolous royalty irked his father, who sent him back to Lucknow in 1879. By this time, the former had developed a talent for narrating imaginative, historical tales with a keen sense of eloquence. Coming in contact with Munshi Nawal Kishore he started writing articles for the *Awadh Akhbar*. In 1887, he launched his own publication, *Dil Gudaz,* becoming a prolific writer with a penchant for historical novels. "Sharar" is best known for his series of articles on Lucknow, published in *Dil Gudaz*, titled *Hindustan Mein Mashriqi Tamaddun Ka Akhri Namuna* or *Guzasta Lakhnau*, in which he described the history of Lucknow as well as the lifestyle of its people, including their religion, education, medicine, ceremonies and etiquette, dress, culinary arts, calligraphy, entertainment and pastimes. These articles were later translated into English and compiled into a single volume called *Lucknow: The Last Phase of an Oriental Culture*. This effectively earned him the honour of being recognised as the cultural biographer of Lucknow, although Abdul Halim had neither personally observed nor lived through the *Lakhnavi* experience, which he detailed so passionately. Abdul Halim "Sharar" died in Lucknow on December 1, 1926.

Agha Mir: He was given the title of "Motamid-ud-Daula" by Ghazi-ud-Din Haider and appointed as *Naib* in the court of Awadh. However, the usual court intrigues resulted in his incarceration for about a year, but he regained his status and was awarded the title of *Wazir* when Ghazi-ud-Din Haider assumed the title of independent King. Nasir-ud-Din Haider retained Agha Mir as his *Wazir*, with extensive financial and administrative authority, but later had him exiled, with British help. Severe penalties were also imposed on him, before his final departure from Lucknow to Kanpur. This entire sequence of events seems to have been master-minded by Badshah Begum, dowager queen of Ghazi-ud-Din Haider, an act that would be repeated subsequently with Hakim Mehndi, Agha Mir's successor.

Ahmadullah "Danka" Shah: Born Saiyid Ahmad Ali Khan in 1789 - the son of Nawab Mohammad Ali Khan of Chinapatam (later Madras), he visited England, and returned to India after performing *Haj*. With a mystical bent of mind, he became a disciple of Saiyad Furquan Ali of the *Qadri* order, who named him Ahmadullah Shah. The *Maulvi* criss-crossed central, northern and eastern India, and in due course reached Faizabad - all the while exhorting his ever-increasing number of armed followers to wage war against the British. Ultimately, he was arrested, imprisoned at Faizabad and sentenced to death. On June 8, 1857, Indian freedom fighters broke open the jail, freed Shah and declared him as their leader. He soundly routed the British, who were led by Henry Lawrence, in the Battle of Chinhat on June 30, 1857. Despite his theological differences with Hazrat Mahal's court, he set up his command from Lucknow's *Taaron Wali Kothi* and proved to be a formidable enemy of the British. Shah was usually accompanied by a drummer during his forays and came to be known as '*Danka Shah*.' Colin Campbell attacked Mohammadi (district of Lakhimpur Kheri) on May 24, 1858 and defeated Shah, who then proceeded towards Puwanyan, north-east of Shahjahanpur, to solicit the support of Jagannath Singh, the Raja of Puwanyan. But the Raja's soldiers started firing at him and one of the bullets hit Shah; he died instantly. The Raja's brother, Baldev Singh, cut off Shah's head and placed it before the Collector, GP Maney, who gave a cash award to the Raja.

Ali Naqi Khan: He held the post of *Wazir* during the period 1847 - 1856. Ali Naqi Khan "Madar-ud-Daula" had become a member of the Nawabi court due to matrimonial alliances and not by dint of merit. Alam Ara Begum, *Khas Mahal* of Wajid Ali Shah was the niece of Ali Naqi Khan; his daughter, Begum Akhtar Mahal was also married to Wajid Ali Shah, and he himself was the descendant of Mir Muhammad Yusuf Ali Khan "Madar-ud-Daula", whose daughter, Begum Afzal-un-Nisa had been the *Khas Mahal* of Sa'adat Ali Khan. Since he was a man of mediocre abilities, without any administrative acumen, he was ably assisted by his deputy, Sharaf-ud-Daula in day-to-day administration. Ali Naqi Khan, on behalf of Wajid Ali Shah, had held a series of meetings with General Outram in 1856, regarding the final annexation orders of Awadh. But Outram had his own orders cut-and-dried from Calcutta,. Was Ali Naqi Khan a willing accomplice to this conspiracy as insinuated by some authors? A perusal of dispatches between the Lucknow Residency and Fort William (now available in public domain) indicate no such subterfuge. Ali Naqi Khan was prevented from accompanying Wajid Ali Shah to Calcutta, but eventually he did join the King, only to be incarcerated in Fort William as the insurrection of 1857 had broken out in Lucknow. He later died of cholera in Lucknow in 1871, having lost his properties and riches.

Almas Ali Khan: Almas Ali started his life as a slave, coming to Faizabad as part of Bahu Begum's dowry. However, he was diligent and sincere in his duties, which impressed both Shuja-ud-Daula and Bahu Begum. As a result of this, with time, he became rich and powerful, as a land-owner and also as a brave and efficient soldier. He refused the post of *Naib* after the death of Elich Khan in 1776 (which was then given to Hasan Raza Khan). Haider Beg, Hasan's deputy unearthed instances of financial impropriety on the part of Almas, which resulted in conflict between the two. Efforts to get Almas removed from the court failed, as he had become immensely rich and powerful with time. Apparently, he also held interests in the Mughal court of Delhi and had become more powerful than Asaf-ud-Daula in the Nawabi court. His love-hate relationship with the British continued unabated all throughout his career. He died in 1808 at Mianganj (Unnao) after a leading a life full of intrigues, confrontations, worldly ambition, defiance and conflict. He had no offspring since he was a eunuch by birth. Naturally a dispute now arose about the inheritance of his wealth and vast properties; this time however, the players were Sa'adat Ali Khan and Bahu Begum. He is also known for usage of larger-than-normal size bricks, named *almasi* bricks, in the monuments built by him, in and around Lucknow.

Auckland Colvin: Lord Colvin was born on March 8, 1838 at Calcutta. Educated at Eton and East India College, he arrived in India on January 17, 1858, fully trained as a "writer" (parlance for "administrator" in the East India Company). Colvin held various assignments during his stay in north India, before moving to Egypt, playing an active role, both during war and peace time. He returned to India as Member of the Viceroy's Council in August 1883. His role in famine relief and revenue policies have not been taken kindly by latter day historians. Colvin was subsequently transferred to Allahabad as Lt. Governor of the NW Provinces and Chief Commissioner of Oudh (Awadh) on November 21, 1887; water supply systems, sanitation, medical and educational facilities received his attention. The Colvin Taluqdars School was established by him at Lucknow in 1889, for imparting education to the children of British administrators and landed aristocracy of Awadh.

As would be obvious, Colvin was against the idea of a free India, which automatically made him hostile to the Congress. Back in England after retirement in 1892, he settled at Framlingham (Suffolk), and kept himself occupied in writing as well as in welfare activities at local level. Colvin died at Surbiton, on March 24, 1908 and was buried at Earl Soham, Suffolk.

Brij Narayan Chakbast: Of Kashmiri origin, Pandit Brij Narayan Chakbast was born in 1882 at Faizabad. His family shifted to Lucknow in 1887 and started residing in *Kashmiri Mohalla* of old Lucknow. Brij Narayan completed his education, obtaining a degree in law and started practicing law in Lucknow. He became popular as a *nazm* poet of the Lucknow school of poetry, being strongly influenced by Mirza Ghalib, Mir Anis and Khwaja Haider Ali Aatish "Lakhnawi." Braj Mohan also participated in the freedom movement, and was actively involved in social and political movements of his time. He would organise all India *mushairas* annually, also initiating and participating in community development programmes for Kashmiri youth. Chakbast's patriotic fervor found its finest expression in his elegies on the deaths of national leaders, e.g. Bal Gangadhar Tilak. Chakbast also dedicated a poem to Mahatma Gandhi who was still working in South Africa at the time.

Chakbast died on February 12, 1926 from a paralytic stroke, at Rae Bareilly. His untimely death left a huge void in contemporary Urdu poetry of Lucknow. Chakbast's path breaking poetry was published posthumously after his death, in a compilation called *Subah Watan.* A road in *Kaiserbagh* area, Lucknow was named Chakbast Road in his honour.

Captain Robert Smith: Captain Smith was a military engineer with the East India Company, having arrived in Calcutta in 1805. His flair for surveying was noticed by the Surveyor General, as "*the best draughtsman I am acquainted with. His masterly rapid pencil particularly qualifies him for survey of the Frontier, as he will be able to delineate the passes and surrounding country with the greatest correctness.*" Between 1812 and 1813

Smith joined the camp of the Commander-in-Chief, Sir George Nugent, for his tour of Upper India. Smith's sketches were appreciated by Lady Nugent, who noted in her diary that "*Just as day dawned, we crossed the Jumna. ... I took the engineer officer, Mr. Smith, with me, and we projected a drawing of the line of march, which will be a treasure to me, if he executes it according to my plan, and I have little doubt of its being quite perfect, by what I have seen of his drawings.*" He was next appointed as Inspecting Engineer to accompany Lord Moira (both Governor-General and Commander-in-Chief) on his tour to the Upper Provinces from May 1814, being "*selected from his character for talents and abilities.*" Smith's panoramas of Lucknow provide fantastic details of the city, including details of structures which are no longer extant. These include the *Sunheri Burj* palace, adjacent to the *Rumi Darwaza* and the front elevation of the *Musa Bagh kothi*. His sketch of *Khurshid Manzil* (1814) provided details of what the building looked like originally (present day La Martiniere College for Girls). He also produced detailed sketches of the marching equipage of the rulers of Awadh, as also their fish shape boats gliding down the Gomti. The cupola atop *Qutub Minar* was also designed by Smith (this was later brought down, and came to be known as Smith's Folly).

Claude Martin: Born in Lyons, France on January 5, 1735, Martin's family background was modest. At the age of 15, he decided to join the French East India Company to seek his fortune in India. He served under Dupleix and de Lally, but when the French were routed by the British, he offered his services to the English East India Company, which was grudgingly accepted. He reached Lucknow in 1776 and was appointed as Superintendent of Nawab Asaf-ud-Daula's arsenal. Martin was a man of multifarious talents, from soldiering to surveying to indigo cultivation; from casting cannons to botany; from astronomy to medicine and several other diverse fields of interest. Most importantly, he was an amateur architect and it was this talent of his, which made him not only indispensable to the then Nawab – his fame reached far and wide due to his charismatic architectural creations, a fame which continues till today.

Martin never married, possibly due to a medical condition, as a result of which, he did not leave any heirs. After his untimely death on September 13, 1800, his enormous fortune and estate remained disputed for several decades, although he had left a detailed, if rather convoluted Will. Martin was buried in his new home, *Constantia*, at Lucknow, in which he never had the good fortune to live in. The prestigious La Martiniere schools in Lucknow, Calcutta (Kolkata) and Lyons and several endowments are symbols of his generous legacy. Martin's motto on life was: *Labore et Constantia*, a motto which he constantly adhered to in his lifetime, and which was adopted and shared by the schools bearing his name today.

Col. SA Abbott: Saunders Alexius Abbott was born in July, 1811, being the fourth son of a retired Calcutta merchant. He joined the Bengal Infantry in 1828, and served under Henry Lawrence in 1836. He fought in the First Anglo-Sikh war of 1845 and also served under Henry Hardinge at the Battle of Ferozeshah, Punjab, where he was seriously injured. Abbot was Deputy Commissioner of Umballa (Ambala), followed by Hoshiarpur. He was Commissioner of Lucknow from 1858 - 1863. In 1863, he and his wife founded the Lucknow Girls School, which would be the nucleus for the La Martiniere Girls' School, later on. After his retirement, Abbott became an agent for a railway company in *Lahore*, before being promoted to its Board of Directors. Alexius died in *Brighton* on 7 February 1894. The present day *Vidhan Sabha Marg* of Lucknow was originally called Abbot Road. The city of Abbottabad in Pakistan, where Osama Bin Laden was killed had been earlier named in honour of James Abbott, elder brother of Alexius Abbott.

Colin Campbell, Baron of Clyde: Colin Macliver was born on October 20, 1792 in Glasgow, Scotland. He was raised by his uncle, Major John Campbell, and hence addressed as "Colin Campbell." He was first commissioned on May 26, 1808 and saw action on several fronts, during which, his bravery was noted by his superiors. Late in life, he was offered command of British forces in India during the 1857 insurrection, with the rank of a full general. He reached Calcutta in August, 1857 and evacuated Lucknow in November 1857, after successfully engaging with Tantia Tope in Cawnpore (Kanpur). Campbell recaptured Lucknow in March 1858, and remained busy thereafter in mopping up operations, involving Begum Hazrat Mahal, who had escaped from Lucknow, Ahmadullah 'Danka' Shah, who was still battling British forces in the hinterlands of Awadh, as well as the local "rajas" and landowners who remained sympathetic towards Hazrat Mahal's cause and continued to wage war against the British in whichever manner they could. Ironically, in 1858, Campbell faced a near rebellion of the troops belonging to the East India Company, which he managed to quell, using troops of the British army. Campbell returned to England in June 1860 and lived a retired life in London with the title, Baron of Clydesdale, Scotland. He died in November 9, 1862 and was buried at Westminster Abbey. His statues adorn Waterloo Palace, London and George Square, Glasgow. Clyde Road in Lucknow had been named in his honour by the colonial government. A Campbell Road is also extant in Haiderganj area of old Lucknow.

CW Gwynne: Major C.W. Gwynne, ICS was Chief Secretary to the Government of the United Provinces. Not much is known about his life and times. A road passing through Aminabad and Maulviganj in Lucknow was named in his honour. The road is famous for its paper market. Surprisingly, Gwynne had produced a detailed *Monograph on the Manufacture of Wire and Tinsel in the United Provinces*, which was published in 1910. The monograph was based on his personal survey work in Benaras (Varanasi), Agra, Bareilly and Lucknow on the various nuances of gold and silver embroidered articles of dress, including *Zardozi, Salma-Sitara, Tarkashi* and *Kamdani.* A hilarious incident occurred when he was appointed as Joint Secretary in the Home Department, but his claim for transport of one horse from Lucknow to Delhi was rejected by the Imperial Government. On a more serious note, since Gwynne was in the Home Department at New Delhi, he got involved in the Penal Settlement at the Andamans, including the fate of its prisoners. Interestingly, the prisoners included the Savarkar brothers, Hrishikesh Kanji Lal and Ganesh Damodar.

Felice Beato: Also known as Felix Beato, he was a well-known photographer of Italian-British origin, who created several panoramas of architecture and landscapes of Asia and the Mediterrranean. Born in 1832 in Venice, he was a prolific traveller and specialised in "war photography", focussing mostly on the destructive effects of war across the globe. He arrived in Calcutta in 1858 and travelled throughout northern India, photographing war torn Delhi, Kanpur, Meerut, Lahore and of course, Lucknow. His works provided authentic photographic evidence of monuments and archaeological details, immediately in the aftermath of the First War of Independence. Many of these ruins would later be torn down; hence Beato's work effectively documented photographic details of structures, which would disappear in due course of time. Beato's evocative treatment of *Sikandar Bagh* is well known in photographic circles across the world. Similarly, his panorama of *Macchi Bhavan* and *Kaiserbagh* would provide details which enable researchers even today to draw conclusive pictures of their architectural details. Beato would later carry out similar works in China, Japan and Burma. He died in Florence in January 1909.

George Beechey: George Duncan Beechey belonged to a family of portrait artists; born on January 1, 1798 at Cavendish Square, London, he arrived in India in 1828 and took up the assignment as court painter during the reign of Nasir-ud-Din Haider and remained so in the court of Awadh, till the death of Mohammad Ali Shah in 1842. Apparently, he married a princess from the royal family, which gave him access to the royal court, facilitating his painting of portraits for royalty. Beechey died in Lucknow on December 6, 1852 and was buried in the Madiaon cemetery of Lucknow. It is said that his demise was due to grief, because the ship carrying his best portraits to England for exhibition, had sunk in the sea, before reaching their destination. For this very reason, his artworks are very rare to find and very expensive also. Beechey's restless spirit reportedly continued to his former house in Madiaon cantonment, which was later occupied by Rev. Polehampton.

George Couper: George Wilson Couper was born on April 28, 1824 in Halifax, Nova Scotia. He joined the Bengal Civil Service in 1846, and was initially posted in Dinajpur. Dalhousie, who was close friend of his father, took a keen interest in George's career. After the annexation of Awadh in 1856, he was appointed as Secretary to the Chief Commissioner, James Outram and then Henry Lawrence. Lord Canning denied Outram's recommendation that Couper should succeed him as Chief Commissioner, as the latter was too junior in the service. After a stint in Allahabad, Couper went back to Lucknow in 1863, this time as Judicial Commissioner. He finally assumed the post of Chief Commissioner in Lucknow in 1873. After the amalgamation of Agra and Awadh, Couper became the first Lieutenant Governor of the United Provinces. Couper has been generally appreciated for his actions and tactful attitude during his pro-active service career. He retired in April, 1882 and returned to England, settling in Camberly, where he died on March 5, 1908. The Hussainabad Clock Tower was built in Lucknow in his honour.

George DeRusset: Popularly known as "The Barber of Lucknow", George Harris Quigley arrived at Calcutta in the 1820s, adopted an exotic name of DeRusset and soon reached Lucknow to seek his fortunes. He was patronised by the then ruling king of Awadh, Nasir-ud-Din Haider, and eventually became his close confidante. In addition to hair-dressing duties of his Majesty, DeRusset quickly assumed the role of major domo-cum-counsellor for the King. Acquiring a notorious reputation, DeRusset managed to amass a considerable amount of wealth through his machinations in the royal household, till his eventual banishment by the King himself. After his unceremonious eviction from the royal court, he escaped to Calcutta and boarded a ship for England. He subsequently settled in London and dabbled in various trades and business ventures, many of which ran into losses.

Gore Ouseley: Ouseley has been described as an entrepreneur (trader), linguist and diplomat. He was born in Limerick, Ireland in June, 1770. 1787 saw Gore Ouseley moving to India, becoming a successful trader, and later establishing a textile factory in Dacca, East Bengal in 1792. During 1795-96, he traveled to Lucknow and became acquainted with the then reigning Nawab, Sa'adat Ali Khan, ultimately becoming his *aide-de-camp*. Ouseley was responsible for designing the *Dilkusha Kothi* for the Nawab, from architectural drawings available in the *Vitruvius Brittanicus*, a collection of copperplate engravings depicting English country houses and public buildings, primarily based on neo-Palladian styles. For *Dilkusha*, he chose the site plan and elevation of Seaton Delavel, a country house in Northumberland, England, which had been John Vanburgh's final work. Ouseley was appointed as Major-Commander and later made a baronet on the recommendations of Lord Wellesley. He was fluent in Sanskrit, Arabic and Persian, becoming President of the Society for the Publication of the Oriental Texts in 1842. Major Ouseley died at Hall Barn Park, Beaconsfield, Buckinghamshire, England in 1844. His widow erected a monument to his memory in Hertingfordbury Church, Hertfordshire.

Haider Beg Khan: Haider Beg served as deputy to Hasan Raza Khan during 1776 - 1796. Originally from Kabul, the joined the services of Shuja-ud-Daula, but due to subsequent differences, he and his brother were imprisoned and tortured. Ultimately, Haider Beg could secure his freedom and survive, firstly because of his landed properties, which yielded him considerable income, and also due to British intervention in his favour. Haider Beg visited Calcutta with Hasan Raza to try and reduce the burden of subsidies on Awadh; he succeeded in his endeavors and also managed to get correct the disbalance due to trade monopolies granted to Europeans earlier. Haider Beg died in 1792.

Hakim Mehndi: Originally from Kashmir, he was close to Asaf-ud-Daula, but his importance increased considerably in the court of Sa'adat Ali Khan. The Residents in the court of Lucknow remained inimical towards him, although, by all accounts, he was an able, but not entirely honest administrator. On the accession of Ghazi-ud-din Haider in 1814, Hakim Mehndi was deprived of all his public offices and much of his property, and he was also imprisoned for sometime. He returned from exile in 1831 during the reign of Nasir-ud-Din Haider; his reforms were duly supported by Lord Bentick. But the good times did not last and he too, like Agha Mir earlier, was replaced by Roshan-ud-Daula. An austerity measure, which proved fatal for his career was the reduction in the stipends of the Awadh begums, and interference in their innovations during *azadari*. This made him a *persona non-grata*, and his eventual dismissal in 1832 was apparently at the instigation of Badshah Begum, dowager queen of Ghazi-ud-Din Haider.

Harcourt Butler: Spencer Harcourt Butler came from a family of distinguished academicians. He arrived at the United Provinces in November 1890 and after various assignments, took over as Lt. Governor of the United Provinces of Agra and Oudh (1918 - 1921) and was later the Governor (1921 - 1922). He took keen interest in restoring Lucknow's importance, as a result of which, the capital of the United Provinces was shifted from Allahabad to Lucknow in 1920. Consequently, the Foundation Stone of the UP Council Chamber (present day *Vidhan Sabha Bhavan*) was laid by him in 1922. He also played an active role in establishing the University of Lucknow in 1920. The present day Harcourt Butler Technical University at Kanpur had been originally established as Government Research Institute in 1920. Butler laid the Foundation Stone of the present main building in 1921. He died in 1938 in London.

Henri Polier: Antoine-Louis Henri de Polier, born in 1741 at Lusanne, Switzerland, was actually of French origin and an engineer by profession. Warren Hasting arranged for him to go to Awadh to work as engineer and architect for Shuja-ud-Daula at Faizabad in 1772. Later, he worked in the courts of Shah Alam – II at Delhi and Asaf-ud-Daula, at Lucknow. While in India, he was an ardent collector of rare Indian manuscripts and antiques. Polier was one of those foreign adventurers in India, who later became "completely native", adopting Indian dress, language and customs. He engaged in a broad range of commercial activities, which included trading in spices, laying of fruit-bearing gardens, trading in liquor, cloth, and even elephants. Being a prolific writer, he wrote several books on the people and customs of India, and was awarded the title of *Arsalân-i-Jang* by the Mughal court. Polier married twice, both time to Indian ladies and was in close touch with Claude Martin in Lucknow. Later in life, with the immense wealth acquired from his stay in India, he left Indian shores, after leaving his two wives in the care of Martin. However, he did not live long to enjoy the fruits of his foreign adventures. During the violence that had erupted in Europe due to the French Revolution, he was assassinated on February 9, 1795, in the town on Avignon.

Henry Havelock: Havelock was born on April 5, 1795 at Bishopwearmouth, North England. He studied military history and the art of war during his active military service in England. Havelock was a deeply religious man, who introduced the concept of distributing bibles to all soldiers, as a sort of missionary activity. His military prowess impressed James Outram, which resulted in him being stationed at Awadh to support Gen. Wheeler at Cawnpore (Kanpur) and Henry Lawrence at Lucknow during the events of 1857. Although he won several victories against Indian freedom fighters, he was stymied inside the Residency for quite some time. He died of dysentery on November 24, 1857 during military operations at *Dilkusha* and was hurriedly buried near the *Alambagh Kothi* in an unmarked grave. Havelock's grave stands today in a small park near *Alambagh Kothi,* having an obelisk and an inscription. This tomb was erected much later on his remains, by his family, consisting of his widow and sons. Nicknamed as "The Hero of Lucknow", his statue adorns Trafalgar Square, London.

Henry Lawrence: Henry Montgomery Lawrence was born on June 28, 1806, in Matara, British Ceylon (now Sri Lanka). He was of Irish origin. He arrived at Calcutta in 1823 and was stationed at Dum Dum. After the Anglo-Burmese war, his health failed him and he returned to England to recuperate. He set sail for Calcutta once again in 1829 and was stationed this time at Cawnpore (Kanpur). After seeing action on various fronts, he was posted at Lucknow as Chief Commissioner in March 1857. Shortly afterwards, he got embroiled in the insurrection, which started in March 1857. He took strategic decisions for the defence of Lucknow and facilitated the retreat of British soldiers, civilians and their families to the Residency, although he faced a humiliating defeat in the Battle of Chinhat on June 30, 1857. July 2, 1857 saw him wounded by a shell which burst into his room while he was resting on a couch; death came quickly on July 4, 1857. Lawrence was buried in the Lucknow Residency cemetery, where he lies in eternal sleep; a Memorial to Henry Lawrence stands at St. Paul's Cathedral, London.

In addition to his duties as a soldier and administrator, Lawrence had established four schools in different hill stations, for providing education to children of serving and deceased British officers and soldiers stationed in India. These include the Lawrence School, Sanawar (HP), Lawrence School, Lovedale, Ooty (TN) and Lawrence College in Murree (now in Pakistan). The premises of the fourth school at Mount Abu (Rajasthan) were later taken over by the Central Reserve Police Force for establishing the Internal Security Academy.

Henry Polehampton: Henry Stedman Polehampton was born in 1824 at Middlesex, England. He obtained his education from Eton and Oxford and as per family tradition, became a pastor in 1848. After marriage with Emily Allnatt, he sailed for India in 1856 abroad the ship *SS Pera*. Later, as

Assistant Chaplain of the fledgling British cantonment at Madiaon, in addition to his duties as priest for Lucknow and its neighbourhood, he also nursed cholera patients, becoming severely ill himself. With the outbreak of the insurrection, he left the cantonment and shifted to the Residency, where, accompanied by Mrs. Polehampton, he remained active in care-giving for the besieged. It is said that "*he never swerved from this self-imposed duty and only left the hospital to go to his meals.*" Polehampton, struck by a stray shot, and further weakened by cholera, breathed his last on July 20, 1857. He was hurriedly buried, sans coffin, in the Residency cemetery. Mrs Polehampton continued to nurse the wounded and ill, throughout her stay in the Residency, a fact which has been documented by several authors. She returned to England, re-married and died in 1905.

Henry Sleeman: William Henry Sleeman was born on August 8, 1788 in Cornwall, England. Financial hardships made him to join the Bengal Army in 1808 and travel to India. He saw action on various fronts, including the Anglo-Nepal (Gorkha) War. Sleeman is known for his mastery over Hindi and Urdu, his comprehensive report on Oudh (Awadh), his interest in anthropology and his suppression of the *Thuggee* cult (bands of organised criminals, responsible for looting and strangulating travelers). Sleeman was Resident at Gwalior (1843 – 1849) and at Lucknow (1849 – 1856). He was not in favour of outright annexation of Awadh, but was convinced that British intervention was necessary to curb the corruption and mismanagement in Awadh, as he perceived it. His health took a downturn and he left India. His journey back home remained incomplete as he died off Ceylon (Sri Lanka) on February 4, 1856, four days after the EIC's annexation of Awadh.

Humphry Ozias: Humphrey or Humphry was born on September 8, 1742 in Honiton, Devon County, and derived his name from his great grandfather, Rev. Ozias Upcott, Rector of Honiton. He studied art in London and Bath and moved to Italy for some time, where there was demand for his works. He became well known for portrait miniatures, oils, pastels and crayons. Ozias was active in India during 1785 - 1787. He produced many miniatures and sketches in Calcutta and then proceeded to Lucknow where he hoped to earn a fortune in Asaf-ud-Daula's court, where he painted water colours miniatures of Haider Beg Khan and an infant Wazir Ali. However, it seems he only got a token payment with a bond (promissory note) for the remainder, which (as it appeared), Asaf-ud-Daula had no intention of honouring. Humphry made other miniatures during his 5 months stay at the house of John Wombwell, the East India Company's Accountant at Lucknow. One such miniature, dated March 13, 1786, depicts boats and elephants along the Gomti river with the *Teele-Wali Masjid* on the opposite bank and the high walls of the *Macchi Bhavan* beyond it, parallel to the river. He left Calcutta in 1787 with an impaired health and without any fortune. Ozias also had a failing eyesight, due to a fall during horse riding in 1772 and went completely blind in 1797. He died in 1810 in Hampstead, north London.

Isabella Thoburn: Of Irish descent, Isabella was born in Ohio, USA on March 29, 1840. Having lost her father at the age of ten, and being subject to related anxieties, she remained firmly rooted to Christianity all throughout her life, which gave her succour and mental strength. After attending the Wheeling Female Seminary, she felt the need for reform in education, particularly female education. She arrived in Bombay on January 7, 1870, accompanied by Clara Swain of New York. Isabella was sent to Lucknow whereas Clara was to work in Bareilly and Rampur. Lucknow remained the home of Ms Thoburn all her life. Her first venture was a small school, with only six students, then moving on to the *Zahur Baksh* compound, and finally to a Nawabi property in *Lalbagh.* In 1873, during an outbreak of cholera in Lucknow, Ms Thoburn proved her mettle, although she had no formal training in patient care. She was responsible for initiating a Christian college exclusively for women in 1886. This college, in a new campus at *Chand Bagh,* would subsequently become the prestigious IT College of today. Ms Thoburn died of cholera on September 1, 1901 after thirty-one years of devoted service to the Methodist Episcopal Church and its missionary work.

James La Touche: James John Digges La Touche was born in Dublin, Ireland on December 16, 1844. He joined the Indian Civil Service in 1867, and spent four years in *Ajmir* (Ajmer) Province and four years in Burma, before moving to the North-Western Provinces. There, he served as a member of the Board of Revenue and Chief Secretary, and in 1897, acted as Lieutenant-Governor for six months, after the breakdown in health of Sir Anthony MacDonnell due to the outbreak of famine in that year. La Touche was a Member of the Council of the Viceroy of India, and was appointed Lieutenant-Governor of the North-Western Provinces and Chief Commissioner of Oudh in November 1901. He continued as Lieutenant-Governor of the United Provinces of Agra and Oudh until December 1906.The following year, he was appointed a Member of the Council of the Secretary of State for India. La Touche was appointed a Companion of the Order of the Star of India (CSI) and promoted to a Knight Commander (KCSI) in the 1901 Birthday Honours List on 9 November 1901. Having served at Burma and India for nearly 39 years, he died in Dublin on October

6, 1921 and was interred in Mount Jerome Cemetery, County Dublin, Ireland. Major roads in colonial Lucknow and Kanpur were named in honour of La Touche.

James Outram: James Outram, son of Benjamin Outram, was born on January 29, 1803, at Derbyshire, England. He was educated in Marischal College, Aberdeen (Scotland), and obtained an Indian cadetship in 1819. After several military victories, which earned him the sobriquet of *Bayard of India*, he was appointed as Resident of Lucknow in 1854. He was described by Sleeman as a 'worthy successor.' However, while Sleeman's views on Oudh (Awadh) were based on personal experience (whatever they might have been), Outram was hampered by his 'absence of any personal experience in this country', as he himself admitted. Ultimately, under the inflexible directions from Calcutta, Outram formally annexed Awadh on February 11, 1856 and took over as its first Chief Commissioner. Subsequent events occurred with terrifying swiftness. Due to a series of administrative blunders, ill-planned reforms and concerted efforts to humiliate the old Nawabi order, Awadh erupted in rebellion within a few months, more aptly termed as the "First War of Independence." Aided by Colin Campbell, Outram managed to free Lucknow from the control of the freedom fighters, but his innings at Lucknow were coming to an end. He returned to England in 1860 and died on March 11, 1863. Outram was buried in Westminster Abbey; his bronze statue stands on the Thames Embankment near Charing Cross, London.

James Quinton: James Wallace Quinton was born in Enniskillen, Ireland in 1834 and graduated from Trinity College, Dublin, in 1853. He joined the Bengal Civil Service in 1856, subsequently serving as a junior officer in Ghazipur and Meerut. His longest stint as an ICS officer was as Deputy Commissioner of Oudh (Awadh) during 1865 - 75. He was Judicial Commissioner in Burma during 1865 - 77 and Commissioner of Jhansi in 1878. He served as Member of the Legislative Council, as Member, Board of Revenue, NW Provinces and as Public Service Commissioner. In 1889, he became Chief Commissioner of Assam. In 1891, he was sent to Manipur to quell civil unrest, due to the death of the Maharaja there, resulting in succession problems among his sons. When Quinton tried to arrest one of the princes, Tikendrajit - who was also the Commander of Manipur's armed forces, trouble spilled over and Quinton, together with other British officials were hacked to death. The disturbances thereafter in the region are often referred to as the Anglo-Manipur war. A road in *Kaiserbagh* area of Lucknow, named in honour of Quinton, is still extant.

Jean-Baptiste Gentil: Jean-Baptiste Joseph Gentil was the French Resident of Nawab Shuja-ud-Daula in Faizabad. Born in Bagnols, Languedoc on June 25, 1726, he served in India under various French generals *viz.* Joseph Dupleix, Charles Bussy, Jean Law de Lauriston and Comte *de* Lally. He saw action and intrigues in Pondicherry, Chandernagore and Murshidabad. Later, he joined the court of Shuja-ud-Daula, literally becoming his *aide-de-camp*, advising the Nawab on diverse matters, and establishing a battalion of 600 French mercenaries. He made detailed maps of Mughal India, wrote treatises on historical matters, collected rare and valuable manuscripts and acted on behalf of the Nawab, particularly when negotiating with the British. His importance can be gauged from the fact that the Mughal Emperor, Shah Alam during his visit to Shuja-ud-Daula at Faizabad, paid a personal visit to Gentil at his house.

Shuja-ud-Daula was under constant pressure from the British to remove Gentil from his court, whom they perceived as a threat. Ultimately, Shuja bowed to their wishes and Gentil returned to Chandernagore, and by October 1777 was back in France. Having lost his military pension, he died in poverty on February 15, 1799 at Bagnol.

Johann Zoffany: Zoffany was born in Frankfurt, Germany on March 13, 1733. He arrived in England in 1760 and was an immediate success. He got many commissions, including work from the Royal Family, but subsequently fell out of favour. The riches of India attracted Zoffany and he boarded ship to Calcutta, where he landed in 1783. Accompanying Warren Hastings to Lucknow in 1784, he came in contact with other Europeans of the Nawabi court, including Martin, Polier and Wombwell. His incredibly detailed painting, "Colonel Mordaunt's Cock Match" was the highlight of his stay in Lucknow, although he made paintings of Mughal Prince Jawan Bakht, Hasan Raza Khan and of Asaf-ud-Daula himself. Zoffany's paintings were extremely detailed and he considered his work to be historical pieces and not just observational scenes. His imagery was always dense, whether they were portraits or landscapes, e.g. the painting entitled "The Embassy of Haider Beg to Lord Cornwallis." Zoffany returned to England in 1789 and continued to produce original art as well as copies of his earlier works. He died on November 11, 1810 and was buried in the churchyard of St Anne's Church, Kew.

John Wingfield: Charles John Wingfield was born on April 16, 1820 and served in the Bengal Civil Service during 1840 - 1866. He was Chief Commissioner of Oudh (Awadh) during February 15, 1859 - April 20, 1860.

Those were troubled times, but it was Wingfield (and to a lesser extent, Robert Montgomery) who convinced Lord Canning that a "clemency" policy would bear fruit, instead of further confrontation and conflict with the traditional landowners of Awadh. The latter responded by proposing to construct a *Wingfield Manzil* at Lucknow in his honour. The first *Lucknow Durbar* was held on October 26, 1859, during the tenure of Wingfield, in which Lord Canning announced his government's noble intentions towards the *ta'aluqdars* of Awadh. In 1860, an old Nawabi garden, called *Banarsi Bagh* was landscaped and developed into a colonial-style park called Wingfield Park in Lucknow in his honour, by George Campbell, Judicial Commissioner of Lucknow. The park was later upgraded as the Prince of Wales Zoological Gardens in 1921 (present day Nawab Wajid Ali Shah Zoological Garden).

A bachelor by choice, Wingfield preferred to remain in active politics late in life, being elected to British Parliament during 1868 - 1874. He died on January 27, 1892, at London.

John Wombwell: Not much is known about Wombwell, except that he was an accountant with the EIC, stationed at Lucknow. He was born in Yorkshire, England, in the year 1755. The artist Humphry Ozias (described elsewhere) had stayed at his house in Lucknow and produced several miniatures, without any commission. Wombwell was one of those who had gone "completely native" during his stay in India and reportedly had an Indian wife or *bibi*. Lucknow was a lucrative posting in those days, with the fledgling court of Asaf-ud-Daula, and apparently Wombwell had used his connections to secure a position in Lucknow as Company Accountant and Paymaster of the troops in 1777. He quickly became friends with both Martin and Polier, due to shared interests of learning about Indian's culture, collecting manuscripts and maintaining libraries. John Bristow's third tenure as Resident at Lucknow, had become tenacious, having "hesitated to obey orders", as a result of which, he was asked to revert to Calcutta in 1783, after giving charge to Wombwell. A series of correspondences between Bristow, Wombwell and Calcutta came to naught as the Governor General seemed adamant to remove immediately Bristow from the scene. Wombwell's responsibilities further increased with Warren Hastings impending visit to Lucknow. Wombwell died in 1795, at the young age of forty years.

LM Jopling: Lindsay Millias Jopling was born on May 19, 1875 at Chesham Bois, England. As an Indian Civil Service officer, he worked in various capacities at Lucknow, from City Magistrate to Officiating

Commissioner, Lucknow Division. He was also *ex officio* President, Provincial Museum Committee of Lucknow, and Chairman, Lucknow Improvement Trust. Jopling was instrumental in the establishment of the Jubilee Girls' School (present day AP Sen Memorial Girls College), Lucknow. He has been described as a "*thin, distinguished looking, ascetic man, who looked young to hold the post, although he was silver haired. A man who commanded respect, reserved and laconic, a fanatically efficient worker, dedicated to promoting the welfare of the people of the famous Lucknow city and district. He had some weakness of the spine and always worked seated on a high stool.*" He married his first wife Nina, in India. His second marriage to Joan was in 1931, in England. Jopling died on March, 14, 1967, at the age of 91. He was interred in the Chesham Bois Burial Ground, Buckinghamshire, England. A road in Lucknow was named in his honour by the then colonial government.

Lousada Barrow: Major General Barrow was officiating Commissioner of Lucknow during 1860 – 61 and Chief Commissioner in 1871. A statue of Barrow - designed by Edwin Roscoe Mullins, was completed in 1883 in London and installed in the *Kaiserbagh* central vista, but was removed post-1947 and has been presently kept on display, with other colonial era statues, in the Lucknow Museum. Barrow also had a road named after him; this Barrow Road ran across *Lalbagh* and *Kaiserbagh*, effectively connecting the two. It was later renamed as JC Bose Marg. Barrow was fortunate in having an unblemished record in India and could die in peace in his motherland – a good fortune which many of his compatriots could not enjoy. He returned to England and died in 1877, being buried at Ryde Old Cemetery on the Isle of Wright.

Major Banks: John Sherbrooke Banks, born in 1811, arrived in India in 1829, where he joined the 33rd Regiment of the Bengal Native Infantry. After an eventful career, he moved to Lucknow in 1855, in connection with the imminent annexation of Awadh. He was appointed as Commissioner of Lucknow, working under Henry Lawrence, who was Chief Commissioner. Bank's resided in the *Kothi Hayat Baksh*, which came to be known as Bank's House. He had the dubious honour of leading a team of soldiers to the *Kaiserbagh*, to unearth and loot the valuables and arms stored there; even the *zenana* had not been spared. After Lawrence's death on July 5, 1857 in the Residency, Banks assumed the charge of Chief Commissioner. He was killed shortly afterwards, by a musket shot on July 21, 1857, while reconnoitering the defence arrangements from atop of Gubbin's House in the Residency. As was the practice, he was hurriedly buried in the Residency Cemetery. Banks was survived by his wife, Elizabeth and one child.

Post-1857, a road between *Hazratganj* to *Kaiserbagh* was later re-named Major Bank's Road in his honour.

Makka Darzi: Makka has been described as a "tailor by caste and a fashion designer by profession." Among all the rulers of Awadh (1722 – 1856), only Nasir-ud-Din Haider (1827 – 1837) had a penchant for western attire and *Mian* Makka satisfied the king's sartorial tastes by way of creating elegant European dresses. For which, he was paid handsomely, of course. Eventually, he fell victim to court intrigues (as did his patron, the King himself) and was banished from Lucknow. He is credited for building a *serai* and garden near *Bakshi ka Talaab*, Lucknow, as well as an ornate *Imambara* and *Qadam Rasul* at Khairabad, Sitapur. The name of the locality, *Makkaganj* in Lucknow is also derived from the name of *Makka darzi* (*darzi* = tailor). A small bridge over the river Gond, in Kasraila, which demarcates Laharpur from Khairabad is also attributed to Makka *darzi.*

Mammoo Khan: Often described as "guide, philosopher and friend" of Begum Hazrat Mahal, Mammoo (or Mammu) Khan *a.k.a.* Ali Mohammad Khan's antecedents are not clear. He had tremendous personal clout in the court of Begum Hazrat Mahal, but otherwise, even as *Daroga* of the *Diwan Khana* (Superintendent of the Hall of Audience), he wielded considerable authority and exercised full powers during the brief reign of Birjis Qadr. Many accounts about his scandalous conduct and cruelty have been written by different authors, a discussion of which is beyond the scope of this book. He was sentenced to life imprisonment by the British for his role in the uprising of 1857.

Martin Gubbins: Martin Richard Gubbins was born to Major General Joseph Gubbins and his wife, Charlotte, in the year 1812. He reached India in 1830 and held various assignments in Delhi, Allahabad, Mathura and finally joined as Financial Commissioner at Lucknow in 1856. He was known as a no-nonsense officer and his conflicts with Henry Lawrence during that critical period are matters of record. The decisions taken by him, as next in Command during Lawrence's illness, were rescinded by Lawrence himself, on his return. It is surmised that the defeat of Lawrence at the Battle of Chinhat could have been averted, had he taken Gubbins into confidence and listened to his advice, since the latter managed the intelligence department at the Residency. In a huff, and in poor health, Gubbins returned to England, only to return in 1858, to discover that the situation was not conducive for him. His actions during 1857 were under scrutiny and his writings on the sequence of events had been rebutted. After a short stint at Agra, as a Judge, he resigned and returned to England in January 1863, committing suicide shortly afterwards on May 6, 1863.

Mirza Hasan Raza Khan: Hasan Raza Khan was *Naib* in the court of Asaf-ud-Daula during 1776 - 1796. Earlier, he had been a loyal courtier to Shuja-ud-Daula, then known as *Mirza Hasnu.* Although illiterate, he was respected for his acumen and hard work by the British Residents of that period, *viz.* Otto Ives and also George Cherry, although Haider Beg Khan and Raja Tikait Rai wielded the actual administrative power, being his deputies. His detractors included Tipur (Tapar) Chand (of *Bakshi ka Talaab* fame), who resented the pro-British leanings of both Hasan Raza and Haider Beg. Researchers have identified Hasan Raza as Asaf-ud-Daula's key official, who actively promoted the practices of Shi'ism in the Awadh court, ultimately resulting in the building of the *Asafi Imambara* and *Masjid* complex at Lucknow. Possibly, he wanted to reduce the importance of the *Sunni* theology emanating from *Firangi Mahal* in those times. Due to his differences with Nawab Sa'adat Ali Khan, Hasan Raza's career and life ended in penury in 1801.

Munshi Nawal Kishore: Munshi Nawal Kishore, originally from Aligarh, was born on January 3, 1836. From an early age, he developed an interest in journalistic writing, and published a weekly newspaper *Safeer-è-Agra* for some time. After briefly serving as Assistant Editor and then Editor of *Koh-i-Noor*, a magazine of the *Koh-i-Noor* Press, he founded a printing press known as Munshi Nawal Kishore Press in Lucknow, on November 23, 1858. From 1859 onwards, he published a weekly newspaper called *Awadh Akhbar* or *Oudh Akhbar*. In his lifetime, Munshi Nawal Kishore published more than 5000 books in Arabic, Bengali, Hindi, English, Marathi, Punjabi, Pashto, Persian, Sanskrit and Urdu. Over almost a century, the Nawal Kishore Press published some 12,000 titles. Approximately 5000 of these were issued during Nawal Kishore's lifetime; 3000 under Prag Narayan and 2000 under Bishan Narayan, his successors. The press was praised by a personality no less then Mirza Ghalib himself, for its role in preserving and reviving the cultural heritage of India. This was achieved by the Munshi's practice of procuring rare manuscripts in various languages, as well as pertaining to different religions and publishing them, in an unbiased manner, devoid of any prejudice. He has often been likened to being a "Caxton of India" (William Caxton was first person to introduce a *printing press* into England in 1476), although the comparison is a misnomer, because printing had arrived in Lucknow, during Nawabi rule itself. A printing press in Lucknow had been set up in 1817 during the reign of Ghazi-ud-Din Haider, called *Matb'e Sultani* or *Royal Press* and the *Haft Qulzum*, a Persian dictionary and grammar of the Persian language in seven volumes, had been published from this press in 1820 - 22. Introduction of lithography by Henry Archer (superintendent of the Asiatic lithographic press at Kanpur) was on the insistence of King Nasir-ud-Din Haider. In 1831, the first lithographed book from Lucknow was titled *Al Bahjah al Mardiya,* which was an Arabic commentary by the famous Quranic commentator, *Abu al-Fadl.*

Munshi *ji* died on February 19, 1895 at Delhi, and was buried, instead of being cremated as per Hindu rites. A postage stamp was issued in his honour by the Government of India in 1970. A road behind Hazratganj was named Nawal Kishore Road in his honour. The author (of this book) has had the privilege of being born and having resided at Nawal Kishore Road, Lucknow, during his early years.

Raja Bal Kishan: A Hindu *kayastha* by caste, the Raja had served under Ghazi-ud-din Haidar and had been the *Diwan* during the reign of Wajid Ali Shah. He was on friendly terms with Martin Gubbins, the Financial Commissioner, which was looked upon by disapproval by Coverly Jackson, the then Chief Commissioner. The Raja was appointed as *Diwan* in the court of Begum Hazrat Mahal without opposition, but he did not play a very active role in the new Nawabi court. His disinterest could have been possibly stemmed from his belief that the new regime would not have long innings. However, he continued to hold the post of *Diwan* as long as the rebel court was functioning and died of illness about three weeks before the reoccupation of Lucknow by the British.

Raja Beni Madho Baksh: Beni Madho was the nephew and adopted heir of Rana Shiv Prasad Singh of Shankarpur estate, near present day Rae Bareilly. He had suffered heavily under the land settlement policy of the British, after their annexation of Awadh. Subsequently, he was appointed as administrator of Jaunpur and Azamgarh, by Begum Hazrat Mahal's court. Not being content with an administrative role, Beni Madho, accompanied with his brother, Gajraj Singh, relentlessly battled against the British on various fronts, even after the Begum and Birjis Qadr had left the city, subsequent to the fall of Lucknow in 1858. Realising the Raja's fighting prowess and patriotism, Major Barrow offered a truce to him in November 1858, which the Raja refused. Beni Madho fled to Nepal, following Colin Campbell's relentless attempts to subjugate him. However, Rana Jung Bahadur of Nepal proved uncooperative and advised the Rajput leader to lay down his arms and surrender to the British, which the brave heart naturally refused to do. Beni Madho's end remains a mystery.

Raja Jai Lal: The Raja and his father had worked with distinction in the former Nawabi court, and due to his personal charisma and goodwill, he was appointed as Superintendent of Begum Hazrat Mahal's court. He enjoyed the confidence of both the Begum and the soldiers, who came from different backgrounds. The Raja had multifarious responsibilities, including the maintenance of the fortifications, organisation of intelligence, care of the wounded and sick, and also liaison between the infantry and the court, although he was a civilian. The Raja was executed by the British for his alleged involvement in the massacre of British officers, Mount Stuart Jackson, Patrick Orr, Lt. Burns, Sgt. Morton and several women and children, during November 1857.

Raja Jhau Lal: Originally a *Saxena kayastha* from Faizabad, he was a *daroga* in the Nawabi stables there, preferring to provide his services to Nawab Begum and Bahu Begum, after the death of Shuja-ud-Daula. Jhau Lal's later intrigues in the court of Asaf-ud-Daula have been documented by many writers. Known earlier as Lalluji, he soon became force to reckon with. His relatives also shared the bounty of his power and wealth. His first run-in was with Haider Beg, who had him imprisoned. He secured his release through the British resident. Jhau Lal seemed to have an interest in cloak-and-dagger operations; after getting Tikait Rai and Hasan Raza dismissed on fabricated charges, he amalgamated the revenue and intelligence departments and assumed control of the police chief (*daroga*) of Luckow city. His intelligence network through messengers (*harkaras*) spread far and wide, from Delhi to Calcutta, which naturally alarmed the British. Lumsden, who succeeded Cherry as Resident, got Jhau Lal banished from the Nawabi court, and replaced by Tafazzul Hussain. This, as expected, was not appreciated by Asaf-ud-Daula. Jhau Lal was a bundle of contradictions; indeed, the British suspected him to be a Muslim, because of his zeal in observing Muslim customs, particularly the observance of Muharram, although he was actually a Hindu *kayastha* by caste. A bridge built by him called *Jhau Lal ka Pul* in Aminabad area, an *Imambara (Shia Bait-ul-Mal)* in Thakurganj area, as well as a market named *Bazar Jhau Lal* are still extant in Lucknow.

Robert Home: Robert Home, born in 1752 in Hull (Eastern Yorkshire), England, was the son of a former army surgeon. From an early age, he displayed no talent for medicine, but began to study art and painting instead. He sailed for India in 1791 and after establishing himself in Calcutta, proceeded to Lucknow, ultimately becoming a celebrated court artist for Ghazi-ud-Din Haider, the first King of Awadh in 1814. In addition to his access to the King himself, he was one of the privileged few who were also privy to the royal household. Along with studio portraits of royalty and nobility, both Indian and British, Home was also responsible for conceptualising and designing a diverse range of articles and objects, from the King's crown, to his dress, regalia, chairs and even the crocodile-shaped barge he traveled in. It has been also suggested that Home was involved in designing the *Chattar Manzil* palace itself, which, if true, lends credence to Home's multifarious talents and his influence in the court of Ghazi-ud-Din Haider. After the King's death in 1827, Home led a retired life in Kanpur with his widowed daughter, Anne Walker. Having spent most of his lifetime in India, Home died at the age of 82, and was interred in the *Kutchery* Cemetery of Kanpur.

Roshan-ud-Daula: Mohmmad Hussain Khan, with the title of "Roshan-ud-Daula Bahadur" succeeded Hakim Mehndi as *Wazir* in the court of Nasir-ud-Din Haider. Although he had impressive antecedents, his ancestors having served in the court of Awadh for several generations, he was not very efficient, despite the fact that sweeping changes in the administration were made during his *wazirat* (tenure as *Wazir)*. He was removed by Nasir-ud-Din's uncle and successor, Mohammad Ali Shah, fined a sum of Rs 20 lakhs and his magnificent home, *Roshan-ud-Daula Kothi* was confiscated. He left Awadh in disgrace and settled in Kanpur till the end of his days. The *kothi* itself was appropriated by Wajid Ali Shah renamed as *Kaiser Pasand*, and incorporated into the Kaiserbagh palace complex.

Sharaf-ud-Daula: An Agarwal Hindu convert, Sharaf-ud-Daula held important administrative assignments in the administration of Muhammad Ali Shah and Amjad Ali Shah, in addition to being a *Mutawasit* (paymaster) for the Hussainabad Trust. However, it appears that there were frequent quarrels between Amjad Ali Shah and Sharaf-ud-Daula, although the latter was a full fledged *Wazir.* Sharaf-ud-Daula was ultimately dismissed by Amjad Ali Shah for no other reason other than the former being of *Sunni* faith. During the reign of Wajid Ali Shah, Ali Naqi Khan being considered to be a weak administrator, Sharaf-ud-Daula was appointed as his deputy. After Wajid Ali Shah was deposed, Sharaf-ud-Daula cooperated with the British and was accused of high-handedness in his dealings with the business community of Lucknow. Subsequent to the coronation of Birjis Qadar, he was appointed as *Naib* in the administration of Begum Hazrat

Mahal, but he was not without enemies. He was murdered by his compatriots in 1857, it appears, at the instigation of the *maulvi* Ahmadullah Shah.

Tafazzul Hussain: Tafazzul Hussain Khan, known as "*Khan-è-Allama*" hailed from Lahore and had been appointed as the tutor of Sa'adat Ali Khan by Shuja-ud-Daula. He remained a close associate of Sa'adat Ali for some time, but ultimately became a British sympathizer, being quite supportive of Warren Hastings, and later, Lord Cornwallis. He contributed behind the scenes to get Sa'adat Ali Khan anointed as Nawab of Awadh by John Shore. Tafazzul extended his services to Haider Beg also, but could not get the support of Tikait Rai or Hasan Raza in the Nawabi court. There is no doubt that he was a well-lettered, learned person, respected by scholars, but his blind support for the British undermined his own importance in the Nawabi court as Jhau Lal's successor. His worldly knowledge could benefit neither himself as an individual, nor Awadh as a whole. There are conflicting accounts of death, which remains shrouded in mystery.

Thomas Longcroft: Longcroft was born in 1760. A "British Old Master" artist, he reached Indian shores in 1783 and visited Lucknow with Zoffany in the following year. Zoffany became a celebrity in the Awadh court (of Asaf-ud-Daula), but Longcroft was less successful. Longcroft was known for producing stunning artworks (Company School) depicting Indian landscapes and life. In fact, his visit coincided with the on-going construction of the *Asafi Imambara* complex at Lucknow, and one of his paintings actually depict the scaffoldings around the under-construction *Asafi Masjid*. His "views" of Lucknow depicting palaces and streets, provide a great deal of detail, in the absence of photography in those days. Particular mention must be made of his depiction of the *Daulat Khana* complex from the river side (discussed elsewhere). However, he was mortified to realise that his works and talents were overshadowed by Zoffany in Lucknow. In 1787, he purchased an indigo estate at Koil, near Aligarh and lived there till the end of his life, having formed a lasting relationship with an Indian lady, Mubarak Jahan. Related to Thomas Twining of the EIC (whose family would later become famous for the marketing of tea and other beverages), who visited him in December 1794, many of Longcraft's artworks passed to the Twining family after his death in 1811.

Tikait Rai: Raja Tikait Rai Bahadur was the *Diwan* of Awadh from 1791-1796, during the regime of Asaf-ud-daula. He belonged to the *Kayastha* community from Rae Bareilly district and had started his career in the Nawabi court as a clerk, attached to Hasan Raza Khan. By dint of merit and hard work, he rose to the position of the Finance Minister but faced later humiliation in his career due to court politics, although he was often supported by Haider Beg and George Cherry, the then Resident in Asaf-ud-Daula's court. Tikait Rai was responsible for building several works of public utility (see Annexure II) in and around Lucknow, as also liaison with the EIC, regarding Asaf-ud-Daula's finances and reforms, which the latter resented. He died in 1800.

Tilly Kettle: Tilly Kettle was born in Silver Street, London on January 31, 1735. He was a portrait artist, active in London and finally leaving for India in 1768. Arriving in Madras in 1769, he spent two years working in Calcutta before receiving a letter of invitation from Shuja-ud-daula who had been told that Mr Kettle 'is a master of his art'. Kettle painted the Nawab and his sons several times during his visit to Faizabad in 1772-73, setting the trend for European artists to visit India to earn their fortunes. Kettle returned to London in 1776, and settled there for some time. Although he was well off, and his wife, Mary had also brought a substantial dowry, it appears that he lost his wealth and fell into debt. This prompted him to set off for India once again in 1786. However, this journey was short-lived and he died, possibly while trying to cross the desert near present day Iraq.

William Marris: William Sinclair Marris was born at Warwickshire, England, on October 9, 1873, being the eldest son of Charles Marris, chartered accountant of Birmingham, and his wife, Jessie. He was educated at Wanganui Collegiate School and Canterbury College in New Zealand, and later studied at Christ Church, Oxford. He qualified for the Indian Civil Service examination in 1895. After various assignments, he was appointed as Governor Assam for a brief period (1921 – 1922), followed by Governorship of the United Provinces (1922 – 1928). His lasting impression can be seen on several places in Lucknow. The college of music established in 1926 in the erstwhile premises of Canning College, *Kaiserbagh* was inaugurated by the then Governor and named as Marris College of Music. Marris Market (and adjacent Saunders Market) at *Kaiserbagh* was envisaged as a proper hygienic market, fit for Europeans to visit, as compared to the disorganised array of shops in the native quarters. March 3, 1927 saw the laying of the Foundation Stone for the Chemistry Department of Lucknow University by Marris.

Marris retired in 1937 and settled in Gloucestershire. As an educationist, he was responsible for the publication of a number of translations of Greek and Latin classics into English verse. He died on December 12, 1945 and was interred in Chesterton Cemetery, Gloucestershire.

William Capper: William Copeland Capper was born in Essex County, England. He was educated at Haileybury and joined the Bengal Civil Service in 1852. Initially, he was posted in Punjab. In 1856, he was transferred to Oudh (Awadh), as the first Dy. Commissioner of Mallawan (Hardoi). He remained there, till the 1857 broke out, after which he moved to the Lucknow Residency, where he was wounded while manning the Anderson's Post. After Lucknow was re-taken by the British, he was made Special Commissioner of Farrukhabad. He returned to England for some time, and on his return, was posted as Deputy Commissioner, Dariabad. He remained there till 1868, followed by becoming Commissioner of Rae Bareilly Division, followed by Commissioner of Faizabad and then Judicial Commissioner in 1877 - 1881. He retired in 1892 and returned to England where he died in Sussex on July 2, 1902. A road in *Kaiserbagh* area of Lucknow, named in honour of Capper is still extant.

Annexures

The human race tends to remember the abuses to which it has been subjected rather than the endearments. What's left of kisses? Wounds, however, leave scars.

—Bertolt Brecht

Cities have the capability of providing something for everybody, only because, and only when, they are crated by everybody.

—Jane Jacobs

Therefore the best fortress is to be found in the love of the people, for although you may have fortresses, they will not save you if you are hated by the people.

—Nicolo Machiavelli

Annexure I

Historical Gateways of Lucknow

(An indicative list in chronological order)

Name	*Year*	*Nature*	*Builder*	*Present Condition*
Akbari Darwaza	1572	Pre-Nawabi	Qazi Mehmood Bilgrami	Extant. Dilapidated condition
Panch Mahalla Gate / Sheikhan Darwaza (Macchi Bhavan Fort)	1590	Pre-Nawabi	Sheikhzada family of Sheikh Abdur Rahim	Not extant. Demolished during colonial rule
Gol Darwaza	1780	Nawabi	Asaf-ud-Daula	Extant. Dilapidated condition
Rumi Darwaza and Bada Imambara Gateways	1790	Nawabi	Asaf-ud-Daula	Extant. Partially restored
Tripolia Gateway	1790	Nawabi	Asaf-ud-Daula	Demolished post 1857
Sheesh Mahal Gateway	1794	Nawabi	Asaf-ud-Daula	Not extant. Demolished during colonial rule
Hazratganj Gateway	1800	Nawabi	Sa'adat Ali Khan	Not extant. Demolished during colonial rule
Moti Mahal Gateway	1800	Nawabi	Sa'adat Ali Khan	Not extant. Collapsed during floods in 1923
Khurshid Bagh Gateway	1800	Nawabi	Sa'adat Ali Khan	Extant. Dilapidated condition
Latkan Darwaza (Clock Tower Gate)	1810	Nawabi	Sa'adat Ali Khan	Not extant. Demolished post 1857
Baillie's Guard Gateway	1814	Colonial	Lt. Col John Baillie	Extant. Restored during colonial rule
Farhat Baksh Gateway	1816	Nawabi	Ghazi-ud-Din Haider	Demolished during 1857
Vilayti Bagh Gateway	1817	Nawabi	Ghazi-ud-Din Haider	Extant. Restored partially post 1947
Shahnajaf Gateway (south side)	1816	Nawabi	Ghazi-ud-Din Haider	Extant. Dilapidated condition
Shahnajaf Gateway (north side)	1816	Nawabi	Ghazi-ud-Din Haider	Extant. Restored post 1947
Sher Darwaza / Neil's Gate	1830	Nawabi / Colonial	Ghazi-ud-Din Haider / Nasir-ud-Din Haider	Extant. Remodelled during colonial rule, and then again post 1947
Hussainabad Gateways	1838	Nawabi	Mohammad Ali Shah	Extant. Partially restored
Malka Gheti Phatak	1845	Nawabi	Amjad Ali Shah	Extant. Dilapidated condition
Sibtainabad Gateway	1846	Nawabi	Wajid Ali Shah	Extant. Partially collapsed recently
Alambagh Gateway	1847	Nawabi	Wajid Ali Shah	Extant. Restored post 1947
Sikandar Bagh Gateway	1848	Nawabi	Wajid Ali Shah	Extant. Restored post 1947
Kaiserbagh Gateways	1850	Nawabi	Wajid Ali Shah	Few extant. Partially restored post 1947
China Gate	1850	Nawabi	Wajid Ali Shah	Extant. Dilapidated condition
Mermaid (Jal Pari) Gate	1850	Nawabi	Wajid Ali Shah	Not extant. Demolished post 1857

Note: Several gateways have been classified as "Nawabi" for convenience, although from Ghazi-ud-Din Haider onwards, the Nawabi rulers had declared themselves as "King."

Annexure II

Monuments, Localities and their Builders

(An indicative list in alphabetical order)

Name	*Designation*	*Monument*	*Locality*
Aafreen Ali Khan	*Khwajasara*		*Inayat Bagh (present Lucknow Christian College and Centennial School)*
Agha Baquir	*Risaldar*	*Imambara Agha Baquir, Musafirkhana*	
Agha Mir	*Wazir*	*Imambara Agha Mir (present Jubilee College), Nur Baksh Kothi (present residence of District Magistrate), Zahur Baksh Kothi and Imambara (demolished; site for present Epiphany / Zahur Baksh Church), Karbala (presently houses Masonic Lodge), Kothi Malika-e-Jahan (now demolished)*	*Dyodhi Agha Mir, Serai Agha Mir, Wazir Bagh, Buland Bagh,*
Alam Ara Begum	*Khas Mahal*	*Alambagh Kothi and Masjid*	*Alambagh* (present Krishnanagar and Chander Nagar)
Almas Mian	*Khwajasara*	*Almas Imambara; Maqbara of Bani Khanum (Bani was the sister-in-law of Bahu Begum), Faizabad*	*Almasbagh*
Ambar Ali Khan	*Khwajasara*		*Ambarganj*
Amjad Ali Shah	*Badshah*	*Begum Kothi, Sibtainabad Imambara, Malka Geti Phatak, Shahi Kothi, Malka Geti Imambara, Iron Bridge* (imported from England)	*Hazratganj*
Anonymous	*Brother of Ashraf Ali Khan, Risaldar*		*Naubasta*
Ashraf Ali Khan	*Risaldar*		*Musharfabad*
Anonymous	*Rani of Girdha Naga, Subahdar to Muhammad Shah*		*Rani Katra*
Anonymous	*French Traders*	*Firangi Mahal*	
Anonymous		*Nadan "Nidan" Mahal and associated cenotaphs, related to Sheikh Ibrahim, a Sufi saint and Sheikh Abdur Rahim, first Subedar of Awadh suba*	
Asaf-ud-Daula (Asif-ud-Daula)	*Nawab Wazir*	*Daulat Khana, Asafi Kothi, Aina Khana /, Gend Khana, Sheesh Mahal, Zenana (Sheesh Mahal) Talab, Pathar Wali Masjid, Kothi Hayat Baksh (originally Martin's powder magazine, later Bank's House and now Raj Bhavan), Asafi (Bada) Imambara, Asafi Masjid, Rumi Darwaza, Bibiapur Kothi, Asafi Kothi (Lucknow), Asafi Kothi (Chinhat), Top Darwaza, Sunheri Burj, Begum Kothi (Residency), Tedhi Kothi; Gulab Bari Masjid, Maqbara of Shuja-ud-Daula and Nawab Begum (Faizabad), Nahar-e-Asafi (Najaf, Iraq)*	*Astabal (stables) at Yahyaganj, Musabagh, Aishbagh, Moti Jheel, Charbagh, Wazirganj (in honor of his son, Wazir Ali), Amaniganj, Fatehganj, Rakabganj, Nakkhas, Daulataganj, Begumganj, Nawabganj, Tirmaniganj, Tikri, Chaoni Hasan-ud-Din Khan, Bhawaniganj, Balakganj, Kashmiri Mohalla, Ahata Surat Singh, Niwazganj, Ambarganj, Mehboobganj, Khayaliganj, Khansama ka Ahata, Nawazganj, Thakurganj, Khudaganj, Tope Darwaza, Mohammad Bagh, Husnbagh, Hussain Bagh*

Contd.

Ashraf Ali Khan	*Risaldar*		*Ashrafabad*
Ashraf-un-Nisan (Tajdar Bahu)	*Shahzadi*	*Masjid Ashraf-un-Nisan*	*Dyodhi Tajdar Bahu*
Aurangzeb	*Mughal Emperor*	*Alamgir Masjid (Teele Wali Masjid)*	*Shahdara-Budheshwaran, Alamnagar*
Azimullah Khan	*Musahib*	*Chaulakhi Kothi, Imambara, Karbala*	
Badshah Begum	*Khas Mahal*	*Badshah Mahal, Rauza-e-Dowazdah Imam (not extant)*	*Badshah Nagar*
Bahu Begum	*Khas Mahal*	*Moti Mahal (Faizabad)*	*Aliganj, Khudaganj, Daulatganj*
Bashir-ud-Daula	*Wazir*		*Bashirganj*
Bi Misri	*Female singer in court of Asaf-ud-Daula*	*Masjid and Karbala Bi Misri*	*Bi Misri ki Bagiya*
Claude Martin	*Hony. Maj. General to East India Company*	*Town House (later Farhat Baksh), Lakhi Pera / Constantia (later La Martiniere Boys' School), Old Martin Kothi / Gori Bibi ki Kothi (later Kakori Kothi), Gori Bibi ka Maqbara, Gori Bibi ki Masjid, Biposi (Najafgarh),*	*Martin Purva, Gori Bibi ka Ahata, Captain Bazar, Martingarh (Najafgarh)*
Darab Ali Khan	*Khwajasara*	*Maqbara of Bahu Begum, Darab Ali Mahalsara (Faizabad)*	
Dayanat-ud-Daula	*Khwajasara*	*Karbala Dayanat-ud-Daula*	
Dhania Mehri	*Darogha*	*Masjid, Imambara, Pul*	
Fakhr-un-Nisan Begum "Mughal Saheba"	*Shahzadi*	*Mahalsara, Imambara, Masjid*	*Dyodhi Mughal Saheba*
Farid Khan	*Sher Shah "Sūr"*		*Taksal*
Fateh Ali (Zafar-ud-Daula)	*Risaldar*	*Maqbara, Kaptan-ka-Kuan (well), Talaab (pond)*	*Fatehganj*
Ghazi-ud-Din Haider	*Nawab Wazir (1814 - 1818) Badshah (1818 - 1827)*	*Shahnajaf, Bada Chattar Manzil, Maqbara Sa'adat Ali Khan, Maqbara Khurshid Zadi, Mubarak Manzil, Shah Manzil, Qadam Rasul, Sher Darwaza, Matba-e-Sultani (printing press), Sultan Manzil*	*Badshahbagh (present Lucknow University), Hazaribagh, Mehndiganj, Hussainganj, Hyderabad, Chini Bazar, Vilayati Bagh*
Ghulam Hussain	*Syce (Suis); Daroga of Astabal*	*Mahalsara, Pili Masjid, Imambara (present LDA's office)*	*Hussainganj, Katganj, Khayalganj*
Haider Beg Khan / Amir-ud-Daula	*Naib*	*Haider Beg ka Talaab*	
Hakim Mehndi	*Wazir*	*Mahalsara, Maqbara, Shitla Devi Temple, Madarsa Sultania*	*Mehndiganj, Mehendi Sarai (Saharanpur)*
Hamid Husain "Goonge Nawab"	*Son of Imdad Ali Amin-ud-Daula*		*Goonge Nawab ka Ahata*
Hasan Raza Khan	*Naib*	*Hasanganj ki Baoli, Imambara (demolished), Baradari (demolished); Chowk Masjid (Faizabad)*	*Hasanganj, Hasanpuriya*
Hasinuddin Khan	*Risaldar*		*Chawni Hasinuddin Khan (Sa'adatganj)*
Hazara	*Baba*	*Shahi Math*	*Bagh Baba Hazara*
Imdad Ali Khan Amin-ud-Daula	*Wazir*	*Kalan Phatak Masjid, Wazir Manzil, Baradari, Karbala Amin-ud-Daula*	*Aminabad, Imdadbagh, Gulab Bari*
Jagannath Agarwal "Sharaf-ud-Daula"	*Official in court of Amjad Ali Shah*	*Rauza Kazmain*	
Jawahir Ali	*Musahib*	*Imambara (Faizabad)*	
Jhunnu Lal "Dilgeer"	*Brother of Raja Jhau Lal*	*Imambara*	
Qazi Mahmud Bilgrami	*Naib of Jawahir Khan, Subahdar of Awadh*	*Akbari Darwaza*	*Shahganj, Mahmudnagar*

Contd.

Maharaj Tej Krishna			*Teji Khera, Ahata Ramzan Ali, Ahata Suraj Singh, Ahata Tulsi Ram, Ahata Fakir Mohammad Khan*
Malka Afaq "Mariam Makani"	*Begum*	*Malka Afaq Karbala, Imambara*	
Malika Jahan	*Begum*	*Karbal Chote Hazrat, Karbala Bade Hazrat, Imambara*	
Malka Kishwar	*Khas Mahal*	*Masjid Malka Kishwar*	*Kishwarganj*
Malka Zamani "Dulari"	*Begum*	*Imambara Malka Zamani, Masjid, Imambara Kaiwan Jah*	
Mashuq Mahal	*Begum*	*Moti Masjid, Imambara*	*Motibagh*
Mian Makka	*Darzi (tailor), later Musahib*	*Makka Darzi Bagh (Lucknow), Makka Serai, Qadam Rasul and Imambara, Makka Pul (Sitapur/ Khairabad)*	*Makkaganj*
Mir Fazal Ali	*Wazir*	*Masjid Etmad-ud-Daula*	
Mir Khuda Baksh Khan	*Musahib*	*Karbala Talkatora*	
Mirza Fazil	*Son of Sultan Ali Shah, Subahdar to Emperor Shah Jahan*		*Fazilnagar*
Mirza Jumma Shaukat-ud-Daulah	*Son of Mirza Qasim Ali (nephew of Bahu Begum)*		*Bagh Mirza Jumma*
Mirza Mansur	*Son of Sultan Ali Shah, Subahdar to Shah Jahan*		*Mansurnagar*
Mirza Qasim Ali Khan	*Nephew of Bahu Begum*	*Maqbara Salar Jung (brother of Bahu Begum), Kala Imambara*	
Mirza Salim (Jahangir)	*Mughal Shahzada*	*Mirzabagh*	*Mirza Mandi*
Mirza Sikander Shikoh	*Mughal Prince*	*Imambara Sikander Shikoh (later Mumtaz College, now demolished)*	*Massaratnagar (now Aminabad)*
Mohammad Ali Mohammad Khan	*Raja of Mahmoodabad*	*Butler Palace*	
Mohammad Ali Shah	*Badshah*	*Hussainia (Chota) Imambara, Sat Khanda, Hussainabad tank, Baradari (present Picture Gallery), Jama Masjid,*	*Hussainabad. Pasandbagh,*
Mohammad Elich Khan	*Daroga*		*Elich ka Maidan*
Moti Begum	-		*Begumkheda*
Muhammadi Khanum (Begum Hazrat Mahal)	*Begum*		*Muhammadinagar*
Mumtaz Mahal (Kangla Mahal)	*Begum*	*Mahalsara, Baradari*	
Munshi Muzaffar Ali Khan	*Wazir*		*Munshiganj*
Musahib-ud-Daula	*Wazir*		*Musahibganj*
Nanduji Kayastha	*Merchant*	*Imambara*	
Nathu Lal	*Contractor*	*Rauza Jannat-ul-Baqi, Imambara*	
Nasir-ud-Din Haider	*Badshah*	*Choti (Khurd) Chattar Manzil, Darshan Bilas Kothi, Gulistan-e-Iram Kothi, Tara Wali Kothi, Iradatganj Karbala, Ghazi-ud-Din Haider Canal, Dar-ul-Shifa (originally owned by Joseph Quieros, trustee of Martin), Chakkar Wali Kothi (King's race course), King's Hospital (Shahi Shifa Khana), Khairat Khana (Poor House), Banarsi Bagh (present Zoo)*	*Vilaytibagh, Pasandbagh, Ganeshganj, Chandbagh (present Chandganj and IT College campus), Chakkar Purva*

Contd.

Naushad Ali	*Raja of Jahangirabad*	*Jahangirabad Palace*	
Newal Rai	*Naib*	*Pucca Pul (Nawabi Pul) / Stone Bridge, completed by Asaf-ud-Daula*	
Pir Khan	*Risaldar*		*Garhi Pir Khan, Garhi Sanjar*
Raja Jhau Lal	*Diwan*	*Jhau Lal ka Pul, Imambara (Shia Baitul Mal) Jhau La, Imli Wali Masjid*	*Bazar Jhau Lal,*
Raja Jiya Lal			*Jiamau, Ahata Khansamah*
Raja Mehra Bhawani			*Bhawaniganj, Balakganj (present Balanagar)*
Rani Jai Kunwar	*Friend of Khadeja Khanum, purported Begum of Burhan-ul-Mulk*	*Pandain ki Masjid*	
Roshan-ud-Daula	*Wazir*	*Roshan-ud-Daula Kothi (later Kaiser Pasand of Kaiserbagh palace complex)*	
Rustam Haider	*Wazir*		*Rustamnagar*
Sa'adat Ali Khan	*Nawab Wazir*	*British Residency, Tehri Kothi, Lal Baradari (Qasr-us-Sultan), Dilaram Kothi (demolished during colonial rule), Dilkusha, Kankar Wali Kothi (demolished; site of PMG office) Khurshid Manzil (now La Martiniere College for Girls), Jarnail Kothi, Badshah Manzil, Chaupar Astabal (stables), Musabagh Kothi, Moti Mahal, Maqbara Janab-e-Alia, Dargah Hazrat Abbas*	*Sa'adatganj, Rakabganj, Jangliganj, Maqboolganj, Golaganj, Maulviganj, Rastogi Mohalla, Barood Khana, Chiria Jhil, Chikmandi, Mashakganj,*
Sa'adat Khan Burhan-ul-Mulk	*Nawab Wazir*	*Haveli Sa'adat Khan, Shahjahanabad*	*Katra Sayyad Hussain Khan, Katra Abu-Turab Khan, Katra Khudayar Khan, Katra Bizan Beg Khan, Katra Muhammad Shah, Katra Khudayar Khan, Katra Bizan Beg Khan, Katra Muhammad Ali Khan, Serai Mali Khan, Katra Jahangir Beg, Bagh Maha Narain*
Sadr-i-Jahan	*Nawab Begum*	*Masjid (Faizabad)*	
Abul-Mansur Khan Safdarjang	*Nawab Wazir*	*Safdarjang "Mansion", originally part of Dara Shikoh Mahal, (Shahjahanabad), Burj-e-Mansur and Baradari (Ashok Vihar, Delhi), "Bangla" (Faizabad), Jalalabad Fort (Bijnor, Lucknow), Macchi Bhavan, Lucknow*	*Wazirpur (Delhi), Safdarbagh (present Sundarbagh), Gulab Bari (Faizabad)*
Saiyed Imam Ali Rafiq-ud-Daula	*Musahib*	*Karbala Abbas Bagh / Rafiq-ud-Daula, Masjid e Kufa*	
Sarji "Raja Mehra"	*Chaudhari (Head) of palanquin bearers in court of Asaf-ud-Daula*	*Kothi (also known as House of Raja Mehra); not extant*	*Raj Ghat*
Sayyid Dildar Ali	*Mujtahid*	*Imambara Ghufran Ma'ab*	
Shah Bihari Lal	*Mahajan*	*Kothi Shah Bihari Lal (presently houses Emma Thompson School)*	*Lalbagh*
Sharaf-un-Nissan (Miss Whearty)	*Foster sister of Vilayati Begum (Emma Walters)*	*Sharaf-un-Nissan Mosque, Imambara at Residency*	
Sheikhzadas		*Panch Mahalla*	
Shuja-ud-Daula	*Nawab Wazir*	*Bayasi ki Masjid (Lucknow); Safdarjang Maqbara and Masjid (Delhi); Dilkusha (later Afeem Kothi under Colonial rule), Fort Calcutta, Moti Mahal (Faizabad)*	*Faizabad city, its Chowk with tripolia gates, Angoori Bagh, Moti Bagh, Lal Bagh*

Contd.

Tehseen Ali Khan	*Nazir*	*Tehseen-ki-Masjid, Tehsin Mian ka Maqbara*	*Tehseenganj*
Tikait Rai	*Diwan*	*Tikait Rai ka Talaab, Tikait Rai ka Pul and Shiv Mandir, Shitla Mata Mandir, Masjid, Tikait Rai ki Haveli, Imambara, Baradari (Bithoor), Patthar Ghat (Bithoor), Takia Sharif (Kakori)*	*Tikaitganj, Bazar Tikait Rai / Raja Bazar, Nishatbagh, Tikait Nagar (Bara Banki), Tikait Ganj (Rae Bareilly)*
Tipur Chand	*Bakshi*	*Bakshi ka Talaab*	
Wajid Ali Shah	*Badshah*	*Kaiserbagh palace complex, including Safed Baradari (Qasr-us-Aza), Pari Khana (demolished and replaced by Canning College / present Bhatkhande Music University), Lanka (demolished and replaced by present Amir-ud-Daula Public Library), Hazratbagh, Chinibagh, Naginewali Baradari (relocated to the Wingfield Park / Zoo), Khas Muqam, Chandiwali Baradari, Shahanshah Manzil, Badshah Manzil, Ishq Manzil, Istrahat Manzil, Vaqar Manzil, Afsar Manzil, Shikoh Manzil, Haziri Manzil, Rahas Manzil, Gulzar Manzil, Aram Manzil, Hayat Manzil, Rahat Manzil, Zard Kothi, Qasr-ul-Khakan, Qasr-ul-Baizavi, Makan-e-Dilpasand, Dil Afza, Kabootar Khana, Makan-e-Chogobiya, Makan-e-Khas, Falak Sair, Bait-ul-Sarur, Jahan Numa, Makan-e-Chaupahlu, Kunj-e-Gulshan, Taskin Baksh, Indrasan, Shah Burj; Also Kabootar Wali Kothi, (present Oel House), Sikchewali Kothi, Dilkusha Astabal, Jinnaton ka Masjid.*	*Sikandar Bagh, Jarnailganj, Sarfarazganj, Sundarbagh, Metia Burz palace complex (in Calcutta)*
Zain-ul-Abidin Khan	*Naib*	*Imambara Zain-ul-Abidin*	
Zakir Ali Khan Saeed-ud-Daula	*Naib*	*Karbala Saeed-ud-Daula*	
Sheikh Mohammad "Shah Mina"	*Qazi*		*Minanagar*
Munawwar-ud-Daula	*Nephew of Hakim Mehndi*	*Maqbara Hakim Mehndi*	
Digbijai Singh	*Raja of Balrampur*		*Digbijaiganj Serai*

Annexure III

Lingua Franca

With the passage of time, in addition to developing a home-grown hybrid architectural style, Awadh in general and Lucknow in particular also adopted the usage of several terms / words, derived from different languages, especially Arabic, *Farsi* (Persian), Hindustani and old English. An indicative, if not exhaustive list of this pidgin *lingua franca* is provided below for general readers as well as for researchers. The colonial inflexions are particularly interesting.

Adawlat	*Adâlat*; Court of Justice
Áalam	World; universe
Aarzii	Interim; provisional
Abr	Cloud
Acbar	Akbar (Mughal Emperor)
Achkan	Knee length coat with circular collar, buttoned at the top
Adaab; Adâb	Salutation
Adab	Courtesy, etiquette
Affghan; Affghanistan	Afghan; Afghanistan
Ahir	Caste of cowherds
Ainawala Kothi	*Ainon Wali Kothi* (demolished; present day *Hindi Sansthan*)
Ajmir	Ajmer, Rajasthan
Ajodhya	Ayodhya (town)
Âla	Superior / senior
Alam	Affliction; grief; torment
Albatta	At least; anyway
Alexander's Garden	*Sikandar Bagh*
Allee	Ali (name)
Allyghur	Aligarh (town)
Almairah; Almirah	Wardrobe
Almasi (bricks)	Larger than *lakhauri* bricks, popularly attributed to Almas Ali Khan, *Khwajasara* in the court of Shuja-ud-Daula
Almorah	Almora (town)
Alum	*Álam;* banner held during Muharram procession
Alumbagh	*Alambagh* (palace complex in Lucknow)

Ameer	*Amir*; a nobleman
Amil	Revenue collector
Andaz	Style; mannerism
Andaz karna	To guess
Anglo-Indian	Eurasian; person of mixed parentage - one European and the other Indian or "native"
Arazi	Area
Áriyat	Loan
Arzi; Arzii	Petition; application
Asil; Aseel	Breed of ferocious fighter cock, rooster
Asmani	Sky blue
Astabal	Stable for horses
Atqiyaa	Pious, virtuous person
Aumeen	*Amin*; trustee
Avval	*Awwal*; outstanding; in first position
Ayah	Maidservant; matron
Azadari; Âzâdâri	Mourning rituals, particularly connected with observance of Muharram
Baadnaa	To stake a wager; to bet
Baandi	Maidservant, female slave
Badami	Almond shaped; coloured
Badarnavisi	Audit
Badnaseeb	Unfortunate
Badshah Salamat	May God Preserve the King (salutation)
Bagheecha	(Fruit) garden
Bagla; bagula	Heron (bird)
Bahadoor	*Bahadur*; brave (honorary title)
Bahrii safar	Journey across the seas
Baksheesh; Backsheesh	Tip, pourboire
Bakshi	Paymaster
Bamba	Tap (water)
Bangash; Bangash Pathan	Tribe of ethnic Pashtuns from Afghanistan
Banyan; Bunnian	*Bania;* native Hindu trader / merchant
Bâqirkhâni	Crisp flat bread made of milk, sugar, flour and butter / clarified butter

Baradari; Baradwari	A building or pavilion with twelve entrances (or more), generally used for religious discourses
Baraitch	Bahraich (town)
Barawafat	12th day of Islamic month *Rabi-ul-Awal*, signifying the death of the Prophet; *Milad-ul-Nabi*
Barek	Barracks (military)
Barkat	Blessing
Barrackpoor; Barrackpore	A military establishment on the outskirts of Calcutta, built by the British in 1772
Basti	Small settlement
Batta	*Bhatta*; allowance
Baug	*Bagh*; garden
Bawarchi	Royal chef / chef / cook
Bayan karna	To relate; relate
Bayli-garad	Baillie Guard gate (of Lucknow Residency)
Bazuband	Armlet
Bedaag	Literally "spotless." Breed of homing pigeon
Begum; Begam	Lady with title
Belaspore	Bilaspur (town)
Beldar	Labourer engaged in digging / excavating works
Beloochi	Thoroughbred horse (from Afghanistan)
Berra	Bearer; steward, as in a restaurant or club
Bhagaruttee	Bhagirathi river
Bharti karna	To enlist
Bhisti	*Bhishti*, goatskin water carrier
Bhoota	*Bhutta;* corn
Bhung	*Bhang*; hemp
Bhurtpore	Bharatpur (town)
Biradari	Clan
Biryani	Rice and meat dish, with the rice being infused by the flavors of the meat
Bismillah	An invocation used by Muslims on the commencement of an auspicious task
Biswa	Twentieth share (of land / property)
Bitur	Bithoor (town)
Boolund;	*Buland; bulandi*; elevated; of eminence

Bowlee; Bowli	*Baoli*; step well
Box-walla	Travelling merchant; peddler with merchandise arranged in a metal box
Brumma	Lord Brahma, the Creator in the Hindu pantheon of Gods
Buckram; Bokeram	Stiffener in clothing e.g. collars and hats; also book covers
Buckree Ede	*Bakra-Eid*; Muslim festival *of Eid-ul-Zuha*
Budmash	Ruffian
Bugeros; Budgerows	Old-style boats, at least 60 feet in length, with a single mast and square sail
Bund	Embankment
Buniyaad	Foundation
Bunneah	*Bania*; Hindu trader
Burkandaaz	Armed guard
Burrah Sahib	The "big boss", typically British, in colonial India
Burrumpooter	Brahmaputra river
Bylee	Native carriage
Byrynji	Made of brass
Cabooli	Thoroughbred horse (from Afghanistan)
Cabul	Kabul (city)
Caesar's Garden	*Kaiserbagh*
Caly Yug; Calyoogum	*Kalyug*; fourth and present stage of civilisation according to Hindu belief
Candela	*Chandela* (Rajput tribe)
Cashmere	Kashmir (state)
Cawnpore	Kanpur (city)
Chabutra	Tower-like structure with octagonal or pentagonal shaped open enclosure, found typically in Rajasthani architecture, later adopted by Mughals
Chajja	An overhanging eave or roof covering, found typically in Rajasthani architecture, later adopted by Mughals
Chaka Kothi; Chukkar Kothi	*Chakkar Wali Kothi*; Nasir-ud-Din Haider's race stand (no longer extant)
Chakla; Chakladar/ Nazim	Administrative division under a province; person heading the *chakla*
Chandernagore	Chandannagar (town) in Hooghly district, West Bengal; formerly French settlement

Chapkan; Chupkan	A tight fitting long coat
Chappa-chappa	Every nook and corner
Chhappar	Thatched
Char-diwari; Chahaar -diwari	Boundary; walled enclosure
Chattri	Elevated, dome-shaped pavilion used as an element in Indo-Islamic architecture
Chauk; Choke	*Chowk*; old market of Lucknow, Delhi; cross-roads
Chaupar	Traditional cross and circle board game; cruciform
Chaupoutre	*Chabutra*; platform
Cheraug	*Chirag*; small Indian lamp
Chick	Curtain made of thread and strips of bamboo
Chikni Dali	Betel nuts boiled in milk
Chilamchii; Chillumchee	Wash stand, basin; wide bowl
Chinam	*Chunam*; lime based plaster; may contain crushed sea shells
Chit	A brief letter or note
Chittel	*Chital;* spotted deer
Chobdar; Chubdar	Attendant bearing a staff
Chokedar	*Chaukidar*; guard
Chokidar; Chowkidar	Watchman
Chokra (boy)	Youngster
Chongli	Conical packing made of metal / fabric / paper, for presenting individual servings of *pân*
Chota Hazry	Early morning breakfast
Choultry; Tschultri; Choltri	Rest house / inn for travellers
Chowpeyra Istubul	*Chaupar Astabal*; Nawabi cruciform stable
Chucker; Chukker	Wheel; circle
Chudder	*Chadar*; (bed)sheet
Chukerbutty	*Chakravarty*; title of Bengali Brahmins
Chupatty	*Chapati*; Indian flat bread, unleavened
Chupkun	*Chapkan*; cassock worn by males in north India
Chuprass; Chuprassy	A metal badge worn by a peon; lowly employee physically delivering files and papers
Chuttur Munzil	*Chattar Manzil* (palace)

Circar	*Sarkar*; government
Civilian	Employee of ECI without military rank
Colney Hatch	A lunatic asylum, term being inspired by a similar asylum near London
Company Gardens; Company Baugh	Colonial-style gardens created by the British, often after modifying existing Mughal-style or Nawabi-style gardens
Compleat	Complete
Connouge; Kanog; Kanouj	Kannauj (town)
Consumah; Khansamah	Steward
Coolie	Porter; labourer
Cootub, The	*Qutub Minar*, Delhi
Country born	Europeans born in India
Culpee	Kalpi (town)
Cummerbund	Waist-cloth
Cutcherry	*Katchery*; courthouse
Cutwal; Katwal	*Kotwal*; police chief
Daad-raasi	Justice; one who seeks justice
Dâk	Mail (postal)
Dali	Basket
Darbar	Court
Daroga; Darogah	Superintendent (of police)
Daroga-e-Bawarchikhana	Incharge of royal kitchens
Dastan	Saga
Dastarkhwan	Tablecloth, which is spread on the ground, floor, or table and is used as a sanitized surface for serving food
Dastpanah	Kitchen tongs
Deccan	*Dakshin*, southern part of the Indian sub-continent
Dekkanee	Belonging to the southern states
Demooltee	*Dhanaulti* (hill station)
Deobund	Deoband, town in Saharanpur district, famous for its Islamic seminary called *Darul Uloom*
Deodhi; Dyodhi	Mansion

Dewan; Diwan	Revenue collector, subordinate to a *Zamindar* or European Collector
Dewanee Khas	Hall of Audience (in a palace)
Dewdwallar	*Doodhwala*; milkman
Dhal	Shield
Dhoon; Deyrah Dhoon; Doon	Dehra Dun (town)
Dhooniya	One who fluffs up cotton, prior to filling it in a mattress
Dilkhusa; Dilkoosha; Dil-Koosha; Dil Koosha	*Dilkusha*: Manor and grounds in Lucknow
Dilli; Dehli	Delhi (city)
Din; Deen; Diin	Faith; religion
Dooli	*Doli*; a covered palanquin; litter
Doorgah Poojah	*Durga Puja;* festival prominent in Bengal and other eastern states of India
Dootee	*Dhoti;* waistcloth
Dowr	*Daur*; period; time
Duph (grass)	*Cynodon dactylon* or *Doob* grass, also known as Bermuda grass
Durbangah	Darbhanga (town)
Durriabad	Daryabad (town)
Durzee	*Darzi;* tailor
Eidgah	Open grounds reserved for Eid prayers
Ekka	Horse drawn carriage for single rider
Fakir	Holy man; travelling mendicant
Fana	Cease to exist / disappear
Farman	*Firman*; an oriental sovereign's edict.; a grant or permit; imperial decree
Farzand	Son; male child / offspring
Fasahat	Eloquence
Fasih; Fasiih	Elegant (of language); eloquent word or phrase
Fasl; Fasli	Harvest (of a year)
Faujdar; Sadr Faujdari	A term of pre-Mughal origins. Under the Mughals, the office combined the functions of a military commander along with judicial and land revenue functions
Firinghi; Firingee	*Firang*; An European

Firni	Sweet dish of rice, milk, sugar and garnished with chopped dried fruits, a kind of rice pudding
Fish Market Fort	*Macchi Bhavan*
Friseur	Hairdresser; barber
Furhut Bux; Furrad Buksh; Furra Bux	*Farhat Baksh*; palace of Nawab Sa'adat Ali Khan, former "country house" of Claude Martin
Furlough	Extended leave period availed by officials of EIC
Furruckabad	Farukhabad (town)
Futteh	*Fateh*, victory
Futtehpur	Fatehpur (town)
Futtyghur	Fatehgarh (town)
Fyzabad	Faizabad (town)
Gaazi; Ghazi	Conqueror
Gali Koocha	Lanes and by-lanes
Ganges	Ganga (river)
Garden of God / God's Acre	*Alambagh*
Garhi	Small mud fort; may also pertain to fortified religious structure
Gate ka Darwaza	Wicket gate
Gentoo	Heathen
Gharana	School; ideology (of dance / drama / music)
Gharri	Carriage, often drawn by animals
Ghaut	*Ghat*; river bank
Ghazal; Guzzel; Gazele	Short poem in Urdu, consisting of couplets, often set to music, describing unrequited love (both spiritual as well as worldly) or the charms of intoxication
Ghera bandi	Enclosure
Ghulam Gardish	Corridor / passageway with cubicles, providing temporary shelter (for travellers / pilgrims)
Gilauri	Betel leave folded in conical shape, with a filling of areca nuts, dried fruits, lime, spices etc
Girabaaz	Famed breed of homing pigeon capable of non-stop flying for 10 - 12 hours
Gogra	Ghagra (river)
Gola	Cannon ball
Gola Kabootar	Feral wood pigeon, grey in colour, without any pedigree

Gomastah; Gomasta	Indian agent of the British East India Company, to sign bonds, to fix prices of agricultural produce
Goomty; Goomtee; Gumti	Gomti (river)
Goorka; Gourkah	*Gurkha*; martial tribe of Nepal
Gora Sahib	Literally "white man"
Gulaab-paash	Rosewater sprinkler
Gumma	Brick
Gungootrie	Gangotri glacier
Gunje; Gunge	*Ganj*; market (typically grain market); can also denote locality
Gurhee	*Garhi*; a small fort
Gurrah	*Ghara*; earthen pot for storing water
Gurreeb	*Garib*; poor
Guzar	Passing through
Guzarat	Gujarat (state)
Gwallah	*Gwala;* cattle herdsman, milkman
Haberdasher	A shopkeeper selling small items used in sewing, such as buttons, zips and thread
Habshi	Negro; person of African origin; Abyssinian
Hackery; Hackerie; Hackri	A two wheeled cart, pulled by humans or bullocks
Hai Rabba	Oh God (exclamation)
Hajipore	Hajipur (town)
Hakim	Physician using traditional remedies in India and Islamic countries
Hammam	Turkish bath
Har-carrier	*Harkara*; messenger or courier
Hasrat	Wistfulness, sense of deprivation
Hata	Enclosure; courtyard
Hauz	Water tank
Hawas	Desire; greed
Hayrat	Wonder
Hazrat	Title prefixed to the name of a prophet, or saint or devout person
Hern Khana	*Hiran Khana;* enclosure for housing deer

Hijr	Separation (from beloved)
Hindoo	Hindu
Hindoo Koosh	*Hindu Kush* mountain range
Hindostan	*Hindustan* (sub-continent)
Hindostanee	*Hindustani*; pertaining to the sub-continent of Hindustan or India; Hindi language
Hissa-e-rasadii	Wealth tax
Hooka; Huqqa; Houkah	*Hookah*; hubble-bubble; water pipe
Hookam	*Hukum*; an order or command
Hoolee	Holi (festival)
Hujum	Crowd
Hukkâm	Official
Hukumran	Ruler
Hundi	Treasury bill
Hurdui	Hardoi (town)
Hurdwar	Haridwar (town)
Hussun	Hasan (as in name)
Huzrutgunge	*Hazratganj* (market)
Hyder	*Haider* (name)
Hysar; Hisar	Battlement; fortified enclosure
Ijaradar	Revenue contractor
Ijarband	Cord of pyjama
Ijtihad	Reasoning / rationalising law on basis of Islamic tenets
Ilm-o-fazl	Learning
Emamburra; Imambargah; Ashurkhana	*Imambara;* a congregation hall for Shi'a religious discourses, especially those associated with Muharram.
Imamdasta	Mortar pestle
Insha	Letter
Ittiqaa	Piety; abstaining from evil
Jagir; Jagirdar	A grant of the public revenues of a district; a person with power to collect the revenue
Jah-o-Jalal	Splendour (as of a royal court)
Jaidad	Landed property
Jajman; Jajmani	Familial patron; patronage

Jalousie	A blind or shutter made of a row of angled slats
Jalwa afroz	Literally "to spread radiance." Can denote "ascending the throne"
Jamghat; Jamghata	Literally "gathering." Kite flying festival observed after Diwali festival
Janab-é-Áliya; Janab-é-Ália	Her Majesty
Jân-é-Álam	Spirit of the World (title)
Janpan	A sort of sedan chair, carried by four bearers
Jarnail	General
Jawab; Jawabi	Facsimile (gateway), to maintain architectural symmetry. The responder during *soz-khwani* is also known as a *jawabi*
Jea Mhow	*Jiamau* (locality in Lucknow)
Jeena	Staircase
Jelalabad; Jalallabad	*Jalalabad* (fort) on outskirts of Lucknow
Jemadar	Servant/solder with rank
Jheend	Jind (town)
Jhil	Lake
Jirga	Circle, ring, group
Jounpur	Jaunpur (town)
Jowaulla Mookhee	*Jwalamukhi;* volcano
Jugdespore	Jagdishpur (town)
Juggernaut	*Jagannath;* denoting something massive (originating from Jagannath temple of Odisha)
Justaju	Search with effort
Kaafir	Idolater; infidel; beloved
Kababchi	One who prepare *kebabs* and barbecued items
Kabootar Baazi	Pigeon racing (sport)
Kabootar Khana	Pigeon house
Kahaar	Palanquin bearer
Kahn	Khan (title)
Kal Sira	Literally "black headed." Breed of homing pigeon
Kala Panee; Kala Pani	'Black Water' or seas
Kamalat	Place of excellence
Kana	*Kanha;* Lord Krishna
Kan-Kaiyya	Kite

Karabala; Kerbala	*Karbala;* Holy city of Iraq and centre of Shi'a Muslim pilgrimage; burial place of Mohammed's grandson Husain; place where *Ta'zîyas* are interred
Karnama	Feat; exploit
Kartus	Cartridge
Kasba; Qasba; Qasbat	Township; settlement
Ke zariye se	By means of
Kebab	Meat patty, fried or grilled
Kernaul	Karnal (town)
Khala	Aunt
Khalifa	Muslim civil and religious ruler; Leader
Khamba	Pillar
Khanaut	Wall of tent
Khanpur	Kanpur (city)
Khanqah	Lodge or rest house where travellers discuss spiritual matters, get saints' blessings and hear *Sufi* music
Khansamah	Steward
Khapanaa	Consume
Khapna	Dried up
Khas Mahal	Senior-most Begum or Queen
Khâsdân	Container or try for presenting *pân* and / or token gifts
Khasta haal	Impoverished
Khatma	The end; conclusion
Khidmat	Service
Khilaut; Kelaut; Killut	*Khilat*; ceremonial robe of honour
Khimadtgar; Khudai Khidmadtgar	Servant; Servant of God
Khud	Precipice
Khurd; Khurd Mahal	Smaller; junior Queen / Begum
Khusuusiyat	Distinctive feature; attribute
Khwajasara	Transgender; often holding high position in the Nawabi court
Khwansama	Butler or Captain, responsible for the serving of food on the *Dastarkhwan* as per accepted norms or directions
Khyrabad	Khairabad (town)
Killar	*Qila;* fortress
Kist; Kisht	Instalment
Kitaab Khana	Library

Kittesan	Parasol
Kookeree	*Khukri*; a type of machete used by *Gurkhas* of Nepal
Kos	Unit of distance; approximately 3.2 km
Kotha	Brothel
Kothie; Kothee	*Kothi*; mansion. Large, imposing building
Kotwall, Kotwali	*Kotwal*, police or military officer responsible for law and order of a fort in medieval times; a police chief in modern times; police station
Kuddum Rusool; Kuddum Russool	*Kadam (Qadam) Rasul;* an elevated building housing impression of the Prophet's foot
Kuskus	*Khus khus*; poppy seeds
Kussowlie	Kasauli (hill station)
Lad Sahib; Lat Sahib	Lordship; Governor General
Lakhauri; Lakhori (bricks)	Flat, thin red coloured burnt clay bricks, popular as a building material in the Indian sub-continent, till early 20th century. Size varied from 100 x 150 x 20 mm to 100 x 150 x 50 mm
Laknow; Lakhnau; Lakhnaw; Lakhnow; Lucnow; Lacnow; Nakhlau	Lucknow (city)
Lâl Sharab	Claret; red wine
Land of Regrets	The Indian sub-continent
Lascar	*Lashkar*; Corps; Battery (of army), typically of artillery
Lawh	Tablet (for inscription - not medicine)
Layla and Majnun	Laila and Majnu; a love story originating from Northern Arabia
Liaquat	Ability
Loab	Oil floating on top of curry dish
Logue	*Log*; people; multitude
Loll	*Lâl*; red colour. Also used for names *e.g. Jhao Loll* for *Jhau Lal* or *Loll Baugh* for *Lal Bagh*
Loodianah	Ludhiana (city)
Lustres	Glass prisms and spherical pendants in chandeliers
Lutf uthana	To enjoy
Lyhaza; Lehaza	Therefore
Machan	Platform erected in a tree, originally for hunting large animals from a vantage position (presently used for watching animals in wildlife reserves)

Madad-e-Ma'ash	Revenue free land often given to learned persons
Madrasa; Madrassa	Islamic centre of learning
Mahajan	Trader
Mahez	Simply; only
Mahi	Fish
Mahman nawazi	Hospitality
Mahomet	Mohammad
Mahrattas	Marathas
Mahvar; mahavari	Monthly allowance
Mahviyat	Engrossed; fascinated
Majlis	Congregation
Maktab	Old fashioned method of education in Islamic countries, focussing mainly on memorising the holy *Koran*
Malli	*Mali*; gardener
Manja	String of kite coated with powdered glass (opposite of *saddi*, or plain string)
Mânqulât	Orthodox science
Mansab	Office, post
Mansabdar	A civil or military officer holding rank (*mansab*) in the Mughal administration
Manzuri	Approval
Maqbara	Tomb, revered as a shrine
Mâqulât	Rational science
Marhaba	Bravo; hail
Markaz	Centre (of learning)
Marsiya; Marsiya-khwani	Elegy; reading of elegies (related to Muharram)
Masalchi	One who prepared spices according to the cook's menu (*Bawarchi*) and instructions
Masnad; Musnad; Masnad nashin	Royal seat; ruler sitting on *masnad* / royal seat
Matam	Mourning
Mauza	Village; also district
Mazar	Grave of a Muslim religious leader or saint
Mazuli	Removal; dismissal (in disgrace)
Mehfil	Cultural gathering

Mehfil; Mahfil	Assembly; congregation, cultural gathering
Mesyu	Monsieur (French)
Metranee	*Methrani*; sweepress; a sweeper's wife
Mihrab	Arch; prayer niche in mosque
Milkiyat	Private land ownership of *Zamindars*, often cultivated by contract or bonded labourers
Mir Atishi	Commander of artillery
Mir Bakshi	Head of military
Mir Manzil	Camp superintendent
Mir Munshi	Head clerk
Mithoolee	Mitauli. A *tehsil* in present day Uttar Pradesh
Mohavrat	Idiomatic expressions
Momin	True believer of Islam; staunch Muslim
Momiya	Coating with wax (waxing)
Moofty; Muftee	*Mufti*; A legal expert who is empowered to give rulings on Islamic religious matters; Eastern style of dressing
Mooltan	Multan (city)
Mooluck	*Mulk;* kingdom; one's country
Moolvee	*Maulvi*; Islamic scholar; a learned and religious man; interpreter of Islamic law
Moon Garden	*Chand Bagh* (present day *Chandganj*), Lucknow
Moonshee	*Munshi*; clerk
Moora	Small stool
Moorshedabad	Murshidabad (town)
Moslem; Mussulman	Muslim
Motee	*Moti;* pearl
Motimahul	*Moti Mahal* (palace)
Muchee Bhowun; Muchi Bawan	*Macchi Bhavan;* old pre-Nawabi fort of Lucknow
Muddat	For a long time; period
Mugger	Crocodile
Mughlai	Pertaining to the Mughals, who ruled the Indian sub-continent for three centuries
Mujahid	Crusader; warrior fighting for his faith
Mujra	Dance performance by female dancers, to the accompaniment of vocal and instrumental music

Mujtahid	Individual who is qualified to exercise *ijtihad* in the evaluation of Islamic law
Mukarrar	Encore, as in a recital of poetry
Mukhtasar	Short; in brief
Mulazammin	Servants; employees
Munsarowar	Mansarovar glacier
Munzil	*Manzil;* generally denotes a large building, although the term has other connotations e.g. destination, floor
Muqarrar	Settle, confirm
Muraqqa	Album of miniature paintings in book form
Musahib	Courtier; friend and advisor
Mushaira	Congregation of poets during which Urdu poetry is recited, typically taking the form of a contest
Musjed	*Masjid;* mosque
Mussooree	Mussoorie (town)
Must	*Musth;* seasonal condition in bull elephants characterized aggressive behaviour and rise in reproductive hormones
Mustaydi	Alertness
Mut'ah	Ancient Islamic practice uniting man and woman as husband and wife for a limited time, on mutual agreement
Mutawasit	Paymaster
Muttra	Mathura (town)
Mynporee	Mainpuri (town)
Naanbai	One who prepares flat breads such as *roti, kulcha*, *sheermal* etc.
Naaz-aafriin	Coquettish lover
Naaziriin	Viewers; spectators
Nabob	*Nawab*; provincial Governor, often *de facto* ruler
Nafa	Profit
Nafs	Body; flesh
Naib; Nayb-e-Khas	Second in command; a deputy
Najib	High born; superior; outstanding
Naqdi; jama	Revenue deposit
Naqqar; Naqqarkhana	Short, flat drum; pavilion where drums are beaten at intervals, or to announce royalty
Nasl	Race

Nath	Nose ring
Nath utarna	Ceremonial sexual intercourse with a virgin prostitute
Nawab Wazir	Person holding dual posts of *Nawab* or provincial governor e.g. Awadh, and also *Wazirat* or Ministership of the Mughal court at Delhi
Nazabaz	Lancer
Nazim	First officer of a province; minister of the department of criminal justice
Nazir	Court official
Nazm	Urdu poetry, that is normally written in rhymed verse and also in modern prose-style
Nazul	Confiscated (estate)
Nibhana	To get along
Nigrani	Keeping watch
Nikah	Matrimonial ceremony under Islam
Nimish; Makhan Malai	Light dessert based on set cream, flavoured with saffron and rose water
Nipal	Nepal (Himalayan country)
Nishapuri	Belonging to Nishapur, Persia
Nizam; Nizamat	A hereditary ruler; territory, office, or authority of the *Nizam*.
Noorani	Shining, conspicuous
Notch girl	Nautch girl; derived from the Hindi word, *Naach*, meaning dance
Nourjehan	*Nur Jahan* (Mughal Empress)
Nullah	Small stream; drain
Nusseeb	*Naseeb;* fate
Nuwabgunge	Nawabganj (administrative sub-division in Bareilly)
Nuzzer	*Nazar*; ceremonial gift presented in court to royalty / nobility
Ooddeen	ud-Din (as in name)
Oonao; Onao	Unnao (district)
Oordoo	Urdu (language)
Oudh; Oude	Awadh (state)
Paalii	A fight of birds
Padre	A Christian priest
Padshah	*Badshah*; king
Paimana	Cup; measure

Palkee; Palankeen	*Palki*, palanquin
Paltan	Battalion; platoon
Pân	A preparation of betel leaves, with condiments such as areca nuts, herbs, lime and dried fruits
Panah lena	To take refuge
Panah-gazin	A refugee
Panapna	To prosper; survive
Pândân	Box for storing *pân* (see above)
Pandy	Derogatory term used by the British for Indian freedom fighters, with reference to Mangal Pandey
Parantha; Paratha	Shallow fried, layered flat bread
Parasol Palace	*Chattar Manzil* palace, Lucknow
Pargana	A revenue unit, consisting of several *mouzas* (smallest unit for collecting revenue)
Pari Khana	Abode of fairies
Parterre	Garden with symmetrical flower beds
Patan; Pathan	Afghan tribesman
Patang Bazi	Kite flying
Patialah	Patiala (town)
Patta	Land deed issued by the government to an individual
Patwari	Village accountant
Paundan	*Pândân* (see above)
Payravi	Follow through
Pehra	Patrol
Pehra dena	To keep watch
Pench ladana	Combat (as in kite flying)
Peon	Footman; foot solder; pawn; lowly employee physically delivering files and papers in an office
Pergola	Outdoor garden with a pillared passageway and / or shaded sitting area, often supporting creepers or climbing plants
Pertabgurh; Pertabghar	Pratapgarh (town)
Peshcush	*Pesh-kash*; an offering; proposal
Phaeton	Four wheeled carriage, drawn by a pair of horses
Phirni	Flavored rice pudding

Phool Sira	Literally "spotted head" (as if with tiny flowers). Breed of homing pigeon
Pindarry	*Pindari;* plunderer; highway robber
Pinjara	Cage
Pir; Peer	A Muslim saint; holy man
Pirich	Saucer
Pishpash	Meat-based rice stew
Plassey	Palashi - site of a decisive war between British East India Company and Nawab of Bengal, fought in 1757. Name derived from the local tree called *Palas* (*Butea monosperma*), bearing red flowers commonly called "Flame of The Forest"
Pleader	An advocate in a court of law
Poojari	*Pujari*; Hindu priest
Poppadam	*Papad*; seasoned dry flatbread
Prophet's Garden	*Mohammad Bagh,* Lucknow
Pucca and Cutcha	*Pakka* and *Katcha*; literally signifying cooked and raw, although meanings could be different, depending on context
Puharree	*Pahari;* inhabitants of hilly regions
Punchayat	*Panchayat;* a village council
Punjaub	Punjab (state)
Punkah; Punkha; Punkah coolie	*Pankha*; fan; a lowly employee who manually operated the fan
Punsaree	*Pansari*; Indian native seller of indigenous medicines
Purdah; Purdahnashin	Literally curtain; religious and social practice of female seclusion prevalent among Muslim and Hindu communities; a woman who practices *purdah*
Purza	Component; part (of mechanical contraption)
Pyke	Night watchman in a village; runner / messenger
Qaahir	Dominant; oppressive
Qahar; Khuda ka qahar	Wrath (of God)
Qaraar denaa	To fix, determine, adjudge
Qasiida	Eulogy
Qatl-e-aam	General massacre
Qaul-o-qarar	Agreement
Qayda; Beqayda	Regular; irregular
Qazi	Magistrate or judge of a *Sharia* court

Qibla	Direction towards *Kaa'ba*
Qil'a-band	Imprisoned (in a fort)
Qil'adaar	Commander of fort
Qil'a-e-Fort Vylyam	Fort William (Calcutta)
Qissa; Qissa goii	Story; recitation of story
Qizilbash	Turkic warriors who settled in Afghanistan in large numbers
Qubuliyat	Acceptance; receipt
Rahgir	Traveller
Rajah	Raja; King
Rajapoot	Rajput
Rakabdaar	The waiter or steward, presenting food, as per the *Khwansama's* instructions. May also be involved in preparation of sweets / desserts
Rampoor	Rampur (city)
Ranee	*Rani*; queen
Raptee	Rapti (river)
Raseed	Receipt
Ratub; Ratib	Food for dogs
Raunaq	Lustre; elegance; cheerfulness
Rauza; Rouza	Tomb of Muslim saint, (with garden) serving as a shrine
Reign of Terror	The period of the Indian Mutiny or First War of Independence (1857 - 58)
Reis	*Rais*; moneyed class; wealthy
Risaldar	Commander of the mounted troop
Rishvat-sitaanii	To get bribe
Riyasat	State
Rob; Raub	Awe, fear
Rora	Pebble; obstruction
Rumali; Roomali Roti	Very thin flat bread, almost like an handkerchief
Rumna; Ramna	Park; hunting ground
Russoulpore	Rasoolpur (town)
Ryasala	Cavalry
Ryot; Ryut	Peasant; tenant farmer
Saalan	Curry; gravy dish
Sada mezaji	Simplicity (of character)

Sahib	A man of authority, typically European
Sajjada Nashin	Descendant of a *Sufi* saint or *Pir*; descendant of disciple of such holy man
Sâlan	Curried (meat) preparation
Santipore	Shantipur city (in present day Nadia district of West Bengal) famous for silk saris
Sardari	Command
Sarzamin	Land; territory
Sataanii	Praise
Saudagar	Merchant
Saz-o-saman	Supplies
Secunder; Secundur	*Sikandar* (as in *Sikandar Bagh*); for Alexander (the Great)
Seda Bearer	*Sardar*; head or leader of palanquin bearers
Seikh	*Sheikh;* typically an Arab chieftain
Sepoy	*Sipahi*; soldier
Serai; Caravanserai; Seraikhana	*Serai; Serai Khana*; shelter for travellers
Shab-é-Baraat	Fifteenth night of the month of *Shaban* (Islamic calendar) when Muslims pray and make offerings in the name of deceased relatives
Shah Nujif; Shan Nujjuff	*Shah Najaf;* tomb of Ghazi-ud-Din Haider in Lucknow
Shahanshahi	Imperial
Shahi Tukda	Sweet dish, made of fried pieces of bread soaked in flavoured sweet milk
Sham-e-Awadh	Colourful evenings of Awadh (Lucknow), often compared with *Subah-e-Banaras* (dawn in Varanasi) and *Shab-e-Malwa* (nights of Malwa)
Shamshir	Sword
Shekarry	*Shikari;* huntsman
Shemianah	*Shamiana;* ceremonial tent, shelter or awning, commonly used for outdoor events
Shervani	A long cloak like garment for males, favoured by Lucknow aristocracy
Shikarnama	Account of a hunting expedition
Shikast	Defeat

Shishmuhull	*Shishmahal* or *Sheesh Mahal;* palace of glass or mirrors
Shroff	*Saraf*; Money changer; banker
Shunkerpore	Shankarpur (town)
Sicca	*Sikka;* coin
Silsila	Link, chain (as in events - not metal chain)
Silsila-e-khair	Social obligation
Silsila-i-Nizamia	Curriculum of Islamic studies of *Firangi Mahal*, Lucknow
Simlah	Simla; Shimla (town)
Sirdar	*Sardar*; Chief; Head - commonly wearing a turban
Sola Topi	A light weight sun hat made from the pith from the *Sola* plant (*Aeschynomene aspera*), formerly worn by the British in India.
Sonnud	*Sanad*; deed, particularly for land holding
Sooltan	*Sultan;* medieval (Muslim) ruler
Soorky	*Surkhi*; pounded brick powder used as mortar
Soubah; Soobah	*Suba*; *Subah* - Province of the Mughal empire
Sowar	*Sawar*; horseman
Soz; Soz-khwani	Dirge; recitation of dirges (related to Muharram)
Srinugger	Srinagar (city)
Subadar / subedar	Provincial governor; army rank
Sudder; Sudder Bazar	*Sadar*; *Sadar Bazar*. Military cantonment; market attached to cantonment
Suer; Soour	Pig; hog
Sultan	Sovereign
Sultan- é-Álam	King of the World (honorific title)
Sultanat-é-Mazia	The past kingdom
Sunderbund	*Sundarban;* delta and mangrove forests of Hooghly river in Bengal
Suraiee	*Surahi*; earthen pitcher for storing water
Surajah Dowla	Siraj-ud-Daula, Nawab of Bengal
Surkunda	*Sarkanda*; reed grass
Sutte	*Sati;* custom of widow burning
Sutuun	Pillar; prop
Syce; Sais	One who grooms horses in a stable
Ta'alluqa; Ta'aluqdar; Talookdar	Connection; land or property over which any kind of right or claim existed; person holding such right

Ta'azim, Takriim	Honour, respect
Tabahi	Destruction
Tabarruk	Blessing; food which is sent to fellow Muslims after a religious ceremony or occasion
Tabasheer	*Tabashir;* medicinal substance from bamboo plant
Tabbaáii	Wisdom; talent
Tabqa	Class, group
Tafrih	Pleasure; entertainment
Tahniyat	Good wishes; to congratulate
Tahzeeb	Culture
Tajurba; Tajurbekar	Experience; Experienced
Takhallus	Pen name; pseudonym
Tamanna	Desire
Tamir karna	To build
Tanga; Tonga	Horse drawn carriage for two or more riders
Taqriiz	Favourable criticism or review
Taqvaa	Fear of God; piety; sanctimonious
Tashtari	Plate; salver
Tatviil	Unnecessary long account, prolonged
Tawaif; tavaaif	Prostitute; dancing girl
Ta'zîya; Tazia	Replica of the tomb of Husain, martyred grandson of Mohammad, carried in processions during Muharram
Tea Cozy / Cosy	Cloth cover for teapot
Teapoy	A small three-legged (tripod) table
Tehalka; Tahalka	Panic; commotion
Tehsil; Tehsildar; Tahsildar	An administrative sub-division in a district; officer or revenue collector in charge of the *Tehsil.*
Thakur	Land owner-cum-local chieftain; ironically may also denote lower caste barbers
Thermantidote	Mechanical contraption which blew a current of air inside colonial homes
Thug; Thuggee	Highway robber who also choked / garrotted his victim to death
Thunder Box	Portable, box-like lavatory seat, manually cleaned by scavengers in colonial India
Til-a-ram	*Dilaram Kothi* in Lucknow (no longer extant)

Tola	Traditional residential area in Lucknow
Tom-Tom	*Tamtam;* native drum
Toofaun	*Toofan;* Storm; hurricane
Toolseepore	Tulsipur (town)
Tope	Cannon
Topkhana	Artillery
Tughra	Calligraphic monogram / seal affixed on official documents like *sanads*, *firmans* etc
Tulwar	*Talwar;* sword; sabre
Tumasha	*Tamasha;* ostentatious display (often with negative connotations)
Tyear	*Tayyar*; ready
Tykhana; Taikhana	*Tehkhana*; basement
Tyrpowliya	Tripolia, a building or gateway with three entrances
Ugaldân	Spittoon
Ulajhna	To get entangled
Umballah; Umballa	Ambala (city)
Urs	Death anniversary of a *Sufi* saint
Usuf	*Yusuf;* Joseph
Vaasta	Connection; also middleman
Vaasta dena	Come in contact; to be concerned; invoking help or mercy
Vaqat; vakat	*Waqt*; time period
Vasiiqa	Affidavit; deed, legal document
Vizir; Vizier; Vizar; Virzeer	*Vazir*; *Wazir;* Prime Minister
Wafat	Death
Wajib	Reasonable
Wali Ahad; Mirza Wali Ahad Bahadur	Crown Prince; Successor designate; heir to the throne
Waqai Navi; Waqai Nigar; Sawanih Nigar	Writer or surveyor providing confidential reports to the ruler
Warq	Foil of silver or gold for edible purposes
Wasifa; Wasiqa	Pension
Waziri	Thoroughbred horse (from Afghanistan)
Wazu; Wazoo	*Wudhu*; cleaning oneself before prayers; ablution

Whitey-brown	See "Anglo-Indian" above
Wazirat	(Prime) Ministership
Writer	Clerk
Yaad taza karna	Recall; refresh memory
Yeshu	Jesus Christ
Zakaat	Alms, charity
Zeminder	*Zamindar*; a landowner, who leases his land to tenant farmers. May not actually own the land, but has tenancy rights, which lapse after his death
Zenana	Seraglio; part of house for the seclusion of women folk
Zihaanat	Intelligence; sagacity
Zille himayat mein	In the protection
Zimma; Zimmedari	Responsibility; obligation
Ziyarat; Ziyarat karna	Pilgrimage; to proceed on a pilgrimage

Afterword:

Idle Musings of the Author

Like Vinod Mehta, I am also a Lucknow boy. A Bengali by community, but a true-blue Awadhi, in character and upbringing. As a schoolboy, I remember my father taking me on visits to the scattered monuments of Lucknow, on Sundays. He would describe wondrous tales about palaces, Nawabs, their begums and their life-styles, while I looked up with shiny eyes. I never came to know from where he got all those snippets of information from. He was the quintessential Daguerre, old-school type, more into hard drinking, clubbing, going to *shikars* to hunt blue bulls, fishing all day long to catch nothing and other similar outdoor activities. As a hobby (never commercial), he bred high pedigree, homing pigeons and fighting roosters, on the roof of the huge crumbling building in Hazratganj, where we resided. I never saw him reading any book on Lucknow. But he did have his share of friends from Lucknow's prominent Nawabi and Anglo-Indian families. I remember a tall, slim and debonair Nawabi-type, who always dressed in a glamorous, bottle-green *shervani*... he looked like a millionaire, resembling Hollywood actor, Christopher Lee, but was in fact a pauper. I recall a beautiful Anglo-Indian lady, whose very mention made my mother start a rant. Sometimes my father took me to his friends' *kothis*, which looked like enormous castles (always run-down), to my innocent eyes. I savored the Awadhi *biryani, sâlan, firni* and *shahi tukda* in these homes, as much as I enjoyed the *kebabs* and *paranthas* from tiny kiosks and hole-in-the-wall pit-stops. My dad knew them all; I was just a dumb, impressionable kid. My mother, who was a Delhite, was equally into tales of old Delhi and its *authentic* Mughlai cuisine. She was slightly contemptuous of the UP *wallas* (including my dad)! We were middle-of-the-road people, concentrating on education, rich food, having an easy-going approach to life, with lots of local culture thrown in. Since both my paternal as well as maternal ancestors had migrated from Bengal shortly after 1857, more than a century later, we - the present generation were regrettably, quite far removed from our original cultural roots of Hooghly district, Bengal. As I write this, sitting in Kolkata, it is but an irony of fate that at least someone from our maverick families could return to his roots, a hundred and sixty years later, albeit temporarily, courtesy an official posting and not because of any emotional attachment *per se*.

For the first two decades of my life, I was confined to Lucknow. I was the idiomatic frog-in-the-well. For my Ph.D, I had to go to big, bad Delhi. In the hostels, I was accosted by student groups of various denominations. But slowly, I developed my own friends' circle, and it was inadvertently populated by Muslim students. One day, I realised that we had two Mirzas, one Khan, an Alam, and a Hasan in our group. I was the only irreverent Hindu around. We happily shared the same language, the food, the interests (*mandir-masjid* issues, *yatras, jihadi* strikes, CAA and NRC were unknown then). I was entranced by old Delhi and was amazed at the sheer size and beauty of Delhi's monuments like Humayun's Tomb, the *Qutub* complex, *Tuglaqabad* and *Shahjahanabad*. Here was a city that if one visited a monument every weekend, he would have to perhaps spend a lifetime to see them all.

My job sent me to our training academy in Hyderabad. I fell in love with old Hyderabad, its sing-song Urdu language, the massive, well preserved fort, palaces, monuments and the rich, tangy Hyderabadi cuisine. I slowly realised that the world was not Lucknow, and there were bigger and more elaborate heritage structures, which needed honest appreciation. I also regrettably realised that Lucknow' monuments were somewhat run-down, and shabby, as compared to those in Delhi or Hyderabad. It was a depressing thought.

Over the years, I toured several cities on official assignments and developed the habit of exploring the old quarters, rather than visiting Malls and glitzy shopping centers. An interesting anecdote here: Or perhaps two. Once I visited Ahmedabad, and took the official day tour in a bus, which left me dissatisfied, as the emphasis on Gandhiji was excessive. The next day, I asked around and ultimately reached the old city by myself, which I explored to my hearts' content. The communal riots had just been over, and in the evening, while describing my explorations to colleagues, I was met with flabbergasted eyes. Ahmedabad left a bad taste in my mouth. Again on being posted at Ranchi, initially, I asked around for the old quarters. What was there to see? Where could I find tasty Mughlai food? I asked my Muslim colleagues about the dates of *Eid*, and what delicacy would they provide me? I was met with a stoic, suspicious silence. The polarisation was complete.

With time, my peripatetic sojourns developed into me, a compulsive obsession for seeing a place from its heritage point of view, as soon as possible, maybe within hours of reaching that particular area. I was on official tour in the outskirts of Calicut, and commenced my usual search as well as authentic *moplah* cuisine. It turned dark, I was 40 kms away from my guesthouse, I got lost, and I was facing a severe language problem. Perhaps I had been over-zealous. But it's not that only Islamic architecture and *Mughlai* cuisine turned me on. Shortly after checking into my hotel in central Panaji, Goa, I asked the receptionist about the availability of authentic Goan cuisine nearby. When he candidly stated that the hotel restaurant specialised in Hyderabadi *biryani* and Chinese dishes, he broke my already fractured heart. But I found the churches and ruins of Old Goa fascinating. If I visit Goa again, it will be for the Portuguese quarter, and not for the *feni* or *bibinca* (I have cholesterol issues) or the over-rated beaches. Similarly, I loved Bhopal (cuisine, monuments, language), I loved Bhubaneshwar / Puri / Konark (ancient temples), I loved Cochin (again the Portuguese quarter). I was entranced by Mysore and the ruins of Tipu Sultan's Seringapatam, where I could trace a connection of the Baillie family with Lucknow.

An extended tour of famed Rajasthan, including its deserts, forts and palaces was another eye-opener for me. Jaipur and Jaisalmer dazzled, Udaipur and Jodhpur impressed, but what struck an emotional chord in me was Chittorgarh. The massive ruins of the fort city reduced to rubble in most places due to repeated invasions and sieges – for a person with a vivid imagination, the visuals were extremely heart-wrenching, saddening and depressing. I encountered living history again in an off-beat place like Murshidabad in West Bengal. Long forgotten names and incidents taught in school suddenly came alive, as one confronted the palaces, tombs, graveyards, and references to people such Warren Hastings, Murshid Quli Khan, Mir Jafar, Siraj-ud-Daula and the Jagat Seths. These were people who had carved the destiny of India as a whole, mostly due to individual and collective greed for power and wealth, and then vanished off the face of the earth, leaving future generations to face the consequences.

Incidentally, I noted the architectural similarity of Susanna Anna Maria's impressive, domed tomb made of marble in Chinsurah with the tomb of Dutch trader, Tamerus Cantes Vischer in Cossim Bazar, Murshidabad. Susanna's first husband, Pieter Bruyes, had been Chief Merchant and Administrator of Chinsurah (1713 – 1783). Since Tamerus had died in 1778 and Susanna died in 1809, it is obvious that someone copied the tomb of Tamerus for the benefit of Susanna. Or did Susanna see the latter's tomb on a visit to Cossim Bazar (about 200 kms away from Chinsurah) and desired that she too should be interred in a similar tomb? Susanna would later be immortalised in the Bollywood film, *7 Khoon Maaf*, starring Priyanka Chopra as Susanna.

Another somber, lost heritage of Bengal explored by me was Gauda or Gaur, near Malda, adjoining the Indo-Bangladesh border. The Muslim rule in Bengal started from here, after Bakhtiar Khilji's sudden depredation of the area. Unlike Awadh, the rulers of Bengal never accepted the suzerainty of the throne of Delhi or later colonial masters of Fort William. Indeed, Siraj-ud-Daula decimated British rule in fledgling Calcutta, and demolished their fort. The present Fort William is in fact a replacement of the original Fort William destroyed by Siraj-ud-Daula. To come back to Gaur, I observed a huge area, dotted with huge mosques, tombs, gateways, pavilions and palace remains, embellished with terracotta ornamentation (stone being in short supply again). Many of the mosques were actually made from materials scavenged from earlier Hindu and Buddhist temples – the images and ornamentation had been chipped away, but not completely, so the intentions of the builders was pretty clear. It was a depressing revelation – the imposition of a new faith by conquerors on the conquered, on fear of the sword. This deliberate demolition of religious structures has no other better example than what I had earlier observed in Kashmir. A look at the crumbling ruins of the once imposing *Avantipora* and *Martand* temples (and many others scattered across the state) due to deliberate vandalism and torture of the native populace by bigots such as Sikander "Butshikan" left an extremely bad taste in the mouth. But of course, history has more of tragic stories and less of "happy endings." From the depredations of home-grown Islamic zealots in Kashmir to the cruel high-handedness of our colonial masters, who set up the notorious penal settlements in Viper Island and Port Blair of the Andamans, my personal visits enabled me to experience, first hand, the more cruel and tragic aspects of our tangible heritage.

However, the cruel imperiousmess of the British did not deter me from becoming an ardent fan of colonial architecture and landscaping. It is no secret that most of the more popular "hill-stations" of India, many with "toy' trains" were established by the British, who wanted an escape from the oppressive heat of the plains. Carved out of unapproachable hilly terrains, these took birth out of tremendous human effort and perseverance, and remain unsurpassed even today. The Victoria Memorial of Calcutta and Bombay VT remain exquisite examples of colonial ambition and grandiose planning. Similarly, Connaught Place of Delhi has no parallel in India, and the India Gate (Delhi) and Gateway of India (Bombay) stand out like beacons in architectural perfection. Central Calcutta (Kolkata) and Madras (Chennai) as well as south Bombay (Mumbai), erstwhile Presidency towns, were akin to European cities in architectural design and landscaping, with towering, gothic style buildings and vast open spaces.

So having had the good fortune of travelling across the length and breath of the country, where does all this leave Lucknow? I was left with the realisation that Lucknow's Nawabi rulers, although creative and extravagant, were hampered by British interference. Palace intrigues and other factors prevented Lucknow's rulers from fully realising their dreams. Their buildings, though unique, were smaller, built with *chunam, surkhi* and *lakhauri* bricks. Often gilded, often decorated with florid ornamentation. The look was complete - from a distance. But the dazzle of marble, and the sturdiness of sandstone were absent. Lucknow also missed out on colonial architecture and town-planning, as a sort of punishment, when, for several decades, Allahabad became the capital of the United Provinces. Post-independence, Lucknow faced a deluge from refugees, which added to its woes, due to lack of infrastructure and opportunities. It also faced political disinterest. The politics of gigantic UP prevailed, the importance of Lucknow, as a city, diminished. Each ruling political party, in a game of political upmanship, tried to undo the good work (if any) of the previous Government. Surprisingly a much maligned political leader took immense interest in the city; not only massive edifices were put up, but several old structures were also beautified, and Hazratganj was given an outstanding make-over. Political affiliations apart, the make-over of Hazratganj alone deserves a ton of accolade from Lucknowites.

With the taking over by another political establishment, Lucknow saw even better days. Old, Nawabi buildings were restored and made ready for re-use. Hitherto forgotten buildings like *Darshan Bilas* and *Gulistan-e-Iram* got a new lease of life. The entire Hussainabad area was spruced up, and the incomplete *Satkhanda* tower got a make-over, albeit an unusual one. Excavations around the *Chattar Manzil* palace revealed hidden floors buried deep underground - the architectural features of these undisturbed floors gave a true picture of what the palace actually was in its hey-days, before it was misused to such an extent, post-1947, that it remained but a shell of its original magnificence in present times. Because a city cannot survive simply on the relics of its past - a 'duplicate' Hardinge bridge was put into place, which physically resembled the original bridge, but was built as per modern engineering principles and materials. This was because the old colonial bridge, built in 1914 across the Gomti river and popularly known as *Hardinge Bridge* (in honor of Lord Hardinge, Viceroy of British

India) proved to be too narrow to bear the load of modern Lucknow's traffic. The UP Council House (*Vidhan Sabha*) too got a clone - a rather disproportionate one, in the form of the UP CM's office. Lucknow got a metro rail, which cleverly avoided overshadowing the heritage areas in its path, by partially going underground. Yet, crowded places such as *Charbagh* and *Hazratganj* became even more congested due to its presence. The bricked-up portico of the colonial-era Divisional Railway Manager's office building was demolished, but a sleeker version was put in place, after prolonged efforts of heritage enthusiasts under the umbrella of *Citizens For Lucknow*. Lucknow was on the path of progress, with massive malls, stadiums, superhighways and of course, a highly ambitious riverfront development project. But fate had other plans. The city which had witnessed so many upheavals, saw yet another change of policy matter in the highest echelons of power; its famed tourist spots were downgraded, the duplicate *Hardinge Bridge* was left unfinished, the riverfront development was put on hold and the focus now shifted to temple tourism. But do iconic structure like the *Taj* in Agra or the *Bada Imambara* at Lucknow really need to be bolstered up through government interventions? Perhaps yes, but only in part. Their reputation as architectural wonders being so prominent, it would be an impossibility that these would wither away, even if neglected. And so stands Lucknow, till the time of writing this book.

So where do we go from here? Individual citizens, various fora and heritage groups have genuine concern for the city. Till today, the cuisine, the *Ganga-Jamuni tahzeeb* and the communal harmony of Lucknow remain unparalleled. It deserves to be preserved further. But ultimately the funds, the resources and the brute physical will, to get things done, lies with the government. Although priorities do change with time, Lucknow should not be allowed to wallow in despair, due to political or administrative disinterest.

Thus, a person on a visit to Lucknow should not be reminded to smile. He should smile on his own accord.

Select Bibliography

Abbas, SA, *Incredible Lucknow, A Visitor's Guide* (2010), Saiyed Anwar Abbas, Lucknow.

Abbas, SA, *Lost Monuments of Lucknow* (2009), Saiyed Anwar Abbas, Lucknow.

Abbas, SA, *Wailing Beauty: The Perishing Art of Nawabi Lucknow* (2010), Saiyed Anwar Abbas, Lucknow.

Abdul Ali, AFM, *The Last Will and Testament of Bahu Begum* (1926), N. Mukherjee, Art Press, Calcutta.

Abidi, HA, "Begum Hazrat Mahal", *Naya Daur*, No. 5 (1966) pp. 45-48.

Abu, TKM, *Tafzihul Ghafilin* [The Disgrace of The Negligent], translated from Farsi by William Hoey, *History of Asafud Daulah, Nawab Wazir of Oudh*, Government Press, Allahabad (Reprint, Pustak Kendra, Lucknow, 1971).

Ahmad, EU, *Formation and End of a Mughal Provincial Civilization: A Socio-Economic and Cultural History of Awadh* (2008), Thesis for Ph.D, Aligarh Muslim University, Aligarh.

Ahmad, MT (translation), *Tarikh Badshah Begam* (1938), The Indian Press, Allahabad.

Ahmad, Safi, Two Kings of Awadh: Muhammad Ali Shah and Amjad Ali Shah, 1837 – 1847 (1971), PC Dwadesh Shreni, Aligarh.

Akhtar, Wajid Ali Shah, *Pari Khana* (1965), Kitab Ghar, Rampur.

Akhtar, Wajid Ali Shah, *Pari Khana*, translated from Farsi by Shakeel Siddique (2017), Rajpal & Sons, New Delhi.

Alam, Muzaffar, *The Crisis of Empire in Mughal North India: Awadh & the Punjab 1707 – 1748* (1991), Oxford University Press, New Delhi.

Alavi, Seema, *Islam and Healing: Loss and Recovery of an Indo-Muslim Medical Tradition, 1600 – 1900 (2008)*, Palgrave Macmillan / Permanent Black, Ranikhet.

Ali, Darogha Haji Abbas, *An Illustrated Historical Album of The Rajas and Taaluqdars of Oudh* (1880), North Western Provinces and Oude Government Press, Allahabad.

Alli, Darogha Ubbas, *The Lucknow Album* (1874), Baptist Mission Press, Calcutta.

Ali, MH, *Observations on the Mussulmauns of India. Descriptive of their Manners, Customs, Habits and Religious Opinions made during Twelve Years Residence in Their Immediate Society* (1832), Humphrey Milford, London, UK.

Almeida, Hermione and Gilpin, GH, *Indian Renaissance: British Romantic Art and the Prospect of India* (2005), Ashgate Publishing Ltd., Aldershot, UK.

Amir, SM, "The Great Uprising and Civil Rebellion in Shahjahanpur: A Study of Anti-British Resistance in 1857", *Shodh Sanchayan*, Vol. 2 (1 & 2) (2011) pp. 1-2.

Anderson, AT, *A Short History of Lucknow* (1913), Pioneer Press, Allahabad.

Anderson, G and Subedar, M, *The Last Days of The Company: A Source Book of Indian History, 1818 – 1858* (1918), AH Wheeler, Bombay.

Anderson, RP, *A Personal Journal of The Siege of Lucknow* (1858), W Thacker & Co, London.

Anon (*ed.*), *Imperial Gazetteer of India, Provincial Series: United Provinces of Agra and Oudh*, Vol. II (1908), Superintendent of Government Printing, Calcutta.

Anon (*ed.*), *Lucknow Ki Rachi Basi Tehzeeb* (2016), Sanatkada, Lucknow.

Anon., "Memorandum of Operations carried out under the Command of Major-General Sir James Outram, GCB, during the Siege of Lucknow", *The Edinburgh Gazette* (1858), London, pp. 1071-1072.

Anon. (*ed.*), *Gazetteer of The Province of Oudh – 3 Vols* (1877), Low Price Publications, Delhi.

Anon., *Vision for Lucknow (2017) Region, Clean, Green and Prosperous Lucknow* (2017), Lucknow Development Authority, Lucknow.

Anon. (*ed.*), *Gazetteer of The Province of Oudh* – Vol. III – *N to Z* (1878), North-Western Provinces and Oudh Government Press, Allahabad.

Anon. (*ed.*), *Hazratganj – A Journey Through The Times* (2011), Bennett & Coleman, Lucknow.

Anon., *Oude: Papers Relating To Presented to both Houses of Parliament by Command of Her Majesty* (1856), Harrison & Sons, London.

Anon., *Personalities, A Comprehensive and Authentic Biographical Dictionary of Men who Matter In India* (1950) Arunam & Sheel, New Delhi.

Anon. (*ed.*), *Report on The Urban Land Price Scenario – Lucknow* (2005), Industrial and Economic Planning Division, Ministry of Urban Development, Govt. of India, New Delhi.

Anon., "Preservation of Monuments: Monuments of National Importance, *Indian Archaeology 2008 – 09: A Review*", Archaeological Survey of India, New Delhi.

Anon., *1857: A Pictorial Representation* (2000), Publications Division, Ministry of Information & Broadcasting, Govt. of India, New Delhi.

Anon., *A Glimpse of The Monumental Heritage of Lucknow* (2009), Archaeological Survey of India, Lucknow Circle, Aliganj, Lucknow.

Anon., *First Master Plan (2009 – 2018/9), Lucknow Zoological Gardens* (2009), Lucknow.

Anon., *Lucknow: The Garden of India* (1928), GW Lawrie, Lucknow.

Anon., *The Modern Traveller. A Popular Description, Geographical, Historical and Topographical of the Various Countries of the Globe. India Vol III* (1828), James Duncan, London.

Anon., *The Story of The Indian Mutiny, 1857 – 58* (1898), Hay & Mitchell, Edinburgh, UK.

Anon., *Updated Final Detailed Project Report for Lucknow Metro Rail Project (Phase – I) (*2013), Delhi Metro Rail Corporation, New Delhi.

Anon., *Copy of The Memorandum and Rules and Regulations of the Association of the Prince of Wales Zoological Garden* (1926), Lucknow.

Anon., "An Account of Colonel Martin's Villa Near Lucknow in the East Indies", *The European Magazine*, Vol. XVII (Jan - June) (1790), pp. 86-87.

Anon., "Recent Notes on Lucknow - A.B.C. House", *The Asiatic Journal and Monthly Miscellany*, Vol. 2 (July - Dec) (1816), pp. 578-581.

Anon., "A Home away from Home", *An Aesthete's Lament* (2011), at: http://aestheteslament.blogspot.com/2011_09_04_archive.html

Anon., "Our Goodly Heritage", *The Lal Bagh Jubilee Book* (1870 - 1920), Lucknow.

Ansari, G, *Transcience of Life* Vol. I (2017), Friesen Press, Victoria, Canada.

Ansari, IH, Qureshi, HA and Aadil, M, *Studies on 1857,* Vol. I (2020), Idarah-i-Adabiyat-I Delli, Delhi.

Ansari, Tahir Hussain, "The Cultural and Literary Contribution of Nawab Wajid Ali Shah", *Int. J. English Language, Literature and Humanities*, Vol. II(III) (2014), pp. 181-189.

Anson, OHSG, *With H.M. 9th Lancers during the Indian Mutiny* (1896), WH Allen, London.

Archer, E, *Tours in Upper India*, Vol. 1 & II (1833) Richard Bentley, London.

Arend, Nicolaas VD, "Architecture: Ancient and Modern", *The Sewanee Review*, Vol. 17(1) (1909), pp. 14-25.

Asher, Catherine, *Lucknow's Architectural Heritage* (2010), University of Minnesota, digital version at: http://history.ncsu.edu/projects/visualCulturc/readings/Asher.pdf

Awasthi, Preeti, *Awadh – Congenial Home for Nurturing Arts – In Historical Perspective of Painting and Music [1722 – 1856]* (2014), Thesis for Ph.D, University of Lucknow, Lucknow.

Azmi, AA, *The Annexation of Awadh and its Consequences* (1973), Thesis for Ph.D, Aligarh Muslim University, Aligarh.

Bajpai, U and Gupta, S, "Use of Solar Passive Concepts in the Avadh Architectural Buildings and their Modified Impact", *Indian J. History of Sc.*, Vol. 50(1) (2015) pp. 163-181.

Barnett, Richard B, "Embattled Begams: Women as Power Brokers in Early Modern India" in Gavin RG Hambly (*ed.*) *Women in Medieval Islamic World: Power, Patronage and Piety* (1998), St. Martin's Press, New York, USA, pp. 521-536.

Bartrum, Katherine, *A Widow's Reminiscences of the Siege of Lucknow* (1858), James Nisbet, London, UK.

Bartsch, K and Scriver, P, "The House of Stars: Astronomy and the Architecture of New Science in Early Modern Lucknow" in *Religion and Art in Islam* (2019), University of Adelaide Press, Adelaide.

Basu, Purnendu, *Oudh and the East India Company: 1785-1801* (1943), Maxwell Company, Lucknow.

Bayly, CA, *Rulers, Townsmen and Bazaars* (1998), Oxford University Press, New Delhi.

Beale, TW, *An Oriental Biographical Dictionary* (1894), WH Allen, London, UK.

Beg, MA, *The Guide to Lucknow* (1911), Asian Educational Services, New Delhi.

Bhasin, Rakesh, *Dastan-e-Awadh: A Momentous Journey from Faizabad to Lucknow* (2018), Notion Press, Chennai.

Bhatnagar, GD, *Awadh Under Wajid Ali Shah* (1968), Arun Press, Varanasi.

Bhatt, Ravi, *The Life and Times of The Nawabs of Lucknow* (2006), Rupa Publications, New Delhi.

Bird, RW, *The Spoliation of Oudh* (1857), Nassau Steam Press, Charing Cross, London, UK.

Blake, SB, *Shahjahanabad: The Sovereign City in Mughal India, 1639 - 1739* (2002), Cambridge, UK.

Blunt, Alison, "Embodying War: British Women and Domestic Defilement in the Indian Mutiny, 1857 – 8, *Journal of Historical Geography*, Vol. 26(3) (2000), pp. 403-428.

Blunt, EAH, *Christian Tombs and Tablets of Historical Interest in the United Provinces of Agra and Oudh* (1911), Govt. Press, Allahabad.

Burgess, J and Spiers, RP (eds), *History of Indian and Eastern Architecture by the late James Ferguson* (1910), John Murray, London, UK.

Butler, Harcourt, *India Insistent* (1931), William Heinemann, London, UK.

Butter, Donald, *Outlines of the Topography and Statistics of the Southern Districts of Oudh* (1839), Guttman, Calcutta.

Caliskan, O, "Urban Gateway: Just a Symbol or More?", *J. Urban Design*, Vol. 15 (1) (2010), pp. 91-122.

Campbell, LD, *Asiatic Annual Register for the Year 1806, History of Awadh* (1809), T Cadell & W Davies, London, UK.

Carnegy, P, Woodburn, J and Noble, CS, *Historical sketch of Tahsil Fyzabad, Zillah Fyzabad, including Parganas Haveli-Oudh and Pachhimrath* (1870), Oudh Government Press, Lucknow.

Casci, Simonetta, Casolari, Marzia and Vittorini, Simona, *Cultural and Political Identities in India* (2002), Casa, Milan, Italy.

Case, Adelaide, *Day by Day at Lucknow: A Journal of the Siege of Lucknow* (1858), Richard Bentley, London, UK.

Castro, G, *Wâjid, Alî Shâh Plays Krishna's Stolen Flute: The Multiplicity of Voices in the King of Awadh's Dramatic Work* (2016), Thesis for Ph.D, University of Washington, Seattle, USA.

Chatterjee, B and Alam, I (*eds.*), *Dictionary of Martyrs: India's Freedom Struggle (1857 – 1947),* Vol. 2 (2013), ICHR, New Delhi.

Chatterjee, Nandlal, *Glories of Uttar Pradesh* (1957), Publications Bureau, Information Department, UP, Lucknow.

Choudhary, Manisha, "Domesticity, Religion and Politics: Exploring Life in Royal Palace of Awadh", *Int. J. Soc. Sc. Tomorrow*, Vol. 1(4) (2012), pp. 1-14.

Clarke, GR, *The Post Office of India and Its Story* (1920), Mayflower Press, Plymouth, UK.

Cole, JRI, Roots of North Indian Shi'ism in Iran and Iraq - Religion and State in Awadh: 1722-1859 (1989), University of California Press, Berkeley, USA.

Crooke, William, *Ethnographical Handbook for the NW Provinces and Oudh* (1890), NW Provinces and Oudh Government Press, Allahabad.

Crumb, James, *The Highland Brigade: Its Battles and Heroes* (1886), Simpkin, Marshall & Co, London.

Curl, JS, *A Dictionary of Architecture and Landscape Architecture* (2006), Oxford University Press, London, UK.

Cupples, G, *Memoir of Mrs Valentine, Jeypore* (1882), James Nisbet, London.

Cuthell, Edith, *My Garden in the City of Gardens: A Memory With Illustrations* (1905), John Lane, London, UK.

Dadlani, Chanchal, "Transporting India: The Gentil Album and Mughal Manuscript Culture", *Art History*, Vol. 38 (4) (2015), pp. 748-761.

Dalrymple, William (*ed.*), *Begums, Thugs and Englishmen: The Journals of Fanny Parkes* (2002), Penguin, New Delhi.

Dalrymple, William, *The Last Mughal* (2006), Penguin, New Delhi.

Dalrymple, William, *White Mughals: Love and Betrayal in Eighteenth-Century India* (2004), Penguin, New Delhi.

Daniell, W and Caunter, H, *The Oriental Annual or Scenes in India, comprising Twenty-Two Engravings from Original Drawings by William Daniell, RA and A Descriptive Account by the Rev, Hobart Caunter, BD* (1835), Bull and Churton, London, UK.

Davidson, CJC, *Diary of Travels and Adventures in Upper India,* Vol. II (1843), Henry Colburn, London.

Davies, CC, *Warren Hastings and Oudh* (1939), Oxford University Press, London, UK.

Davies, Philip, *British Architecture in India 1660 – 1947: Splendours of The Raj* (1987), Penguin, Middlesex, UK.

Davis, John Francis, *Vizier Ali Khan: A Chapter in British Indian History* (1871), Spottiswoode & Co., London.

Dewar, D, *A Handbook to the English Pre-Mutiny Records in the United Provinces* (1920), Government Press, Allahabad.

Dodd, George, *The History of the Indian Revolt and of the Expeditions to Persia, China and Japan: 1856-7-8* (1859), W & R Chambers, London, UK.

Dodson, David Scott, *General Views & Special Points of Interest of the City of Lucknow: From Drawings Made on the Spot: With Descriptive Notices* (1860), Day, London, UK.

Dronah, *Unesco Creative Cities Network: Inclusion of Lucknow - Interim Report* (2019), Deptt. of Culture, Govt. of Uttar Pradesh, Lucknow.

Dwarris, Robert, *My Escape from The Mutinies in Oude,* Vol. II (1858), Richard Bentley, London, UK.

Eaton, Natasha, "Between Mimesis and Alterity: Art, Gift and Diplomacy in Colonial India, 1770 – 1800", *Comparative Studies in Society and History*, Vol. 46(4) (2004), pp. 816-844.

Eaton, RM, *The Rise of Islam and the Bengal Frontier, 1204 – 1760* (1993), University of California Press, Berkeley.

Eden, Emily, *Up The Country* (1867), Richard Bentley, London, UK.

Edwardes, Michael, *Orchid House: Splendours and Miseries of the Kingdom of Oudh, 1827 – 1857* (1960), Cassel, London, UK.

Evelegh, James, "To What Extent was 1857 An Example of Colonial Genocide? A Study of Colonial Violence During the Indian Uprising of 1857 – 59", *The South Asianist*, Vol. 3(1) (2014), pp. 209-238.

Fergusson, James, *History of Indian and Eastern Architecture*, Vol 3 (1876), John Murray, London, UK.

Finn, M and Smith, K (*eds.*), *The East India Company at Home, 1757 – 1857* (2018), UCL Press, London.

Fisher, Michael H, *A Clash of Cultures*: *Awadh, the British, and the Mughals (1987)*, Manohar Publishers & Distributors, New Delhi; *Idem.*, *The Dynastic History of Lucknow*, http://www.academia.edu/4139086/The_Dynastic_History_of_Lucknow.

Fonia, RS, *Monuments of Lucknow* (2013), Archaeological Survey of India, New Delhi.

Forbes, James, *Oriental Memoirs: A Narrative of Seventeen Years Residence in India* Vol. 2 (1834), Richard Bentley, London, UK.

Forbes-Mitchell, William, *Reminiscences of the Great Mutiny 1857 – 59* (1910), DK Publishers Distributors, New Delhi.

Forrest, GW (*ed.), Selections from the Letters Dispatches and Other State Papers Preserved by The Military Department of The Government of India: 1857 – 58,* Vol. I (1893), Military Department Press, Calcutta.

Forrest, GW, *A History of The Indian Mutiny Reviewed and Illustrated from Original Documents,* Vol. I (1904), William Blackwood & Sons, Edinburgh, UK.

Forster, G, *A Journey from Bengal to England: Through the Northern Part of India, Afghanistan and Persia, and into Russia by the Caspian Sea* (1808), R. Faulder, London, UK.

Foster, William, "George Duncan Beechy", *Bengal Past & Present*, Vol. XLI (81 - 82) (1931), pp. 101-104.

Franklin, Michael J, *Romantic Representations of British India* (2006), Routledge, Oxford, UK.

Freitag, Sandra, "A Visual History of Three Lucknows", *J. South Asian Studies*, Vol 37 (2014), pp. 431-453.

Freitag, Sandra, "Postscript. Interdisciplinary Dialogue and Lucknow's Cultural System", *S. Asia Multidisciplinary Academic Journal*, Vol .11 (2015) pp. 1-16.

Fuhrer, A, *The Monumental Antiquities and Inscriptions of the North-West Provinces and Oudh* (1891), Archaeological Survey of India, Allahabad.

Gamon, RB, *Warren of Oudh* (1926), Erskine MacDonald, London, UK.

George, Viscount Valentia, *Voyages and Travels to India, Ceylon, the Red Sea, Abyssinia and Egypt*, Vol. I (1809), William Miller, London, UK.

Germon, Maria Vincent, *A Diary Kept by Mrs RC Germon at Lucknow, Between the Months of May and December, 1857* (1870), Waterlow & Sons, London, UK.

Gill, RS, Indegenous Spectres, *Subversive Lilas: Encounters Between Nawabi Authority, Colonialism and Popular Ritual in Lucknow* (2003), Thesis for MA, University of British Columbia, Vancouver, Canada.

Gilliat, Edward, *Heroes of The Indian Mutiny* (1914), Seeley, Service & Co., London.

Gomez, Fernando T, *Cities of Dreams: Examining the Ideology of Colonial Architecture in India* (2009), Thesis for Ph.D, St. Lawrence University, New York, USA.

Gordon, Sophie, *Monumental Visions: Architectural Photography in India, 1840-1901* (2010), Thesis for Ph.D, School of Oriental and African Studies, University of London, London, UK.

Graff, Violette (*ed.*), *Lucknow: Memories of A City* (1999), Oxford University Press, New Delhi.

Groom, Helen (*ed.*), *With Havelock from Allahabad to Lucknow* (1894), Sampson Low Marston & Co., London, UK.

Gubbins, Martin R, *An Account of the Mutinies in Oudh and the Siege of the Lucknow Residency* (1858), Richard Bentley, London, UK.

Haider, Sanobar, *Sibtainabad Through The Lens of Time* (2017), APP Press, Lucknow.

Hannavy, John (*ed.*), Encyclopedia of Nineteenth-Century Photography Vol. I (2008), Taylor & Francis, New York, USA.

Harcourt, ES and Hussain, Fakhir (translation), *Lucknow: The Last Phase of an Oriental Culture by Abdul Halim Sharar* (1989), Oxford University Press, New Delhi.

Harris, Georgina Maria, *A Lady's Diary of the Siege of Lucknow* (1858), Rupa Publications, New Delhi.

Hasan, Mushirul, *From Pluralism to Separatism: Qasbas in Colonial Awadh* (2012), Oxford University Press, New Delhi.

Hasnain, Nadeem, *The Other Lucknow* (2016), Vani Prakashan, New Delhi.

Hay, Sidney, *Historic Lucknow* (1939), Asian Educational Services, New Delhi.

Herbert, Eugenia W, *Flora's Empire: British Gardens in India* (2011), Penguin, New Delhi.

Heber, R, *Narrative of A Journey Through The Upper Provinces of India*, Vol. II (1849), John Murray, London.

Hill, Samuel Charles, *The Life of Claud Martin, Major-General in the Army of the Honorable East India Company* (1901), Thacker, Spink & Co., Calcutta.

Hilton, Edward H, *The Tourists Guide to Lucknow* (1894), Murray & Co and Peake, Allen & Co., Lucknow.

Hodges, W, *Travels in India during The Years 1780, 1781, 1782 & 1783* (1793), J. Edwards, London, UK.

Husain, Shaikh Tasadduq, *Begmat-i-Awadh* [Royal Women of Awadh] (1945), Kitab Ghar, Lucknow.

Hutchinson, G, *Narrative of The Mutinies in Oude, Compiled from Authentic Records* (1859), Cranenburgh, Calcutta.

Inglis, Julia Selina T, *The Siege of Lucknow: A Diary* (1892), McIlvaine, London, UK.

Innes, McLeod, *Lucknow & Oude in The Mutiny, A Narrative and A Study* (1895), AD Innes, London.

Irvine, William, *Later Mughals,* Vol. II: 1719-1739 (1922), MC Sarkar & Sons, Calcutta.

Irwin, HC, *The Garden of India: Chapters on Oudh History and Affairs* (1880), WH Allen, London.

Islam, Arshad, "The Backlash in Delhi: British Treatment of the Mughal Royal Family following the Indian "Sepoy Mutiny" of 1857", *J. Muslim Minority Affairs*, Vol. 31 (2) (2011), pp. 197-215.

Jafri, SZH, *Studies in the Anatomy of a Transformation: Awadh from Mughal to Colonial Rule* (1998), Gyan Publishing House, New Delhi.

Jafri, SZH (*ed.*), *Delhi and Awadh During 1857, Studies, Images and Documents* (2020), Gyan Publishing House, New Delhi.

Jones, Justin, "Urban Mythologies and Urbane Islam: Refining the Past and Present in Colonial-Era Lucknow", *S. Asia Multidisciplinary Academic Journal*, Vol. 11 (2015) pp. 1-20.

Kabir, N, Naz, N and Qayyum, A, "The Contribution of British Engineer Architect Colonel Samuel Swinton Jacob (1867 – 1902): Proponent of European Indo-Islamic Architecture in Colonial India", *Pakistan J. Science*, Vol. 66 (3) (2014), pp. 282-290.

Kamleh, Elise, *Architectural Exchange in the Eighteenth Century: A Study of Three Gateway Cities: Istanbul, Aleppo and Lucknow* (2012), Thesis for Ph.D, University of Adelaide, Australia.

Kataria, I, *Railway Heritage: Indian Railways* (2019), INTACH, New Delhi.

Kaye, JW, *Lives of Indian Officers* Vol. I & II (1867), Strahan & Co, London.

Keene, HG, *A Handbook for Visitors to Lucknow: with Preliminary Notes on Allahabad and Cawnpore* (1875), Asian Educational Services, New Delhi.

Keshani, Hussein, "Architecture and the Twelver Shi'i Tradition: the Great Imambara Complex of Lucknow", *Muqarnas: An Annual on the Visual Culture of the Islamic World*, Vol. XXIII (2006), pp. 219-250.

Keshani, Hussein, *Strangers, Lovers, and Kin: Gender Roles and Their Interplay with the Architecture of Awadh* (2003-2004), in *Studies on Architecture, History and Culture,* Aga Khan Program for Islamic Architecture, Massachusetts Institute of Technology, Cambridge, USA.

Khan, AA, *Glimpses of The Arts of Awadh* (1989), State Museum, Lucknow.

Khan, Iqbal Ghani, "The Awadh Scientific Renaissance and the Role of the French", *Indian J. History of Science*, Vol. 38(3) (2003) pp. 273-301.

Khan, RK, *The Known and the Unknown / Monuments, Places & Persons of Awadh* (2020), New Royal Book Company, Lucknow.

Khan, Vijaya, "Glimpses into the life and times of the Begums of Avadh", *The India Magazine*, Vol. 3(9) (1983), digital version at: http://oudh.tripod.com/oudhbegam/vnawab.htm

Khorakiwala, A, "Staging the Modern Ruin: Beato's Sikander Bagh, Lucknow", *Thresholds*, Vol. 41 (2013) pp. 138 - 145.

Knighton, William, *The Private Life of an Eastern King Together with Elihu Jan's Story or the Private Life of an Eastern Queen* (1921), Oxford University Press, London, UK.

Krishna, Ashima, *The Urban Heritage Management Paradigm: Challenges from Lucknow, An Emerging Indian City* (2014), Thesis for Ph.D, Cornell University, New York, USA.

Kumar, A and Rai, RB, "Nawabi Kothies and Shekhawati Havelis: Comparative Study of Deserted Architectural Marvels", *J. Basic and Appl. Engg. Res*. Vol. 2 (23) (2015) pp. 2014-2020.

Kumar, Vijay, "Archaeological Gazetteer of District Sitapur (Part -1)", *Indian J. Archaeology*, Vol. 1 (2) (2016), pp. 119-329.

Laird, MA (ed), *Bishop Heber in Northern India: Selections from Heber's Journal* (1971), Cambridge, UK.

Lal, SN, *Azadari & Avadh. 135 Years of History of Azadari* (2016), Humkalam, Lucknow.

Lang, John, *Wanderings in India and Other Sketches of Life in Hindostan* (2015), Rupa Publications, New Delhi.

Latif, BI, *Forgotten* (2010), Penguin (India), New Delhi.

Lawson, Charles, *The Private Life of Warren Hastings* (1895), Swan Sonnenschein, London, UK.

Laws, RA, *Lucknow: Society and Politics* (1979), Thesis for Ph.D, University of New South Wales, Sydney, Australia.

Lethbridge, Roper, *The Golden Book of India* (1893), Macmillan & Co., London, UK.

Lewin, Malcolm, *Has Oude Been Worse Governed By Its Native Princes Than Our Indian Territories By Leadenhall Street?* (1857), James Ridgway, London, UK.

Llewellyn-Jones, Rosie (*ed.*), *Lucknow: City of Illusion* (2006), Prestel Publishing Ltd., London, UK.

Llewellyn-Jones, Rosie, "The Monuments, the Makers and the Real City", *The India Magazine* (1984), digital version at: http://www.india-seminar.com/2007/575/575_rosie_llewellyn_jones.htm

Llewellyn-Jones, Rosie, *A Fatal Friendship: The Nawabs, the British, and the City of Lucknow* (1992), Oxford University Press, New Delhi.

Llewellyn-Jones, Rosie, *A Very Ingenious Man: Claude Martin in Early Colonial India* (1999), Oxford University Press, New Delhi.

Llewellyn-Jones, Rosie, *Engaging Scoundrels: True Tales of Old Lucknow* (2000), Oxford University Press, New Delhi.

Llewellyn-Jones, Rosie, *Lucknow: Then and Now* (2006), Marg Foundation, Mumbai.

Llewellyn-Jones, Rosie, *The Great Uprising in India 1857-58: Untold Stories, Indian and British* (2007), The Boydell Press, Woodbridge, UK.

Llewellyn-Jones, Rosie, *The Last King in India: Wajid Ali Shah* (2014), Random House India, Gurgaon.

Losty, JP, *Pictursque Views of India: Sita Ram* (2015), Roli, New Delhi.

Low, Ursula (*ed.*), *Fifty Years with John Company* (1936), Murray, London, UK.

Lumsden, T, A Journey from Meerut in India, to London, through Arabia, Persia, Armenia, Georgia, Russia, Austria, Switzerland, and France during 1819-20 (1822), London & Edinburg, UK.

Mackenzie, ARD, *Mutiny Memoirs Being Personal Reminiscences of the Great Sepoy Revolt of 1857* (1891), Pioneer Press, Allahabad.

Mahmud, Aslam, *Awadh Symphony: Notes on a Cultural Interlude* (2017), Rupa Publications, New Delhi.

Majendie, Vivian Dering, *Up Among The Pandies: A Year's Service in India* (1859), Routledge, London, UK.

Malleson, George Bruce (ed.*)*, Kaye's and Malleson's History of the Indian Mutiny of 1857-8 (1889-92), Allen, London, UK.

Malleson, George Bruce, *The Indian Mutiny of 1857* (1891), Seeley & Co., London, UK.

Mann, Sukhbir, *Archaeology of Lucknow: An Investigation into the Culture of Lucknow* (1983), Thesis for PhD, Deccan College Postgraduate & Research Institute, University of Poona, Pune.

Manners, V and Williamson, GC, *John Zoffany, RA. His Life and Works* (1944), John Lane, London.

McPherson WC (ed.), *Soldiering in India, 1764 – 1787, Extracts from Journals and Letters left by Lt. Col. Allan MacPherson and Lt Col. John MacPherson of the East India Company's Service* (1928), William Blackwood, London, UK.

Maude, Francis C, *Memories of The Mutiny*, Vol. II (1894), Remington, London, UK.

Mecham, Clifford Henry, *Sketches & Incidents of the Siege of Lucknow* (1858), Day & Son, London, UK.

Metcalf, Thomas R, *An Imperial Vision: Indian Architecture and Britain's Raj* (2002), Oxford University Press, New Delhi.

Mishra, Amaresh, *Lucknow: Fire of Grace* (2004), Rupa Publications, New Delhi.

Mohammed, J, *Revenue Free Land Grants in Mughal India. Awadh Region in the Seventeenth and Eighteenth Centuries [1658 – 1765]* (2002), Manohar, New Delhi.

Molesworth, FC and Leslie, JH, "The Diary and Letters of Arthur Moffat Lang", *J. Soc. Army Historical Research*, Vol. 11(41) (1932), pp. 1-25.

Mookherji, PC, *Pictorial Lucknow* (1883), Asian Educational Services, New Delhi.

Mount, Ferdinand, *The Tears of The Rajas: Mutiny, Money and Marriage in India 1805-1905* (2015), Simon & Schuster, London.

Mukherjee, Rudrangshu, *Awadh in Revolt: 1857 – 1858* (2001), Permanent Black, Delhi.

Mukherjee, Rudrangshu, *The Rebellion in Awadh, 1857 – 58: A Study in Popular Resistance* (1980), Thesis for Ph.D, University of Oxford, Oxford.

Mundy, Capt, *Pen and Pencil Sketches from the Journal of a Tour of India* (1833), John Murray, London, UK.

Nagar, Amritlal, *Gathering The Ashes* (2014) (translated by Mrinal Pande), Harper Perennial, New Delhi.

Nagpal, S and Sinha, A, The Gomti Riverfront in Lucknow, India: Revitalisation of a Cultural Heritage Landscape, *J. Urban Design*, Vol. 14 (4) (2009), pp. 489-506.

Neville, HR (*ed.*), *District Gazetteers of The United Provinces of Agra and Oudh*, Vol. XXXVII (1904), Govt. Press, Allahabad.

Neville, HR (*ed.*), *District Gazetteers of The United Provinces of Agra and Oudh,* Vol. 4 (1922), Govt. Press, Lucknow.

Newell, HA, *Lucknow -The Capital of Oudh* (1934), HA Newell, Bombay.

Oak, PN, *Lucknow's Imambaras are Hindu Palaces* (2010), Hindi Sahitya Sadan, New Delhi.

Oldenburg, Veena Talwar, *Sham-e-Awadh: Writings on Lucknow* (2007), Penguin, New Delhi.

Oldenburg, Veena Talwar, *The Making of Colonial Lucknow* (1984), Princeton University Press, New Jersey, USA.

Orlich, LP, *Travels in India including Sinde and the Punjab,* Vol. II (1845), Longman, London, UK.

Page, JA, *List of Muhammadan and Hindu Monuments,* Vol. 2: Delhi Zail [Excluding Shahjahanabad] (1918), Govt of India Press, Calcutta.

Parkes, F, *Wanderings of A Pilgrim in Search of the Picturesque* (1850), Pelham Richardson, London, UK.

Patel, A and Leonard, K (*eds.*), *Indo-Muslim Cultures in Transition* (2011), Brill Academic, Leiden, The Netherlands.

Pello, Stefano, "Literary Mirrors and the Reconstruction of the Holy Places of Shiism in Nawabi Lucknow: A Few Topological Asides from Qatil to Ghalib", *Annali di Ca'Foscari: Serie Orientale*, Vol. 53 (2017), pp. 171-183.

Pemble, John, *The Raj, the Indian Mutiny and the Kingdom of Oudh 1801 – 1859* (1977), Harvester Press, Sussex, UK.

Polehampton, Henry Stedman, *A Memoir, Letters and Diary of the Rev. Henry S. Polehampton: Chaplain of Lucknow* (1858), R. Bentley, London, UK.

Praveen, Yogesh, *Lucknow Monuments* (1989), Pnar, Lucknow.

Sharma, PM, "Lucknow: A Walk through History", *J. Tourism: A Contemporary Perspective*, Vol. 1(1) (2014) pp. 7-12.

Qaisar, Ahsan Jan, Verma, Som Prakash and Habib, Mohd. (*eds.*), *Art and Culture: Endeavors in Interpretation*, Vol. 2 (1996), Abhinav, New Delhi.

Qidwai, Ikramuddin, "The Begams of Awadh and their Establishment", *Quarterly Journal of Pakistan Historical Society*, Vol. 38 (1990) pp. 309-328.

Qureshi, HA (*ed.*), *Memoirs of Faizabad – I, William Hoey* (2004), New Royal Book Company, Lucknow.

Qureshi, HA (*ed.*), *Memoirs of Faizabad – II, William Hoey* (2005), New Royal Book Company, Lucknow.

Qureshi, HA (*ed.*), *The Mutiny Records, Awadh and Lucknow 1857- 59 of Edward H. Hilton* (2010), New Royal Book Company, Lucknow.

Qureshi, HA, *Sources on Awadh* (2004), New Royal Book Company, Lucknow.

Qureshi, HA, *The Mughals, The English & The Rulers of Awadh from 1722 AD to 1856 AD. A Kaleidoscopic Study* (2003), New Royal Book Company, Lucknow.

Rai, DC and Dhanapal, S, "Bricks and Mortars in Lucknow Monuments of c. 17 – 18 Century", *Curr. Sci.*, Vol. 104 (2) (2013), pp. 238-244.

Rathore, Nisha, *The Awadh Tenant Struggle, 1917-1939: A History From Below* (1993), University of Hyderabad, Hyderabad.

Reddy, AB, Ravindra, C and Maitra, S, *Cantonments: A Transition from Heritage to Modernity* (2017), Directorate General Defence Estates, New Delhi.

Rees, LER, *Personal Narrative of the Siege of Lucknow* (1858), Longman, London.

Richards, DS, *Cawnpore and Lucknow: A Tale of Two Sieges* (2007), Pen & Sword Books, Barnsley, South Yorkshire, UK.

Rizvi, SAA and Bhargava, ML (*eds.*), *Freedom Struggle in Uttar Pradesh,* Vol. II: Awadh 1857-59 (1958), Publications Bureau, Information Department, Uttar Pradesh.

Rizvi, SNR and Jafri, SZH (*eds.*), *The Great Uprising of 1857: Commentaries, Studies and Documents* (2009), Anamika Publishers, New Delhi.

Roberts, Frederick, Forty One Years in India: From Subaltern to Commander-in-Chief (1901) Macmillan, London.

Rookmaaker, K, "The Royal Menagerie of the King of Oudh", *Back When, and Then*, Vol. II (1) (1997), 10.

Roy, P and Choudhury, S, *Cellular Jail: Cells Beyond Cells* (2016), Farsight, Delhi.

Roy, Shampa, "Inside the Royal *Zenanas* in Colonial India: Avadhi and other *Begums* in the travel accounts of Fanny Parkes", *Studies in Travel Writing*, Vol. 16(1) (2012) pp. 47-63.

Russel, WH, *My Diary in India In The Year 1858 - 9,* Vol. 2 (1860), Routledge, London.

Sanderson, G, *List of Muhammadan and Hindu Monuments,* Vol. 1: *Shahjahanabad* (1916), Govt of India Press, Calcutta; *ibid, idem (1915)*, Illustrations.

Santha, K. Srinivasa, *Begums of Awadh* (1980), Bharati Prakashan, Varanasi.

Sarkar, PC, "Green Technologies in Nawabi and Colonial Architecture", *Tree Take*, September (2016), pp. 16-18.

Sarkar, PC, *Lucknow: Buildings, Begums and The British* (2015), Kalpaz, New Delhi.

Sarvadhikari, Rajkumar, *The Taluqdari Settlement in Oudh* (1882), Thacker, Spink & Co, Calcutta.

Scriver, P and Prakash, V, *Colonial Modernities: Building, Dwelling and Architecture in British India and Ceylon* (2007), Routledge, London, UK.

Sen, SN, *Eighteen Fifty-Seven* (1957), Publications Division, Govt. of India, New Delhi.

Shah, Pankaj, "Lake Buried Under Smrit Upvan", *Times of India*, November 7 (2008), Lucknow.

Sharma, AK, *Begum Hazrat Mahal* (2015), Gyan, New Delhi.

Sharma, JP, *Colonial Intervention and Urban Transformation: A Case Study of Shahjahanabad / Old Delhi* (2005), Thesis for Ph.D, De Montfort University, Leicester.

Sharma, Madhu, *Nawabi Architecture of Awadh* (2000), Thesis for M.Phil, Aligarh Muslim University, Aligarh.

Sharma, VC (*ed.*), *Uttar Pradesh District Gazetteers,* Vol. XXXVIII: Lucknow (1959), Govt. of Uttar Pradesh, Lucknow.

Sheeba, J and Dhas, JTM, "A Study on Indo-Saracenic Architectural Heritage", *Int. J. Pure and Applied Mathematics*, Vol. 118 (22) (2018) pp. 1737-1742.

Shepherd, Kevin RD, "The Indian Mutiny and Civil War 1857-58" at https://www.citizenthought.net/Indian_Mutiny.html

Shorto, S, "Hybrid Accommodations: David Ochterlony, the First Residency and the Mubarak Bagh" in *British Houses in Late Mughal India* (2018), Boydell & Brewer, Rochester, USA, pp. 25-54.

Singh, AA, *Role of Awadh Taluqdars* (2020), New Royal Book Co, Lucknow.

Singh, DP, *Study of Lucknawi Hybrid Architecture* (2001), Thesis for M.Arch, University of Roorkee, Roorkee.

Singh, KA and Bakshi, Pawan, *Ta'alluqdars of Oudh* (2013), Bloomsbury, New Delhi.

Singh, Malvika, *Lucknow: A City Between Cultures* (2011), Academic Foundation, New Delhi.

Singh, P and Ahmad, LA, "Adaptive Reuse – A Case of Lal Baradari, Lucknow", *Int. Res. J. Engg. Technol.*, Vol 6 (2019) pp. 7097-7105.

Singh, Shalini, *Cultural Tourism In The Awadh Region with Special Reference to Lucknow* (1992), Thesis for Ph.D, University of North Bengal, Darjeeling.

Singh, Shilendra K, "Minto and the Begums of Oudh", *Proc. of the Indian History Congress*, Vol. 14 (1951) pp. 295-301.

Singh, SN, *The Kingdom of Awadh: Its History, Polity and Administration* (2003), Mittal, New Delhi.

Sinha, Amita, "Bungalows of Lucknow Cantonment, India", *Open House International*, Vol. 24(2) (1999) pp. 56-63.

Sinha, Amita, "Colonial and post-colonial memorial parks in Lucknow, India: shifting ideologies and changing aesthetics", *J. Landscape Architecture*, September (2010) pp. 61-70.

Sinha, Amita, "Greener Pastures", *Indian Architect & Builder*, (2009) pp. 65 - 67.

Sinha, Amita, "Decadence, mourning and revolution: facets of the 19th Century landscape of Lucknow, India, *Landscape Research*, Vol. 21(2) (1996) pp. 123-136.

Sinha, Amita, "Restoration of the Gomti Riverfront in Lucknow: Claude Martin's Legacy, *Marg (Focus)*, Vol. 65 (2014) pp. 78-87.

Sinha, Amita, *Musa Bagh Conservation Plan* (2011), University of Illinois, Urbana-Champaigne.

Sinha, Arunav, "Nawabi story of Avadh temples' glory", *The Times of India* (Lucknow City), July 5 (2016).

Sinha, S, "Rediscovering Gaur: A Medieval Capital of Bengal," *J. Asian Soc. Bangladesh*, Vol. 58 (1), pp. 27-65.

Sleeman, William H, *A Journey Through the Kingdom of Oudh in 1849 – 185,* Vols. 1 & 2 (1858), Richard Bentley, London, UK.

Sleeman, William H, *Rambles and Recollections of an Indian Official* (1915), Oxford University Press, London, UK.

Snook, AL, *The Counter-Colonial Travel Writing of Fanny Parkes and EM Forster* (2010), Thesis for MA, East Carolina University, Greenville, USA.

Speirs, Malcolm, *Lucknow: Families of The Raj* (2013), CreateSpace, USA.

Speirs, Malcolm, *The Wasikadars of Awadh* (2008), Rupa Publications, New Delhi.

Spry, HH, *Modern India, with Illustrations of the Resources and Capabilities* of *Hindoostan* (1837) Whittaker and Co, UK.

Srivastava, AL, *Shuja-ud-Daulah* Vol. I: 1754 – 1765 (1961), SL Agarwala, Agra.

Srivastava, AL, *Shuja-ud-Daulah* Vol. II: 1765 – 1775 (1945), Minerva, Lahore.

Srivastava, AL, *The First Two Nawabs of Awadh* (1954), SL Agarwala, Agra.

Srivastava, Manish, *Architecture and Development as Instruments for Political Control and Marginalisation in Lucknow, India* (1997), Thesis for MS, Massachusetts Institute of Technology, Cambridge, USA.

Subramanian, Lakshmi, *History of India, 1707-1857* (2012), Orient BlackSwan, New Delhi.

Suryavanshi, SS, *Gadar ki Ankahi Kahani: Awadh ke Antim Badshah - Birjis Qadr* (2016), Pawar Offset, Lucknow.

Susewind, R and Taylor, CB, "Introduction. Islamicate Lucknow Today: Historical Legacy and Urban Aspirations", *S. Asia Multidisciplinary Academic Journal*, Vol. 11 (2015) pp. 1-23.

Talha, Parveen, *Fida-e-Lucknow* (2013), Niyogi, New Delhi.

Tandan, Banmali, *The Architecture of Lucknow and its Dependencies, 1722-1856. A Descriptive Inventory and Analysis of Nawabi Types* (2001), Vikas, New Delhi.

Tandan, Banmali, *The Architecture of Lucknow and Oudh 1722 - 1856: Its Evolution in an Aesthetic and Social Context* (2008), Zophorus, London.

Taylor, CB, "Madrasas and Social Mobility in the Religious Economy: The Case of Nadwat-al-'Ulama in Lucknow", *S. Asia Multidisciplinary Academic Journal*, Vol. 11 (2015) pp. 1-19.

Taqui, Roshan (*ed.*), *Images of Lucknow* (2000), New Royal Book Company, Lucknow.

Taqui, Roshan, *Lucknow 1857. The Two Wars at Lucknow – Dusk of An Era* (2019), New Royal Book Company, Lucknow.

Taqui, Roshan, "Lucknow Monuments, Problems & Solutions", *Indian J. Archaeology*, Vol. 1 (2) (2016), pp. 361-377.

Taiyab, Mohammad, *Subah of Awadh Under The Mughals [1582 - 1724]* (1980), Thesis for Ph.D, Aligarh Muslim University, Aligarh.

Tennant, W, *Indian Recreations, Consisting Chiefly of Strictures on The Domestic and Rural Economy of the Mahommedans & Hindoos*, Vol. II (1803), C. Stewart, Edinburg.

Thorn, Adam, *The Upper Ten Thousand: A Biographical Handbook of All the Titled* (1875), George Routledge, London, UK.

Thornton, Edward, *History of The British Empire in India,* Vol. III (1842), WH Allen, London, UK.

Thornton, JH, *Memories of Seven Campaigns* (1895), Westminster, London.

Tieffenthaler, J, *Description historique et géographique del'Inde,* Vol I (1786–89), CS. Spener, Berlin, pp. 256-57.

Tribunus, "Some Notices of General Claud Martin", *Bengal Past & Present*, Vol. II (Part II) (1908), pp. 280-287.

Trivedi, DB, *Law and Order in Upper India. A Story of Oudh: 1856 - 1877* (1990), Northern Book Center, New Delhi.

Trivedi, Madhu, *The Making of the Awadh Culture* (2010), Primus Books, Delhi.

Trotter, LJ, *A Leader of Light Horse: Life of Hodson of Hodson's Horse* (1901), William Blackwood, London.

Trotter, LJ, *The Bayard of India – A Life of General Sir James Outram by Captain Lionel* (1909), JM Dent & Company, London, UK.

Twining, Thomas, *Travels in India: A Hundred Years Ago* (1893), James Osgood, London.

Varshney, Vipul, *Lucknow: The City of Heritage & Culture. A Walk through History* (2017), Niyogi, New Delhi.

Varshney, Vipul, *Shaam-e-Awadh: A Visual Journey of Lucknow* (2017), Bloomsbury, New Delhi.

Versaikar Godshe, Vishnu Bhatt, *1857: The Real Story of The Great Uprising* (1907), (translated by Mrinal Pande, 2011), Harper Perennial, New Delhi.

Villiers Stuart, CM, *Gardens of The Great Mughals* (1913), Adam & Charles Black, London.

Watson, Bruce, *The Great Indian Mutiny: Colin Campbell and the Campaign at Lucknow* (1991), Praeger Publishers, Santa Barbara, California, USA.

Welch, A, Segger, M and DeCaro, N, "Building for the Raj: Richard Roskell Bayne", *Revue d'art Canadienne / Canadian Art Review*, Vol. 34(2) (2009), pp. 74-86.

Welter, Volker M, "Arcades for Lucknow: Patrick Geddes, Charles Rennie Mackintosh and the Reconstruction of the City", *Architectural History,* Vol. 42 (1999) pp. 316-332.

Wickins, P and Cadell, P, "The Indian Mutiny Journal of Private Charles Wickins of the 90th Light Infantry", *J. Soc. Army Historical Research*, Vol. 35(143), pp. 96-108.

Williamson, GC and Manners, V, *John Zoffany RA. His Life and Works: 1735-1810* (1920), John Lane, London.

Wood, Evelyn, *The Revolt in Hindustan: 1857 - 59* (1908), Methuen, London.

Wymann, FF, *From Calcutta to the Snowy Range* (1866), Tinsley Bros, London.

Yadav, KC, *1857: The Role of Punjab, Haryana and Himachal Pradesh* (2008), National Book Trust, New Delhi.

Yadav, S, *Lucknow's Tourism in Transition: A Stakeholder's Perspective* (2013), Thesis for Ph.D, Lucknow University, Lucknow.

Zastoupil, *Lynn, John Stuart Mill and India* (1994), Stanford University Press, Palo Alto, California, USA.

Plates

There are no rules of achitecture for a castle in the clouds.

—GK Chesterton

Splendid architecture, the love of your life, an old friend... they can all go drifting by unseen, if you are not careful.

—Ian Mckellan

It frustrates and fascinates me that we'll never know for sure, that despite the best efforts of historians and scientists and poets, there are some things we'll just never know.

—Isaac Marion

Plate 1: Mughal Pavilion of Safdarjang, Delhi, NP Singh (2021)

Plate 2: Ruins of *Jalalabad Fort,* Lucknow, Unidentified Photographer (1857)

Plate 3: Ramparts of *Macchi Bhavan* with *Teele Wali Masjid*, Lucknow, RC Tytler & H Tytler (1858)

Plate 4: Interior of the *Macchi Bhavan* Palace Complex, Lucknow, William Daniell (1788)

Plate 5: View of Lucknow: *Daulat Khana* from river side -1 Thomas Longcroft (1790)

Plate 6: View of Lucknow: *Daulat Khana* from river side -II, Thomas Longcroft (1790)

Plate 7: *Aishbagh*, Lucknow, William Daniell (1789)

Plate 8: *Alambagh Kothi*, Lucknow, Unidentified Photographer (1858)

Plate 9: *Alambagh Kothi* grounds with Havelock's unmarked grave under a mango tree, Felice Beato (1858)

Plate 10: Early 20th Century Image of *Lalbagh* School building, incorporating Old Nawabi Kothi, Unidentified Photographer

Plate 11: Wajid Ali Shah Riding Through Kaiserbagh, Lucknow, Unidentified Artist (1856)

Plate 12: Ruins of *Shahi* Well and Water Supply in *Badshah Bagh*, Lucknow, PC Sarkar (2016)

Plate 13: *Mohammad Bagh Club,* Lucknow, Unidentified Photographer (1880)

Plate 14: Wingfield Park, Lucknow, Unidentified Photographer (1863)

Plate 15: Gateway in Faizabad, Unidentified Photographer (1880)

Plate 16: Gateway of *Shahanajaf*, Lucknow, Unidentified Photographer (1890)

Plate 17: Ruins of *Imamo Ka Dargah* and *Sher Darwaza*, Lucknow, Beato (1858)

Plate 18: Ruins of *Moti Mahal* Gateway, Lucknow, Unidentified Photographer (1920)

Plate 19: Ruins of *Latkan Darwaza* (background) and Baillie Guard Gate (foreground), Lucknow, Beato (1858)

Plate 20: Unidentified Turreted Gateway, *Hussainabad*, Lucknow, Beato (1858)

Plate 21: *Hussainabad Imambara* Gateway, Lucknow, Unidentified Photographer (1915)

Plate 22: *Kaiserbagh* (Western) Gateway (*Lakhi Darwaza*), Lucknow, Beato (1858)

Plate 23: Ruins of Mermaid Gateway of *Kaiserbagh*, Lucknow, Unidentified Photographer (1858)

Plate 24: North East Gateway of *Kaiserbagh* Complex, Lucknow, S. Bourne (1867)

Plate 25: Vintage View of Gateway near *Sher Darwaza*, possibly *Dar-e-Daulat*, Lucknow, Unidentified Photographer (1880)

Plate 26: Vintage view of *Sikandar Bagh* Gateway, Lucknow, Unidentified Photographer

Plate 27: *Alambagh* Gate, Lucknow, Lt. Col. OM Lanyon (1857)

Plate 28: A View of *Chattar Manzil* Palace, Lucknow, Unidentified Photographer (1880)

Plate 29: A View of *Chota Chattar Manzil* palace complex including *Darshan Bilas*, *Gulistan-e-Iram* and *Lal Baradari*, Lucknow, Unidentified Photographer (1858)

Plate 30: Ruins of the Water Pavilions near *Chattar Manzil*, Lucknow, Unidentified Photographer (1858)

Plate 31: Ruins of the *Lanka* Pavilion, *Kaiserbagh,* Lucknow, Unidentified Photographer (1858)

Plate 32: Ruins of *Kaiserbagh*, Lucknow, RC Tytler and H Tytler (1858)

Plate 33: A View of *Kaiserbagh*, Lucknow, Edward Sache (1870)

Plate 34: Terrace of Old Martin House, Lucknow, PC Sarkar (2016)

Plate 35: Circular Room of Old Martin House, Lucknow, PC Sarkar (2016)

Plate 36: Panorama of *Daulat Khana* and *Hussainabad*, Lucknow, Beato (1858)

Plate 37: Vintage View of *Dilkusha Kothi*, Lucknow, Unidentified Photographer (1870)

Plate 38: *Musa Bagh Kothi* (North Facade), Lucknow, J. Milliken (1858)

Plate 39: Ruins of *Satkhanda* Tower, Lucknow, Unidentified Photographer (1910)

Plate 40: View of second St. Joseph's Cathedral, Hazratganj, Lucknow, demolished in late 1960s, Unidentified Photographer

Plate 41: Vintage View of Isabella Thoburn College, Chandganj, Lucknow, Unidentified Photographer

Plate 42: Bungalow in *Dilkusha* Cantonment, Lucknow, Lieut. Stanley Percy Ashby (1905)

Plate 43: Vintage View of Lucknow Council Chamber, Unidentified Photographer

Plate 44: Vintage View of Balrampur Hospital, Lucknow, Unidentified Photographer

Plate 45: Vintage View of Carlton Hotel, Lucknow, Unidentified Photographer

Plate 46: Vintage View of *Begum Kothi*, Lucknow, in use as General Post Office, Unidentified Photographer

Plate 47: Post Master General's Office, Lucknow, Unidentified Photographer (1917)

Plate 48: Vintage View of Old Lucknow Railway Junction, Unknown Photographer

Plate 49: Vintage View of Victoria Memorial, Lucknow, Unidentified Photographer (1890)

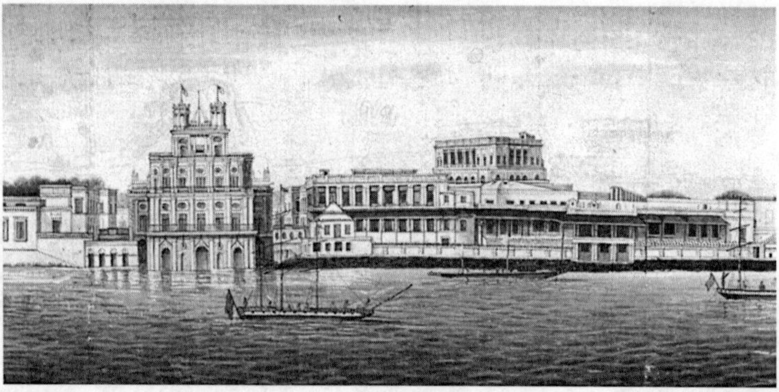

Plate 50: Lucknow Panorama - I, *Farhat Baksh* and neighbouring palaces, Unidentified Artist (1826)

Plate 51: Lucknow Panorama - II, *Macchi Bhavan* and *Panch Mahalla* Gate, Unidentified Artist (1826)

Plate 52: Lucknow Panorama - III, *Shahnajaf* and *Kadam Rasul*, Unidentified Artist (1826)

Plate 53: Lucknow Panorama IV, *Bibiapur Kothi* and *Vilayati Bagh*, Unidentified Artist (1826)

Plate 54: Lucknow Panorama - V, Water Pavilion with jetty and other unidentified palaces, Unidentified Artist (1826)

Plate 55: Lucknow Panorama - VI, *Chattar Manzil* Palace side, *Moti Mahal* gateway and fish-shape royal barge in the river, Unidentified Artist (1826).

"Lucknow on the Goomty", Reid & Johnson (1857)

Plate 56: View of deposed King, Wajid Ali Shah's *Metia Burz* palace complex, Calcutta, from across the Hooghly River, Lala Deen Dayal (1886)

Index

N